CODICES BOETHIANI I

T0346504

WARBURG INSTITUTE SURVEYS AND TEXTS

Edited by Jill Kraye

XXV

CODICES BOETHIANI

A CONSPECTUS OF MANUSCRIPTS
OF THE WORKS OF BOETHIUS

I. GREAT BRITAIN AND THE REPUBLIC OF IRELAND

EDITED BY
M. T. GIBSON and LESLEY SMITH
with the assistance of Joseph Ziegler

THE WARBURG INSTITUTE
UNIVERSITY OF LONDON
LONDON 1995

Margaret Templeton Gibson died on 2 August 1994, when
the volume was substantially complete and ready to enter the
final stages of editing and production.

©WARBURG INSTITUTE 1995
Codices Boethiani = ISBN 0 85481 087 0
Vol. I = ISBN 0 85481 088 9
ISSN 0 85481 088 9

Designed and computer typeset at the Warburg Institute and the University of London Computer Centre
Printed by Henry Ling, The Dorset Press, Dorchester, Dorset

Contents

Acknowledgements

No conspectus such as this could exist without the generosity and kindness of many people. We owe especial thanks to: B. C. Barker-Benfield; Martin Brett; Charles Burnett; Alan Coates; Christopher de Hamel; A. C. de la Mare; A. C. Dionisotti; Richard Gameson; Joan Greatrex; Charles Hope; Caroline Hull; Kristian Jensen; Martin Kauffmann; Sigrid Krämer; Brian Lawn; Elisabeth Leedham-Green; Alistair Minnis; Lodi Nauta; Roger Norris; Giulio d'Onofrio; Nigel Palmer; Alan Piper; Nigel Ramsay; Jayne Ringrose; Fiona Robb; P. Robinson; Brian Scott; Andrew Watson; Tessa Webber; Ian Wintersgill.

In addition, we would like to give our warmest thanks to the librarians of: Aberdeen University Library, Cambridge University Library; Corpus Christi College Cambridge; Emmanuel College, Cambridge; Fitzwilliam Museum, Cambridge; Gonville and Caius College, Cambridge; Jesus College, Cambridge; King's College, Cambridge; Pembroke College, Cambridge; St John's College, Cambridge; Sidney Sussex College, Cambridge; Trinity College, Cambridge; Canterbury Cathedral; Durham Cathedral; Durham University; Edinburgh, National Library of Scotland; Eton College; Glasgow, University Library; Hereford Cathedral; Holkham Hall; Lichfield Cathedral; Lincoln Cathedral; London, British Library; London, Lambeth Palace; London, Sion College; London, University Library; London, Wellcome Institute; Maidstone, Kent County Record Office; Manchester, Chetham's Library; Oscott, St Mary's College; Oxford, Bodleian Library, especially the staff of the Duke Humfrey Reserve; All Souls College, Oxford; Balliol College, Oxford; Corpus Christi College, Oxford; Exeter College, Oxford; Jesus College, Oxford; Magdalen College, Oxford; Merton College, Oxford; New College, Oxford; Queen's College, Oxford; St John's College, Oxford; Trinity College, Oxford; Worcester Cathedral; York Minster.

Our greatest debts are to Jill Kraye for overseeing publication, to Susan Hall for making the index and to the British Academy for making the project possible.

List of Plates

Pl. 1. MS Cambridge, Trinity College, O. 3. 7, fol. 2^r.
c. 1000. *DCPhil.* (Reproduced by permission of Trinity College, Cambridge.)

Pl. 2. MS London, British Library, Add. 19585, fol. 11^r.
s. xiv. Trivet's commentary to *DCPhil.* I. m. 1–8. Northern Italian. (Reproduced by permission of the British Library.)

Pl. 3. MS London, British Library, Add. 19968, fol. 113^r.
s. xii. Continuous commentary on *DCPhil.*, with lemmata. (Reproduced by persmission of the British Library.)

Pl. 4. MS London, British Library, Egerton 628, fols 103^v–104^r.
s. xiii 2/2. Intercalated commentary of Ps.-William of Conches on the *DCPhil.* (Reproduced by permission of the British Library.)

Pl. 5. MS London, British Library, Harley 3082, fols 45^v–46^r.
s. xii 2/2. *Op. Sac. II*, with gloss of Gilbert of Poitiers. (Reproduced by permission of the British Library.)

Pl. 6. MS London, British Library, Harley 3095, fol. 46^v.
s. ix. *DCPhil.* III. ix. 1–17, with at least two layers of Carolingian gloss. French. (Reproduced by permission of the British Library.)

Pl. 7. MS Oxford, Bodleian Library, Auct. F. I. 15, fol. 6^v.
c. 1000. *DCPhil.*, with extensive gloss. St Augustine's, Canterbury. (Reproduced by permission of the Bodleian Library.)

Pl. 8. MS Oxford, Bodleian Library, Laud Lat. 54, fol. 24^r.
s. xiii. *Arith.* with diagrams in red, blue and ochre. (Reproduced by permission of the Bodleian Library.)

Pl. 9. MS Oxford, Bodleian Library, Laud Misc. 457, fol. 145^v.
s. xii 4/4: St Mary, Eberbach. Carolingian commentary on the *Op. Sac.* (Reproduced by permission of the Bodleian Library.)

Pl. 10. MS Oxford, Bodleian Library, Rawlinson G. 187, fol. 3^r.
s. xiv 2/2. *DCPhil.* in two columns, with Trivet's commentary surrounding. (Reproduced by permission of the Bodleian Library.)

Abbreviations

1. BOETHIUS

Arith.	*De arithmetica*, ed. Friedlein, 1867.
Cat.	*Categories, AL*, i.1–2.
DCPhil.	*De consolatione philosophiae*, Loeb, 1973.
De Int.	*De interpretatione, AL*, ii.1.
Div.	*De divisione, PL*, 64:875–92.
Epitaph	*Epitaphs*, Teubner, 1871.
in Cat.	Commentary on *Categories, PL*, 64:159–294.
1 in Int.	First commentary on *De interpretatione*, Teubner, 1877.
2 in Int.	Second commentary on *De interpretatione*, Teubner, 1880.
1 in Isag.	First commentary on *Isagoge, CSEL*, 48.
2 in Isag.	Second commentary on *Isagoge, CSEL*, 48.
in Topica Cic.	Commentary on Cicero, *Topica, Ciceronis Opera*, ed. J. C. Orelli and J. G. Baiter, Zurich, 1833, V.i.269–388; reprinted in *PL*, 64: 1039–174.
intr. Syll. Cat.	Introduction to *Categorical syllogisms, PL*, 64:761–94.
Isag.	Porphyry, *Isagoge, AL*, i.6.
Mus.	*De musica*, Teubner, 1867.
Op. Sac.	*Opuscula sacra*, Loeb, 1973.
Post. Anal.	Aristotle, *Posterior analytics, AL*, iv.1–4; not Boethius.
Prior Anal.	Aristotle, *Prior analytics, AL*, iii.1–2.
Soph. Elench.	Aristotle, *De sophisticis elenchis, AL*, vi.1.
Syll. Cat.	*De syllogismis categoricis, PL*, 64:793–832.
Syll. Hyp.	*De syllogismis hypotheticis, PL*, 64:831–76.
Topica Aris.	Aristotle, *Topica, AL*, v.1.
Top. Diff.	*De differentiis topicis, PL*, 64:1173–1216, and Nikitas, pp. 1–92
Vita	*Vitae*, I–VII.

2. SELECT BIBLIOGRAPHY

AL	*Aristoteles Latinus*, ed. G. Lacombe and L. Minio-Paluello, 2 vols, Rome, 1939 & Cambridge, 1955; *supplementa altera*, ed. L. Minio-Paluello, Bruges etc., 1961. Editions are cited thus: page/line.

For editions of texts within the series, see introduction.

AT	J. J. G. Alexander and E. Temple, *Illuminated Manuscripts in Oxford Libraries, the University Archives and the Taylor Institution*, Oxford, 1985.
Avicenna	*Avicenna Latinus*, ed. S. van Riet and G. Verbeke, 9 vols, Louvain-la-Neuve, 1972–89.
Bergmann	R. Bergmann, *Verzeichnis der althochdeutschen und altsächsischen Glossenhandschriften*, Berlin etc., 1973.
Bernard, *CMA*	E. Bernard, *Catalogi librorum manuscriptorum Angliae et Hiberniae*, Oxford, 1697.
Bernhard and Bower	M. Bernhard and C. M. Bower, *Glossa maior in institutionem musicam Boethii*, Munich, 1993, I.
BHL	*Bibliotheca hagiographica latina antiquae et mediae aetatis*, Brussels, 1898–1901; Supplements 1911 and, ed. H. Fros, 1986.
Bishop, *English Caroline*	T. A. M. Bishop, *English Caroline Minuscule*, Oxford, 1971.
Bolton	D. K. Bolton, 'The Study of the *Consolation of Philosophy* in Anglo-Saxon England', *Archives d'histoire doctrinale et littéraire du Moyen Age*, 44, 1977, pp. 33–78.
Bower	C. M. Bower, 'Boethius' *De institutione musica*: a handlist of manuscripts', *Scriptorium*, 42, 1988, pp. 205–51.
Bubnov	N. Bubnov, *Gerberti postea Silvestri II papae opera mathematica*, Berlin, 1899.
Burnett, *Adelard*	*Adelard of Bath*, ed. C. Burnett, Warburg Institute Suveys and Texts XIV, London, 1987.
Burnett, *Glosses*	*Glosses and Commentaries on Aristotelian Logical Texts: The Syriac, Arabic and Medieval Latin Traditions*, ed. C. Burnett, Warburg Institute

	Surveys and Texts XXIII, London, 1993.
Cappuyns, 'Boèce'	M. Cappuyns, 'Boèce', *Dictionnaire d'histoire et géographie ecclésiastique*, ix, Paris, 1937, pp. 358–61.
Cappuyns, 'Opuscula sacra'	M. Cappuyns, 'Le Plus Ancien Commentaire des "Opuscula Sacra" et son origine', *Recherches de théologie ancienne et médiévale*, 3, 1931, pp. 237–72.
CBMLC	Corpus of British Medieval Library Catalogues.
CCSL	*Corpus Christianorum, Series Latina.*
Colophons	Bénédictins du Bouveret, *Colophons de manuscrits occidentaux des origines au XVIe siècle*, 6 vols, Fribourg, 1965–82.
Conches	*Guillaume de Conches, Glosae super Platonem*, ed. E. A. Jeauneau, Paris, 1965.
Courcelle	P. Courcelle, *La Consolation de Philosophie dans la tradition littéraire*, Paris, 1967.
CPL	*Clavis Patrum Latinorum*, Steenbrugge, 1961.
CSEL	*Corpus scriptorum ecclesiasticorum Latinorum.*
CTC	*Catalogus translationum et commentariorum: Mediaeval and Renaissance Latin Translations and Commentaries*, ed. P. O. Kristeller et al., Washington DC, 1960–.
Delisle	L. Delisle, *Le Cabinet des manuscrits de la Bibliothèque Impériale [et] Nationale*, 4 vols, Paris, 1868–81.
Emden, *BRUC*	A. B. Emden, *A Biographical Register of the University of Cambridge to 1500*, 2 vols, Cambridge, 1963.
Emden, *BRUO*	A. B. Emden, *A Biographical Register of the University of Oxford to A.D. 1500*, 3 vols, Oxford, 1957–59.
Emden, *BRUO 1501–40*	A. B. Emden, *A Biographical Register of the*

	University of Oxford A.D. 1501 to 1540, Oxford, 1974.
Folkerts	M. Folkerts, *'Boethius' Geometrie II: Ein mathematisches Lehrbuch des Mittelalters*, Wies baden, 1970.
Gerbert, *Scriptores*	M. Gerbert, *Scriptores ecclesiastici de musica*, 3 vols, St Blasien, 1784.
Gibson	*Boethius: His Life, Thought and Influence*, ed. M. T. Gibson, Oxford, 1981.
Gibson, *Timaeus*	M. T. Gibson, 'The Study of the *Timaeus* in the Eleventh and Twelfth Centuries', *Pensamiento*, 25, 1969, pp. 183–94.
GL	*Grammatici latini*, ed. H. Keil, 6 vols and supplement, Leipzig, 1857–80.
Glorieux, *Arts*	P. Glorieux, *La Faculté des arts et ses maîtres au XIIIᵉ siècle*, Paris, 1971.
Glorieux, *Théologie*	P. Glorieux, *Répertoire des maîtres en théologie de Paris au XIIIᵉ siècle*, Paris, 1933.
Goff	F. R. Goff, *Incunabula in American Libraries: A Third Census of Fifteenth-Century Books Recorded in North American Collections*, New York, 1973.
Goy	R. Goy, *Die Überlieferung der Werke Hugos von St Viktor*, Stuttgart, 1976.
GW	*Gesamtkatalog der Wiegendrucke*, Leipzig etc., 1925–
Häring	N. Häring, 'Handschriftliches zu den Werken Gilberts, Bischof von Poitiers (1142–54)', *Revue d'histoire des textes*, 8, 1978, pp. 133–94.
Häring, *Gilbert*	N. Häring, *The Commentaries on Boethius by Gilbert of Poitiers*, Toronto, 1966.
Hauréaux	B. Hauréaux, *Initia operum scriptorum latinorum medii potissimum aevi*, 8 vols, Turnhout, 1974.

Hervieux	L. Hervieux, *Les Fabulistes latins*, 5 vols, Paris, 1893–99.
Hunt Memorial Exhibition	*Manuscripts at Oxford: An Exhibition in Memory of R. W. Hunt*, eds A. C. de la Mare and B. C. Barker-Benfield, Oxford, 1980.
James, *ALCD*	M. R. James, *The Ancient Libraries of Canterbury and Dover*, Cambridge, 1903.
Kauffmann	C. M. Kauffmann, *Romanesque Manuscripts 1066–1190. A Survey Romanesque of Manuscripts Illuminated in the British Isles 3*, London, 1975.
Ker, *Anglo-Saxon*	N. R. Ker, *A Catalogue of Manuscripts containing Anglo-Saxon*, Oxford, 1957, reprinted with supplement 1990.
Ker, *MLGB*	N. R. Ker, *Medieval Libraries of Great Britain*, 2nd edn, London, 1964.
Ker, *MMBL* I–III	N. R. Ker, *Medieval Manuscripts in British Libraries*, 3 vols, Oxford, 1969–83.
Ker, *Pastedowns*	N. R. Ker, *Pastedowns in Oxford Bindings*, Oxford, 1954.
Ker and Piper, *MMBL* IV	N. R. Ker and A. J. Piper, *Medieval Manuscripts in British Libraries IV*, Oxford, 1992.
Kottler	B. Kottler, 'The Vulgate Tradition of the *Consolatio Philosophiae* in the Fourteenth Century', *Mediaeval Studies*, 17, 1955, pp. 209–14.
Krämer	S. Krämer, *Handschriftenerbe des deutschen Mittelalters*, Mittelalterliche Bibliothekskataloge Deutsch lands und der Schweiz, Ergänzungsband 1, 3 vols, Munich, 1989–90.
Kristeller	P. O. Kristeller, *Iter Italicum*, 6 vols, London etc., 1963–92
Leonardi	C. Leonardi, 'I Codici di Marziano Capella', *Aevum*, 34, 1960, pp. 1–99, 411–524 (nos 1–241).

Manitius

M. Manitius, *Geschichte der lateinischen Literatur des Mittelalters*, 3 vols, Munich, 1911–31.

Minnis, *Chaucer*

A. J. Minnis, *Chaucer's Boèce and the Medieval Tradition of Boethius*, Cambridge, 1993.

Minnis, *Medieval Boethius*

The Medieval Boethius: Studies in the Vernacular Translations of the 'De consolatione philosophiae', ed. A. J. Minnis, Cambridge, 1987.

Nikitas

D. M. Nikitas, *Boethius' 'De topicis differentiis' und die byzantinische Rezeption dieses Werkes*, Paris etc., 1990; pp. 1–92 contain a complete critical edition of *Top. Diff.*

Obertello

L. Obertello, *Severino Boezio*, 2 vols, Genoa, 1974.

PA

O. Pächt and J. J. G. Alexander, *Illuminated Manuscripts in the Bodleian Library*, 3 vols, Oxford, 1966–73.

Passalacqua

M. Passalacqua, *I Codici di Prisciano*, Rome, 1978.

Peiper

R. Peiper, *Anicii Manlii Severini Boetii Philosophiae Consolationis libri quinque*, Leipzig, 1871.

PL

J.-P. Migne, *Patrologiae Latinae cursus completus*, 221 vols, Paris, 1844–64.

Proctor

R. G. C. Proctor, *An Index to the Early Printed Books in the British Museum: From the Invention of Printing to the Year MD. With Notes of Those in the Bodleian Library*, 2 vols, London, 1898.

Registrum Anglie

R. H. and M. A. Rouse, *Registrum Anglie de libris doctorum et auctorum veterum*, CBMLC, London, 1991.

Robinson

P. R. Robinson, *Catalogue of Dated and Datable Manuscripts c. 737–1600 in Cambridge Libraries*, 2 vols, Cambridge, 1988.

Saxl and Meier

F. Saxl and H. Meier, *Verzeichnis astrologischer und mythologischer illustrierter Handschriften des lateinischen Mittelalters,* III: *Handschriften in englischen Bibliotheken,* 2 vols, London, 1953.

Schaller	D. Schaller and E. Könsgen, *Initia carminum latin orum seculo undecimo antiquiorum,* Göttingen, 1977.
Schenkl	H. Schenkl, *Bibliotheca Patrum latinorum Britannica,* Vienna, 1891–1908.
Schneyer	J. B. Schneyer, *Repertorium der Lateinischen Sermones des Mittelalters für die Zeit von 1150–1350,* 11 vols, Münster i. W., 1973–90.
Silk, *Commentarius*	E. T. Silk, *Saeculi noni auctoris in Boetii Consolationem Philosophiae Commentarius,* Rome, 1935.
Survival	*The Survival of Ancient Literature,* Bodleian Library Exhibition Catalogue, Oxford, 1975.
Temple	E. Temple, *Anglo-Saxon Manuscripts 900–1066. A Survey of Manuscripts Illuminated in the British Isles 2,* London, 1976.
Thorndike/Kibre	L. Thorndike and P. Kibre, *A Catalogue of Incipits of Mediaeval Scientific Writings in Latin,* rev. edn, London, 1963.
Troncarelli, *Boethiana*	F. Troncarelli, *Boethiana Aetas,* Alessandria, 1987.
Troncarelli, 'Opuscula'	F. Troncarelli, 'Aristoteles Piscatorius. Note sulle opere teologiche di Boezio e sulla loro fortuna', *Scriptorium,* 42, 1988, pp. 3–19.
Troncarelli, *Tradizioni*	F. Troncarelli, *Tradizioni perdute: La 'Consolatio Philosophiae' nell' alto medioevo,* Padua, 1981.
Verfasserlexikon	*Die deutsche Literatur des Mittelalters: Verfasserlexikon,* ed. K. Illing and C. Stöllinger, Berlin, 1978–.
Walther	H. Walther, *Initia carminum ac versuum medii aevi posterioris latinorum,* 2nd edn, Göttingen, 1969.

Watson, *London*   A. G. Watson, *A Catalogue of Dated and Datable Manuscripts c. 700–1600 in the Department of Manuscripts, the British Library*, 2 vols, London, 1979.

Watson, *MLGB*   A. G. Watson, *Medieval Libraries of Great Britain: Supplement to the Second Edition*, London, 1987.

Watson, *Oxford*   A. G. Watson, *A Catalogue of Dated and Datable Manuscripts c. 435–1600 in Oxford Libraries*, 2 vols, Oxford, 1984.

Weijers   O. Weijers, *Pseudo-Boèce, 'De disciplina scolarium'*, Leiden etc., 1976.

Wittig   J. S. Wittig, 'King Alfred's *Boethius* and its Latin Sources', *Anglo-Saxon England*, 11, 1983, pp. 157–98.

Wormald I   F. Wormald, *English Kalendars before A.D. 1100*, London, 1934.

Wormald II   F. Wormald, *English Benedictine Kalendars after A.D. 1100*, London, 1939.

Introduction

i. THE CENSUS

Codices Boethiani is a conspectus of Boethius's works—including his commentaries on Porphyry and Aristotle, and his translations of Aristotelian logic—as these survive in manuscripts throughout the world. As in *Aristoteles Latinus*, the order is geographical, thus:

I	Great Britain and the Republic of Ireland.
II	Austria, Belgium, Denmark, Holland, Netherlands, Sweden, Switzerland
III	Czech Republic, Slovakia, Hungary, Poland, Portugal, Russia, Slovenia, Spain; Australia, Japan, New Zealand, United States of America
IV	Italy, Vatican City
V	Germany
VI	France
VII	General Index

We include fragments, as witnesses to manuscripts that once existed complete. We do not include excerpts and quotations, relevant though these are to the reception and knowledge of Boethius as an author. Neither do we include the wide vernacular tradition of the *De consolatione philosophiae*, even when it has a Latin component. Commentaries are noted only when they are accompanied by the *complete* text commented. For instance, some manuscripts of Nicholas Trivet do incorporate the complete *Consolation*; others (the majority) are continuous commentaries with lemmata.

Individual works of Boethius exist in various printed editions, few of which satisfy all the canons of modern scholarship. Often a sound critical text has been established on a narrow manuscript base. A new edition of the Boethian corpus, thoughtfully executed, would tell us a great deal about the learning and literature of the sixth century and the latinity of the Middle Ages. *Codices Boethiani* will contribute to the identification of useful manuscripts. But any census has its underlying rationale. We are concerned not primarily with searching out the best manuscripts for an editor, but with the transmission and use of the works of Boethius. How are they deployed on the page? For whom, by whom? What company do they keep? The *Opuscula Sacra*, for example, drift away from the *Consolation of Philosophy* towards the theologians: Augustine and Hugh of St Victor. The *Consolation* itself has several forms: a Carolingian philosophical text, an element in a school primer, along with the *Disticha Catonis*; a Carthusian paper

manuscript heavy with German and Latin apparatus; an illuminated 'coffee-table'
volume for a wealthy patron in France or England. A few manuscripts defy
classification. They are unusual in their conception, construction, physical
appearance or provenance. In our descriptions we have tried to articulate the
normal types of manuscript, so that these exceptions may be recognized more
easily.

Each entry consists of six parts: (1) material, structure, measurements and
script, (2) summary of contents, (3) annotation to the text, (4) illumination and
initials, (5) provenance, (6) bibliography. Notabilia—e.g., fluency in Greek—and
characterization of the manuscript, if any, follow (1). As to (3) the fundamental
distinction is between a gloss provided by the original scribe and notes added by
subsequent readers. In (4) we are more concerned with the role of the coloured
initial in organizing the text than with localizing style or identifying artists. Where
an original or early provenance (5) is clear, we have named the owner and / or
quoted the *ex libris*. When in doubt, we have given the *ex libris* or remained silent.
More recent owners are cited if they contribute to the history of a collection—e.g.,
Graevius at Cologne—or if they caught our attention. Eighteenth- to twentieth-
century owners have often been omitted. The prudent reader will bear in mind that
in describing manuscripts in major collections in the British Isles we have returned
often to check details, whereas other descriptions are based on a single visit to (let
us say) Worcester cathedral or Holkham Hall. Manuscripts for which we rely
entirely on catalogue descriptions will be asterisked—there are only six (Lichfield,
London, Seilern and Dublin) in the present volume. Finally, we were delighted to
be able to include the Oscott fragment of the *Topica Aris.*, the only known
manuscript of this text prior to the twelfth century.[1]

ii. THE TRIVIUM

The **logica vetus** (1–12)

The *logica vetus* was well characterized by A. van de Vyver, 'Les Étapes du
développement philosophique du haut Moyen-Age', *Revue belge de philosophie
et d'histoire*, 8, 1929, pp. 425–52. Boethius is a major author, translator and
commentator, but not the only one; tenth- and eleventh-century collections would
still include the relevant pages of Isidore and Martianus Capella, and those useful
ignoti, Ps.-Apuleius and Ps.-Augustine. The 1930s saw the establishment of
Aristoteles Latinus: first the census of manuscripts (*AL*) and then the editions (here

---

[1] We are indebted to Fr David Evans, the Librarian of Oscott College, for his assistance, and
to Nicholas Brooks, for verifying the measurements.

AL i.1–6, ii.1, iii.1–2, v.1, vi.1). Boethius's translations of Aristotelian logic were disentangled and put on a sound textual footing by Lorenzo Minio-Paluello, whose work in the 1960s, and the image that he presented to younger scholars,[2] maintained *Aristoteles Latinus* as an active concern to the present day. The twelve Boethian texts in the *logica vetus* consist of translations (1, 4, 6 below), commentaries (2–3, 5, 7–8) and monographs (9–12).

1. Porphyry, *Isagoge*, 1 bk, trans. Boethius: **Isag**.
inc. Cum sit necessarium, Chrisaorie; *expl*. sed sufficiant etiam haec ad discretione-m eorum communitatisque traditionem.
Edition: L. Minio-Paluello, *AL*, i.6, Bruges etc., 1966.

2. Boethius, *First commentary on the 'Isagoge'*, 2 bks: **1 in Isag**.
Boethius's analysis of the translation of the *Isagoge* by Marius Victorinus.
inc. Hiemantis anni tempore in Aureliae montibus concesseramus; *expl*. diligentiore postea consideratione tractabitur.
Edition: S. Brandt, CSEL, 48, Vienna etc., 1906.

3. Boethius, Second commentary on the 'Isagoge', 5 bks: **2 in Isag**.
Boethius's analysis of his own translation of the Isagoge.
inc. Secundus hic arreptae expositionis labor nostrae seriem translationis expediet; *expl*. quinque rerum disputationem et ad Praedicamenta seruanti.
Edition: S. Brandt, CSEL, 48, Vienna etc., 1906.

4. Aristotle, *Categoriae*, 1 bk, trans. Boethius: **Cat**.
also called 'Praedicamenta'.
inc. Aequiuoca dicuntur quorum nomen solum commune est; *expl*.qui autem solent dici paene omnes sunt annumerati [or, mixed recension] sed qui consueuerunt dici paene omnes enumerati sunt.
Edition: L. Minio-Paluello, *AL*, i.1–2, Bruges etc., 1961.

5. Boethius, *Commentary on the 'Categoriae'*, 4 books: **in Cat**.
inc. Expeditis his quae ad praedicamenta Aristotelis Porphyrii institutione digesta sunt; *expl*. quod sub se aliquas partes speciesque contineat.
Edition: *PL*, 64: 159–294.

6. Aristotle, *De interpretatione*, 1 bk, trans. Boethius: **De Int**.
Also called 'Peri hermenias'.
inc. Primum oportet constituere quid sit nomen et quid uerbum; *expl*. simul autem eidem non contingit inesse contraria.

---

[2] See the memoir by W. Kneale, *Proceedings of the British Academy,* 72, 1987, pp. 441–54; and for an exposition of Minio-Paluello's scholarly method his own *Opuscula: The Latin Aristotle,* Amsterdam, 1972.

Edition: L. Minio-Paluello, *AL*, ii.1, Bruges etc., 1965.

7. Boethius, *First Commentary on the 'De interpretatione'*, 2 bks: **1 in Int**.
inc. Magna quidem libri huius apud Peripateticam sectam probatur auctoritas; *expl*.
tractatus edoceat secundae editionis series explicabit.
Edition: C. Meiser, Teubner, Leipzig, 1877.

8. Boethius, *Second Commentary on the 'De interpretatione'*, 6 bks: **2 in Int**.
inc. Alexander in commentariis suis hac se inpulsum causa pronuntiat sumpsisse
longissimum expositionis laborem; *expl*. et si non proderit obloquitur.
Edition: C. Meiser, Teubner, Leipzig, 1880.

9. Boethius, *Introductio in syllogismos categoricos*, 1 bk: **Intr. Syll. Cat**.
Also called 'Antepraedicamenta'.
inc. Multa ueteres philosophiae duces posteriorum studiis contulerunt; *expl*.
easdem lector inueniet praetereundum uidetur.
Edition: *PL*, 64:761–94.

10. Boethius, *De syllogismis categoricis*, 2 bks: **Syll. Cat**.
inc. Multa Graeci ueteres posteris suis in consultissimis reliquere tractatibus; *expl*.
in rebus mendaciumque meditabitur.
Edition: *PL*,64: 793–832.

11. Boethius, *De syllogismis hypotheticis*, 2 bks: **Syll. Hyp**.
inc. Cum in omnibus philosophiae disciplinis ediscendis atque tractandis summum
uitae positum solamen existimem; *expl*. hic operis longitudinem terminemus.
Edition: *PL*, 64: 831–76; L. Obertello, *A. M. Severino Boezio, De hypotheticis
syllogismis. Testo critico, traduzione, introduzione e commento*, Brescia, 1969.

12. Boethius, *De diuisione*, 1 bk: **Div**.
inc. Quam magnos studiosis afferat fructus scientia diuidendi; *expl*. introductionis
breuitas patiebatur diligenter expressimus.
Edition: *PL*, 64: 875–92.

The **logica nova** (13–15, 21)

Four 'new' translations of Aristotelian logic were current from the mid-twelfth
century. The translation of the *Posterior Analytics* (21) is not thought to be by
Boethius. We should remember that only on the discovery of the *logica nova*
could the familiar texts be seen as the corpus of *logica vetus*.

13. Aristotle, *Sophistici Elenchi*, 1 bk, trans. Boethius: **Soph. Elench**.
inc. De sophisticis autem elenchis et de his qui uidentur quidem elenchi; *expl*.
inuentis autem multas habere grates.

Edition: B. G. Dod, *AL*, vi.1, Leiden etc., 1975.

14. Aristotle, *Priora Analytica*, 2 bks, trans. Boethius: **Prior Anal**.
inc. Primum dicere circa quid et de quo est intentio (Florentine recension) [or]
Primum dicere oportet circa quid et cuius est consideratio (Chartres recension);
expl. si autem non, non erit unum unius signum.
Edition: L. Minio-Paluello, *AL*, iii.1–2, Bruges etc., 1962.

15. Aristotle, *Topica*, 8 bks, trans. Boethius: **Topica Aris**.
inc. Propositum quidem negotii est methodum inuenire a qua poterimus syllogizare
de omni problemate ex probabilibus; *expl.* ad quas habundare difficile est continuo.
Edition: L. Minio-Paluello, *AL*, v.1 Brussels etc., 1969.

Rhetoric (16–18)

Cicero's *Topics* was a common constituent of Carolingian manuscripts of the
logica vetus, and Boethius's commentary, though something of a rarity was
certainly available by the 840s.[3] The *De differentiis topicis* did not come into
regular use before the late tenth century.[4] From the thirteenth century bk IV often
circulated on its own.

16. Boethius, *In Topica Ciceronis*, 6 bks: **in Topica Cic**.
inc. Exhortatione tua, Patrici,[5] rhetorum peritissime, quae et praesentis honestate
proposti et futurae aetatis utilitate coniuncta est; *expl.* fortuitarum concursio est.
Edition: *Ciceronis Opera*, ed. J. C. Orelli and J. G. Baiter, Zurich, 1833,
V.i.269–388; reprinted in *PL*, 64: 1039–174.

17. Boethius, *De differentiis topicis*, 4 bks: **Top. Diff**.
inc. Omnis ratio disserendi quam logicen Peripatetici ueteres appellauere in duas
distribuitur partes; *expl.* quos in Aristotelis Topica a nobis translata conscripsimus
expeditum est.
Editions: *PL*, 64:1173–1216; critical text by D. Z. Nikitas, *Boetius, De topicis
differentiis*, Corpus Philosophorum Medii Aevi: Philosophi Byzantini 5, Paris etc.,
1990, pp. lxxviii and 1–92. See also trans. and commentary by E. Stump, Ithaca,
N.Y., 1978.

---

[3] Lupus of Ferrières was angling for a papyrus (sic) manuscript of the *in Topica Cic.* c. 842/6:
Letter 16 to the archbishop of Tours, ed. P. K. Marshall, Leipzig, 1984, pp. 23–24.
[4] Van de Vyver, pp. 443–46.
[5] Perhaps *quaestor palatii* in Italy 534–35: J. Martindale, *Prosopography of the Later Roman
Empire*, Cambridge, 1980, ii.839–40.

Related Texts

18. Cicero, *Topica*, 1 bk.
inc. Maiores nos res scribere ingressos C. Trebati; *expl.* ornamenta quaedam uoluimus non debita accedere.
Edition: A. S. Wilkins, 2nd edn, Oxford, 1935.

19. Ps.-Apuleius, *Peri Hermenias*, 1 bk.
inc. Studium sapientiae, quod philosophiam uocamus, plerisque uidetur tres species seu partes habere; *expl.* praeterea eorum non potest numerus augeri.
Edition: P. Thomas, Teubner, Leipzig, 1908.

20. Ps.-Augustine, *Categoriae decem*, 1 bk.
inc. Cum omnis scientia disciplinaque artium diuersarum non nisi oratione tractetur; *expl.* iam doctos aut indoctos manifestius erudire.
Edition: L. Minio-Paluello, *AL*, i.5, Bruges etc., 1961. The status of the *Categoriae decem* in the Carolingian era is well characterized by J. Marenbon, *From the Circle of Alcuin to the School of Auxerre: Logic, Theology and Philosophy in the Early Middle Ages*, Cambridge, 1981, pp. 16–18 et passim.

21. Marius Victorinus, *De definitionibus*, 1 bk.
inc. Dicendi ac disputandi prima semper oratio est, etiam dialecticis auctoribus et ipso M. Tullio saepius admonente; *expl.* satis esse duxi.
Edition: *PL*, 64: 891–910. Critical text by T. Stangl, *Tulliana et Mario-Victoriniana*, Munich, 1888, pp. 12–48; reprinted by P. Hadot, *Marius Victorinus: recherches sur sa vie et ses oeuvres*, Paris, 1971, pp. 329–65.

22. *Liber sex principiorum*, 1 bk.
inc. Forma uero est compositioni contingens, simplici et inuariabili essentia consistens; *expl.* secundum naturam moueri ut ignis.
Edition: L. Minio-Paluello, *AL*, i.7, Bruges etc., 1966.
A mid-twelfth century text of unknown authorship, which was incorporated in the *logica vetus*. The erroneous attribution to 'Gilbertus Porretanus' is first made by Albert the Great c. 1250.[6]

23. Aristotle, *Posteriora Analytica*, 2 bks: *Post. Anal.*
inc. Omnis doctrina et omnis disciplina intellectiua ex preexistente fit cognitione; *expl.* hoc autem omne similiter se habet ad omnem rem.

---

[6] See L. Minio-Paluello, 'Magister Sex Principiorum', *Studi medievali*, 3 ser., 6, 1965, pp. 123–51; reprinted in Minio-Paluello, *Opuscula: The Latin Aristotle*, Amsterdam, 1972, pp. 536–64.

Edition: L. Minio-Paluello and B. G. Dod, *AL*, iv.1–4, Bruges etc., 1968.

24. Ps.-Boethius, *De disciplina scolarium*, 1 bk.
inc. Vestra nouit intencio de scolarium disciplina compendiosum postulare tractatum; *expl.* ultima tamen alterius saporis inquinamenta permanebunt.
Edition: O. Weijers, *Pseudo-Boèce,'De disciplina scolarium'*, Leiden etc., 1976. An anonymous text, written c. 1230–40, probably in Paris.

25. *De unitate et uno*, 1 bk.
inc. Unitas est qua unaquaeque res dicitur esse una; *expl.* et est id quod est.
A twelfth-century text, perhaps by Gundissalinus, that is often found with *Op.Sac*.
Edition: *PL*, 63: 1075–78; critical text by P. Correns, Beiträge zur Geschichte der Philosophie des Mittelalters, i.1, Münster i.W., 1891, pp. 1–56 (text at 3–11).

iii. THE QUADRIVIUM

1. *De arithmetica*, 2 bks: **Arith**.
inc. pref. In dandis accipiendisque muneribus; *expl.* censebitur auctor merito quam probator.
inc. text Inter omnes priscae auctoritatis uiros; *expl.* huius descriptionis subter exemplar adiecimus.
Edition: G. Friedlein, Teubner, Leipzig, 1867; reprinted Frankfurt, 1966.

2. *De musica*, 5 bks, of which the fifth lacks caps xx-xxx: **Mus**.
inc. Omnium quidem perceptio sensuum ita sponte ac naturaliter quibusdam uiuentibus adest; *expl.* ut in diatonicis generibus nusquam una.
Edition: G. Friedlein, Teubner, Leipzig, 1867; reprinted Frankfurt, 1966.

Related Texts

3. *Geometria*
Boethius's *Geometria* seems to have been a translation or a paraphrase of Euclid's *Elements* I–V, possibly even the entire text of Euclid.[7] Although it has not survived as an independent text, it may well have contributed to several anonymous treatises *De geometria* of the eighth to tenth centuries.[8]

---

[7] See Cassiodorus, *Variae* I.xlv.4, ed. A. J. Fridh and J. W. Halporn, CCSL, 96, Turnhout, 1973, p. 49: 'Euclidem translatum Romanae linguae idem uir magnificus Boetius edidit'; cf. Cassiodorus, *Institutiones* II.vi.3, ed. R. A. B. Mynors, Oxford, 1937, p. 152.
[8] Pingree, in Gibson, pp. 155–61.

4. Ps.-Boethius, *Geometria* I

inc. Geometria est disciplina magnitudinis immobilis, formarumque descriptio contemplatiua; *expl.* variable.
Edition: Books I–II, *PL*, 63: 1352–64; I and II–IV excerpts, ed. C. Lachmann, *Gromatici veteres*, Berlin, 1848, pp. 377–92.

5. Ps.-Boethius, *Geometria* II

inc. Quia uero mi Patrici,[9] geometrum exercitissime, Euclidis de artis geometricae figuris obscure prolata te adhortante exponenda et lucidiore aditu expolienda suscepi; *expl.* Nos uero haec ad praesens dicta dixisse sufficiat.
Edition: M. Folkerts, *'Boethius' Geometrie II: Ein mathematisches Lehrbuch des Mittelalters*, Wiesbaden, 1970.

iv. OPUSCULA SACRA I–V   Op. Sac. I–V

The five *Opuscula Sacra*, long regarded as *dubia*, were conclusively accepted as genuine when Heinrich Usener published the Cassiodoran account of Boethius's family and writings, the *Ordo generis Cassiodororum* (1877).[10] Their first modern edition is Rudolph Peiper's Teubner of 1871.[11] We have used the Loeb edition, by H. F. Stewart and E. K. Rand (1918), revised by S. J. Tester (1973), citing the *Opuscula* by number I–V and the line number of the 1973 Loeb edition.

I *De trinitate* – *inc.* Inuestigatam diutissime; *expl.* uota supplebunt.

II *De trinitate ii* – *inc.* Quaero an pater et filius; *expl.* rationemque coniunge.

III *De hebdomadibus* – *inc.* Postulas ut ex hebdomadibus nostris; *expl.* aliud omnia bona.

IV *De fide catholica* – *inc.* Christianam fidem noui ac ueteris testamenti; *expl.* laus perpetua creatoris.

V *Contra Eutychen* – *inc.* Anxie te quidem; *expl.* causa perscribit.

---

[9] *Pace* Folkerts, p. 113, and Pingree, in Gibson, p. 157, this is not a reference to Symmachus as 'patricius', but to Patrick, the recipient of Boethius's *in Topica Ciceronis* (no. 16 of the *Trivium*).
[10] The text of the *Ordo*, also known as the *Anecdoton Holderi*, is now conveniently available in the Corpus Christianorum edition of Cassiodorus's *Variae* (n. 7 above), pp. v–vi.
[11] R. Peiper, ed., *Boetii Philosophiae consolationis libri quinque*, Leipzig, 1871.

Commentaries on the 'Opuscula Sacra'

1. s. ix[mid]. *The Auxerre commentary on Op. Sac. I–V*
Carolingian manuscripts of the *Opuscula Sacra* usually have marginal glosses, and such annotation can also be found *seriatim*, as a continuous commentary with lemmata. One such commentary was published by E. K. Rand in 1906, with an over-confident attribution to John Scottus Eriugena.[12] Maieul Cappuyns, in a classic article, showed that this commentary, found in twenty Carolingian manuscripts (some marginal in format, some continuous) extended to all five treatises, that it existed in two recensions and that its likely author was Remigius of Auxerre.[13] Cappuyns also found an internal date of 867/91.[14] See most recently C. Jeudy, 'L'oeuvre de Remi d'Auxerre: état de la question', in *L'École carolingienne d'Auxerre: de Muretach à Remi 830–908*, ed. D. Iogna-Prat et al., Paris, 1991, pp. 373–97 (379–80). Whether or not Auxerre was the principal point of dissemination, this type of broadly Carolingian commentary on the *Opuscula Sacra* persisted throughout Europe into the late twelfth century.[15] Fine examples in the present volume are MS Cambridge, King's College, 3 and MS Oxford, Bodleian Library, Laud Misc. 457.
inc. Quinti dicebantur uel a kalendario, quo aut nati fuerant aut memorabile aliquid egerant, uel quod quinquies consulatum meruerant. *Aurelius* dicitur ab aura, id est a claritate, quam pro sapientia et nobilitate meruerat. Aura enim dicitur splendor; *expl.* sed illud specialius bonum est, quod per iustitiam boni operis deo placet quodque et a deo bonum est et a se iustum est, deo tamen donante. *Praescribit.* approbat, commendat.

s. xii[mid]. *The Schools of Northern France (2–4)*

2. 1140. Gilbert of Poitiers (Gilbert de la Porrée), *Commentary on 'Opuscula Sacra' I–III, V*
First prologue *inc.* Libros questionum Anicii quos exhortationibus precibusque

---

[12] E. K. Rand, *Johannes Scottus*, in *Quellen und Untersuchungen zur lateinischen Philologie des Mittelalters*, ed. L. Traube, I.ii, Munich, 1906, pp. 30–80.
[13] M. Cappuyns, 'Le plus ancien commentaire des "Opuscula Sacra" et son origine', *Recherches de théologie ancienne et médiévale*, 3, 1931, pp. 237–72.
[14] Ibid., p. 262.
[15] G. d'Onofrio, 'Giovanni Scoto e Remigio d'Auxerre: a proposito di alcuni commenti altomedievali a Boezio', *Studi medievali*, n.s. 22, 1981, pp. 587–693; F. Troncarelli, 'Aristoteles Piscatorius: note sulle opere teologiche di Boezio e sulla lora fortuna', *Scriptorium*, 42, 1988, pp. 3–19 [= Troncarelli, 'Opuscula'].

multorum suscepimus explanandos; *expl.* incommutabili proposito sue uoluntatis perscribit.

Second prologue *inc.* Omnium que rebus percipiendis suppeditant rationum alie communes sunt multorum generum; *expl.* proprias rationes theologicis communicauerunt esse deceptos.

inc. Premittit prologum in quo quamuis illud de quo locuturus est obscurum sit et plurimis ad cognoscendum difficillimis rebus implicitum minime tamen uerbis apertis sese locuturum promittit; *expl. causa* incommutabili proposito sue uoluntatis *prescribit.*

Edition: N. M. Häring, *The Commentaries on Boethius by Gilbert of Poitiers*, Toronto, 1966. We have included all manuscripts of Gilbert's commentary that contain the complete text of *Opuscula Sacra* I–III, V.

3. 1145. Clarembald of Arras, *Commentary on 'Opuscula Sacra' I–III, V*
Prefatory letter *inc.* Cum regimini scolarum accitus ab episcopo Laudunensi, qui nunc urbi praesidet; *expl.* opus istud supposui.

introduction *inc.* Tria sunt quae hominum uitam ita uicissim occupant; *expl.* sine diuino afflatu fuit.

Op. Sac. I inc. Virgilius in libro Georgicorum res humiles, id est apes, quadam amplificatione conatur extollere; *Op. Sac. V expl.* nullum bonum criminamur.

Edition: N. M. Häring, *Life and Works of Clarembald of Arras: A Twelfth-Century Master of the School of Chartres*, Toronto, 1965.

4. 1148+. Thierry of Chartres, *Commentary on 'Opuscula Sacra' I, III, V*
inc. I Inchoantibus librum hunc de trinitate primo uidendum est que sit auctoris intentio; *expl.* I saltem uoluntas supplebit. Thierry's exposition of III is extant only as a fragment and as a late abridgement; his exposition of V is extant as a 'reportatio' (Häring) and as a late abridgement.

Edition: N. M. Häring, *Commentaries on Boethius by Thierry of Chartres and His School*, Studies and Texts 20, Toronto, 1971.

5. 1256. Thomas Aquinas, *Commentary on 'Opuscula Sacra' I.i-ii and III*
I. Prologue inc. Naturalis mentis humane intuitus, pondere corruptibilis corporis aggrauatus; *expl.* et abscondita produxit in lucem.

Text *inc.* Huic ergo operi prohemium premittit. In quo tria facit; *expl.* 'Omne namque esse ex forma est' (I.ii.21, p.10)…quamuis enim homo naturaliter inclinetur in finem ultimum, non tamen potest naturaliter illum consequi set solum per gratiam; et hoc est propter eminentiam illius finis.

III. *inc.* Habet hoc priuilegium sapiencie studium quod operi suo prosequendo magis ipsa sibi sufficiat; *expl.* et tamen 'omnia' sunt 'bona' in quantum deriuantur a primo bono.

Edition: *S. Thomae de Aquino Opera omnia*, Leonine edition, Rome etc., 1992, 50, pp. 75–171, 267–82.

Symbolum Boethii

inc. Credimus sanctam trinitatem id est patrem et filium et spiritum sanctum unum deum omnipotentem et unius substancie unius essencie unius potestatis; *expl.* cuius uisio eterna erit omnium sanctorum beatitudo et gloria. Gratia et pax a deo patre et filio Iesu Christo domino nostro sit ista confitenti in omnia secula seculorum. Amen.

Edition: *PL*, 101: 56D–58C.

An early Carolingian creed, perhaps the work of Alcuin, which is attributed to Boethius by the Augustinian friar, John Capgrave (d. 1464).[16] In his *De fidei symbolis* Capgrave gives the text of nineteen creeds from the Apostles' Creed onwards; Boethius succeeds Augustine. See MS Oxford, All Souls College, 17, fols 38^r–39^r (catalogue: Watson, pp. 43–45), Capgrave's autograph; and MS Oxford, Balliol College, 190, fols 40^v–42^v (catalogue: Mynors, pp. 190–92). The dedicatory epistle to William Gray, bishop of Ely, is printed by F. C. Hingeston, *Johannis Capgrave Liber de illustribus Henricis*, London, 1858, pp. 213–17. Compare the collection in MS Karlsruhe, Badische Landesbibliothek, Aug. XVIII (s. ix^{in}), in which *Op. Sac.* I–II do duty as 'the creed of Boethius'.[17]

v. DE CONSOLATIONE PHILOSOPHIAE, 5 bks: DCPhil.

Peiper's Teubner edition of 1871 was in principle replaced by Stewart and Rand for Loeb (1918), by Weinberger for CSEL (1934),[18] by the revised Loeb edition of 1973 and by Ludwig Bieler for CCSL (1984).[19] We have again used Loeb, referring to the proses and metres by the continuous line-numbering of the 1973 edition. We have noted the presence of elaborate *tituli* and colophons, as a likely guide to the textual group to which a manuscript may belong.[20] Rhetorical 'labels' in the margins of some (generally older) manuscripts identify the rhetorical strategy in the text to which they refer: e.g., apostrophe, question, definition.

---

[16] Emden, *BRUC*, pp. 121–22.

[17] Note Capgrave's reference to another creed found 'in quodam antiquo codice' (MS Oxford, Balliol College 190, fol. 52^r: Mynors, p .191). We are indebted here to Fiona Robb for sound advice.

[18] G. Weinberger, *Anicii Manlii Severini Boetii Philosophiae consolationis libri quinque*, CSEL 67, Vienna and Leipzig, 1934.

[19] L. Bieler, ed., *Anicii Manlii Severini Boetii Philosophiae Consolatio*, CCSL 94, Turnhout, 1984.

[20] Details in the editions of Weinberger and Bieler. A thorough analysis is planned in the Introduction to vol. IV, *Italy and Vatican City*.

inc. Carmina qui quondam studio florente peregi; *expl.* ante oculos agitis iudicis cuncta cernentis.

Commentaries on the 'De consolatione philosophiae'

Pierre Courcelle's remarkable study of the *Consolation* 'dans la tradition littéraire' (1967) includes twenty-six commentaries from the earlier ninth century to the late fifteenth.[21] Most are unpublished, and few have been fully examined. Yet they confirm the essential pattern of commentary on the *De consolatione philosophiae*: Carolingian, scholastic and humanist. In 1977 Diane Bolton published an article on glossed manuscripts of the *Consolation* written in pre-conquest England; in 1981 Fabio Troncarelli brought to general attention several manuscripts with late antique features in their *mise-en-page*, and marginal annotation that was distinctly prior to the 'Remigian' norm; in 1983 Joseph S. Wittig showed that King Alfred's vernacular 'Boethius' had drawn on continental material that was again distinctly earlier than that commonly ascribed to mid-century Auxerre.[22] There is still much to do. We have where possible identified or characterized glosses accompanying the text of the *Consolation*. Continuous commentary with lemmata (i.e., without the full text of the *Consolation*) is noted only where it appears in a manuscript with which we are already concerned.

s. ix-x. *Carolingian commentary* (1–8)

1. s. ix^mid. *The basic commentary, current in Laon and Auxerre.*
inc. Carmina qui quondam. Sensus est talis: qui olim carmina iocunda et delectabilia feci *florente*, id est laeto, *studio* sed digno labore *cogor*; *expl.* imperf. (V.m.iv.1) id est circumcalco. inde peripatetici.
Edition: E. T. Silk, *Saeculi noni auctoris in Boetii Consolationem philosophiae commentarius*, Rome, 1935. See also H. F. Stewart, 'A Commentary by Remigius Autissiodorensis on the *De consolatione philosophiae* of Boethius', *Journal of Theological Studies*, 17, 1916, pp. 22–42; Courcelle, pp. 405–6 (Remigius of Auxerre); and C. Jeudy 'L'oeuvre de Remi d'Auxerre: état de la question', in *L'École carolingienne d'Auxerre: de Muretach à Remi 830–908*, ed. D. Iogna-Prat et al., Paris, 1991, pp. 373–97 (388). This is the only Carolingian commentary to have been published in full. Several dozen further manuscripts, perhaps more, are witness to the complexity of the tradition.

---

[21] P. Courcelle, *La Consolation de philosophie dans la tradition littéraire*, Paris, 1967.

[22] J. S. Wittig, 'King Alfred's Boethius and Its Latin Sources: A Reconsideration', *Anglo-Saxon England*, 11, 1983, pp. 157–98.

2. s. ix. *The St Gall commentary*

inc. Studio, id est doctrina; *florente*, laeto, id est dum flore iuuentutis gauderem. Ennius et Lucretius flores dicunt omnes quod nitidum est; *expl.* id est uere uel feliciter.

Unpublished; extant in about a dozen manuscripts, wholly or in part. See Courcelle, pp. 403–4.

3. s. ix. *The Vatican commentary*

inc. Carmina, cantus delectabiles; *peregi*, perfecte feci; *flebilis*, lacrimabilis; *expl.* indicta instructa.

Unpublished; extant only in MS Vatican City, Biblioteca Apostolica Vaticana, Vat. lat. 3363 (s. ix). See Courcelle, p. 404, and F. Troncarelli, 'Per una ricerca sui commenti altomedievali al *De consolatione* di Boezio', in *Miscellanea in memoria di Giorgio Cencetti*, Turin, 1973, pp. 363–80, giving excerpts, and idem, *Tradizioni*, pp. 150–96.

4–8. s. ix-x. *Various commentaries on III.m.ix, 'O qui perpetua'*

Editions: R. B. C. Huygens, 'Mittelalterliche Kommentare zum "O qui perpetua", *Sacris erudiri*, 6, 1954, pp. 373–427, with further references. See also Courcelle, pp. 406–8.

Pre-scholastic commentary

9. s. xii$^{2/4}$: Paris. *William of Conches*

inc. Boetius tractaturus de philosophica consolatione primitus ostendit se talem qui indigeat consolatione, ostendens se miserum; *expl.* variable. See MS Troyes, Bibliothèque municipale, 1381, and in the present volume MS London, BL, Harley 2559.

Edition: C. Jourdain, 'Des commentaires inédits de Guillaume de Conches et de Nicolas Triveth sur la Consolation de la philosophie de Boèce', *Notices et extraits*, 22.2, 1862, pp. 40–82 (extensive excerpts); edition forthcoming by H. Westra and L. Nauta. See also Courcelle, pp. 408–10; Minnis, *Chaucer*, pp. 6–11.

William of Conches confirmed the status of the *Consolation* as a classroom text. His commentary was thus still being rewritten and expanded long after his death.

Carolingian and pre-scholastic commentary persists into the later twelfth century, and perhaps beyond. In this category we include the four anonymous commentaries listed by Courcelle, pp. 410–12; cf. also Minnis, *Chaucer*, p. 8 n. 28. Further unexamined examples may be seen in the present volume.

s. xii-xv. *Scholastic and humanist commentary* 10–22

10. s. xiii[1/2]. *Ps.-William of Conches*
inc. Boecius tractaturus de philosophica consolatione primitus se ostendit talem qui indigeat consolatione. uidelicet ostendendo se miserum.
Unpublished: see MS Dijon, Bibliothèque municipale, 254 and in the present volume MS London, BL, Royal 15 B.III.
Formerly regarded as a 'second recension' by William of Conches himself, this commentary has now been conclusively redated to the early thirteenth century (Minnis, *Chaucer*, Appendix I, by L. Nauta).

11. s.xiii[2/2]. *William of Aragon*
inc. Sicut scribit Philosophus primo Politicorum, omnia appetunt bonum. Quod non tantum auctoritate Philosophi sed ratione; *expl.* tibi laus sit honor et gloria in saecula saeculorum. Amen.
Unpublished. See Courcelle, p. 414; C. I. Terbille, 'William of Aragon's Commentary on Boethius's *De consolatione philosophiae*' (unpublished PhD thesis, University of Michigan, 1972); Minnis in Gibson, pp. 312–61 (314–33); Minnis, *Chaucer*, p. 33, whose earlier dating (following Crespo) we accept.

12. c. 1300. *Nicholas Trivet, O.P.*
inc. pref. Explanationem librorum Boecii de consolatione philosophica aggressur-us, uotis quorundam fratrum satisfacere cupiens qui me censentes ex ordinis predicatorum professione tam maioribus quam minoribus apostolico debito obligatum; *expl. pref.* dicta sufficiunt.
inc. comm. 'Consolaciones tue letificauerunt animam meam.' (Ps. 93.19). Inter letare et letificari interesse uidetur quod letari dicimus … ut patet per Boecium in prologo musice sue. Volens igitur Boecius agere de consolacione philosophica primo indicit; *expl.* iudicio *cernentis cuncta* (V. pr.vi.176), qui est dominus deus noster Iesus cui est honor et gloria in secula seculorum. Amen.
Unpublished: see C. Jourdain, 'Des commentaires inédits de Guillaume de Conches et de Nicolas Triveth sur la Consolation de la philosophie de Boèce', *Notices et extraits*, 22.2, 1862, pp. 40–82 (extensive excerpts). E. T. Silk's 'complete but unfinalized edition' (Minnis, *Chaucer*, p. 35) has been made available to Minnis and other scholars. See also Courcelle, pp. 412–13.
Trivet's is the classic scholastic commentary. His text remained very widely known, and apparently stable, for two centuries. Curiously, it failed to attract the attention of Renaissance editors and publishers.

13. flor. 1309–16. *William Wheteley*
Introduction: *inc.* Philosophie seruias ut tibi contingat uera libertas. Ista propositio

scripta est a Seneca in quadam epistola ad Lucillum; *expl.* natura est indestructibile et inauferribile quid.

Text: *inc.* Hic est sciendum quod Boetius hic non ponit prohemium. Cuius causa potest esse quia hoc subito mutatus de magna felicitate; *expl.* excellencie sue deitatis possimus pertingere.

Unpublished: see H. F. Sebastian, 'William of Wheteley's (fl. 1309–16) Commentary on the Pseudo-Boethius's Tractate *De disciplina scolarium* and Medieval Grammar School Education' (unpublished PhD thesis, Columbia University, 1971); Minnis, in Gibson, pp. 312–61 (315, 354). A grammar school adaptation of Trivet, extant in a few fine English manuscripts, but never widely current. Not to be identified with 22 below.

14–21. s. xiv–xv. Nine later scholastic and humanist commentaries, including those of Pierre d'Ailly and Denis the Carthusian, are discussed by Courcelle, pp. 415–18.

22. s. xv. *Ps.-Aquinas*

inc. Philosophie seruias oportet ut tibi contingat uera libertas; *expl.* Sicut enim scribitur ad hebreos, quarto. Omnia nuda et aperta sunt oculis eius qui est deus benedictus in secula seculorum.

Edition: A. Koberger, Nuremberg, 1473 (*GW* 4573, Proctor 1966, Goff B–816). Ps.-Aquinas is a fifteenth-century German tradition of commentary, which achieved considerable circulation as a printed edition. Courcelle, pp. 322–23, 414–15; but see Minnis, in Gibson, pp. 312–61 (354); and Palmer, ibid., pp. 362–409 (363 and 399).

vi. VITAE BOETII

In some manuscripts a *Vita Boetii* either precedes the *Consolation* or is set as a marginal gloss to the *titulus* of Book I. Thus ANICII MANLII SEVERINI BOETII triggers an account of Boethius's family, his literary achievements and / or his role in politics, his imprisonment and martyr's death. In substance the *Vita* is pre-Carolingian, and perhaps sixth-century; but in form it survives as at least seven interrelated *Vitae*, each with its merits and none manifestly superior to the rest. To Peiper's six *Vitae* we add *Vita VII*, as associated with the commentary of William of Conches (c. 1130). The later history of this material is as an item in the *Accessus ad auctores*,[23] and as the introductory chapter in any commentary on the

---

[23] R. B. C. Huygens, *Accessus ad auctores: Bernard d'Utrecht, Conrad d'Hirsau*, Leiden, 1970, pp. 47–48.

Consolation, whether scholastic or humanist.

Vita I: *inc*. Tempore Theodorici regis insignis auctor Boetius claruit; *expl*. nec Virgilio in metro inferior floruit.
List of twenty-six MSS in Silk, *Commentarius*, pp. lvi–lviii.

Vita II: *inc*. Iste Boetius consul fuit Romanorum Theodorico duce, eo tempore inuaserunt Gothi Romam et abstulerunt libertatem eorum; *expl*. amicis eius circumstantibus gladiis interemptus est.

Vita III: *inc*. Boetius iste de familia fuit Manlii Torquati nobilissimi uiri; *expl*. de instabilitate et mutabilitate fortunae.

Vita IV: *inc*. Queritur a nonnullis quo tempore fuit iste Boetius. Dicunt enim quidam quod fuit tempore Marciani imperatoris; *expl*. nec Homero in metro inferior uideatur.

Vita V: *inc*. Hic liber componitur quinque partibus. id est de genere specie differentia de proprio et accidenti; *expl*. habens etiam qua gradatim ad summum gradum perueniebat.

Vita VI: *inc*. Anno dominicae incarnationis quadringentesimo quinto Odoacer quidam rex barbarus inuasit Italiam; *expl*. et uocatur sanctus Seuerinus a prouincialibus quod ei prenomen fuit.

I–VI ed. R. Peiper, *Boetii Philosophiae consolationis libri quinque*, Leipzig, 1871, pp. xxix–xxxv.

Vita VII: *inc*. Iste Boecius nobilissimus ciuis Romanus et fide catholicus extitit, qui contra Nestorium et Eutychen duos maximos hereticos comprobauit; *expl*. quia facit in hoc opere de philosophica consolatione dicitur tractare.
ed. C. Jourdain, *Notices et extraits*, 22.2, 1862, from MS Troyes, Bibliothèque municipale 1101; text here from MS London, BL, Harley 2559, fol. 34^r.

vii. EPITAPHS

I. Boethius:
inc. Hic iacet interpres et alumpnus philosophie; *expl*. nomen per secula uiuit.
Edition: R. Peiper, *Boetii Philosophiae consolationis libri quinque*, Teubner, Leipzig, 1871, p. xxxv.

II. Helpis, his reputed first wife:
inc. Helpis dicta fui Siculae regionis alumna; *expl.* nectat uterque cinis.
Edition: Peiper, pp. xxxvi-xxxvii.
Tradition had it that Boethius married first Helpis, daughter of Festus, and by her had two sons, both future consuls: Hypatius and Patricius.[24]

III. Boethius:
inc. Heu mallus ille sapor, quo uenit mortis amaror.
Walther 7765: an unpublished epitaph that occurs only in MS Oxford, Balliol College, 141, fol. 50^{r-v} (s. xv).

viii. LUPUS OF FERRIÈRES, *DE METRIS*

Quite a common adjunct to the *Consolation* (and a very helpful one) is Lupus's exposition of the twenty-seven verse-forms that Boethius uses in the *metra*.
inc. Quinque libros philosophicae consolationis insignis auctor Boetius xxvii uarietatibus carminum respersit; *expl.* eiusque initium est: 'Quam uariis terras animalia permeant figuris'. Several MSS add: Obserua autem quisque legeris finalem sillabam in omnibus metris indifferenter accipi. Dimetrum uero uel trimetrum uel tetrametrum in metris iambicis trochaicis et anapesticis per duplices. In reliquis uero per simplices computari.

Edition: R. Peiper, *Boetii Philosophiae consolationis libri quinque*, Teubner, Leipzig, 1871, pp. xxiiii-xxviiii; discussed by V. Brown, 'Lupus of Ferrières on the Metres of Boethius', in *Latin Script and Letters A.D. 400–900: Festschrift presented to Ludwig Bieler on the Occasion of his 70th Birthday*, ed. J. J. O'Meara and B. Naumann, Leiden, 1976, pp. 63–79.

ix. VERNACULAR TRANSLATIONS

The *Census* does not include the multifarious vernacular translations of the *Consolation of Philosophy*. We have even omitted manuscripts containing the complete Latin text as an element in a vernacular 'package': e.g., MS London, BL, Harley 43, Walton's English translation of the *De consolatione philosophiae* with the Latin original in the margin; and MSS Harley 4335–39, the five-volume pocket set of *Le Livre de Boece de Consolation*, with luxury illumination by the workshop

---

[24] Martindale, *Prosopography* (n. 5 above), ii.537–38; iii.581.

of Jean Colombe.[25]

1. **English** (a-c)

a. c. 890. The earliest vernacular translation by nearly half a millenium is the prose version attributed to King Alfred or to his immediate patronage in the court of Wessex. This Anglo-Saxon text remained current and consulted into the fourteenth century.

Edition: *King Alfred's Old English Version of Boethius' 'De consolatione philosophiae'*, ed. W. J. Sedgefield, Oxford, 1899.

M. Godden, in Gibson, pp. 419–24, confirming Alfred's authorship; J. S. Wittig, 'King Alfred's Boethius and Its Latin Sources', *Anglo-Saxon England*, 11, 1983, pp. 157–98; B. S. Donaghey in Minnis, *Medieval Boethius*, pp. 1–31.

b. c. 1380. Chaucer's *Boece* is a prose version of Boethius's Latin text, with help from Nicholas Trivet (c. 1300: see above) and from *Li Livres de Confort* of Jean de Meun (c. 1305: see below).

Edition: *The Riverside Chaucer*, ed. L. D. Benson, Oxford, 1988, pp. 395–469.

Minnis, in Gibson, pp. 312–61 (341); idem, *Chaucer's 'Boece' and the Medieval Tradition of Boethius*, Cambridge, 1993.

c. 1410. John Walton's verse translation of the *Consolation* is fundamentally dependent on Chaucer's *Boece*. It was quite widely current in the fifteenth century. First edition: Tavistock, 1525 (Gibson, pl. XIII); *Boethius: De consolatione philosophiae translated by John Walton Canon of Osney* (*Short Title Catalogue*, no. 3200); critical text by M. Science, Early English Texts Society, Old Series 170, London, 1927; Minnis, in Gibson, pp. 312–61 (343–47).

2. **French** (a-c)

For a succinct overview see R. A. Dwyer, *Boethian Fictions: Narratives in the Medieval French Versions of the 'Consolatio philosophiae'*, Cambridge, Mass., 1976, pp. 129–31.

a. c. 1305. Jean de Meun's prose translation of Boethius's text, *Li Livres de Confort*, was influential throughout the fourteenth and fifteenth centuries, without

---

[25] *Renaissance Painting in Manuscripts: Treasures from the British Library*, 1983–84 at J. Paul Getty Museum, Pierpont Morgan Library and the British Library, exhibition catalogue, ed. T. Kren, New York etc., 1983, pp. 157–62.

being the 'standard' edition (b below).
Edition: V.-L. Dedeck-Héry, 'Boethius' *De consolatione* by Jean de Meun',
Medieval Studies, 14, 1952, pp. 165–275. See G. L. Cropp in Minnis, *Medieval Boethius*, pp. 63–88.

b. c. 1360. The anonymous *Livre de Boece de Consolation* (also known to scholars as 'The Anonymous Verse-Prose Translation') makes use of both *Li Livres de Confort* and the Latin commentary of William of Conches in its revised form (s. xiii[1/2]: see above).
Unpublished edition by J. K. Atkinson and G. M. Cropp: see Cropp in Minnis, *Medieval Boethius*, p. 64 n. 10.

c. s. xiv. For other French versions see Cropp, as above, and J. K. Atkinson in Minnis, *Medieval Boethius*, pp. 32–62.

3. German (a-f)

a. s. ix-x. Old High German glosses to the *Consolation* and to other works of Boethius testify to his role as a school author in northern Europe.[26]

b. c. 1000. Notker III of St Gall, 'der Deutsche'.
Edition: J. C. King and P. W. Tax, *Boethius, 'De consolatione philosophiae'*, Altdeutsche Textbibliothek, 94, 100 and 101, Tübingen, 1986–90. See S. Sonderegger, *Althochdeutsche Sprache und Literatur*, Berlin etc., 1974, pp. 106–11; Palmer in Gibson, pp. 362–409, with references; E. Hellgardt, 'Notker Teutonicus: Überlegungen zum Stand der Forschung', *Beiträge zur Geschichte der deutschen Sprache und Literatur*, 108, 1986, pp. 190–205 and 109, 1987, pp. 201–221; N. Henkel, *Deutsche Übersetzungen lateinischer Schultexte: ihre Verbreitung und Funktion in Mittelalter und in der frühen Neuzeit, mit einem Verzeichnis der Texte*, Münchener Texte und Untersuchungen 90, Munich, 1988, pp. 223–24. Notker is discussed in the introduction to *Codices Boethiani* II.

The translation of 1401 by the Benedictine Peter von Kastl has not been identified.[27] This is a very early instance of the German vernacular rendering of a major classical text, second only to the German Valerius Maximus by Heinrich von Mügeln.[28] From the mid-fifteenth century three translations (c, d, e) survive

---

[26] F. J. Worstbrock, 'Boethius', in *Verfasserlexikon*, i.919–27.
[27] Ibid., i.921–2.
[28] See K. Stackmann, in *Verfasserlexikon*, iii.815–27.

in manuscript and another (f) in the bilingual printed edition of 1473. None had a wide circulation.

c. s. xv^{mid}. Münster fragments (Middle Low German).
Edition: A. Bömer, 'Fragmente einer gereimten deutschen Boetiusübersetzung', *Zeitschrift für deutsches Altertum*, 50, 1908, pp. 149–58. See Palmer in Gibson, pp. 362–409.

d. 1465. MS Oxford, Bodleian Library, Hamilton 46.
Apparently the translator's original copy, possibly made in the Charterhouse at Erfurt; associated in the manuscript with the name Rotger Scheffer; unedited. See Palmer in Gibson, pp. 362–409.

e. by 1467. Konrad Humery.
Unedited. Proto-humanist translation.[29] See F. J. Worstbrock in *Verfasserlexikon* iv.301–4.

f. 1473. Anton Koberger's edition of the *De consolatione philosophiae* (22 above) includes a complete German translation, anonymous and distinct from c, d, e, in addition to the commentary of Ps.-Aquinas.
GW 4573; Goff B-816.

Versions in other vernaculars, notably Spanish and Italian, will be noted in later volumes of *Codices Boethiani*.

x. INTERIM REPORT

The 247 manuscripts in the present volume do not constitute a coherent *fonds*, relatively undisturbed since the Middle Ages. For that we must look to St Victor, St Gall or the monastic libraries that were transferred to Munich in 1803 lock, stock and barrel. The manuscripts in Great Britain and the Republic of Ireland represent fragments of medieval libraries and longer sequences of aristocratic collections in the seventeenth and eighteenth centuries. As to the cultural inferences that may be drawn from the manuscripts here described, three may be chosen as illustrative. The logic in Gonville and Caius College, Cambridge, is witness to Boethius's status as an author studied by undergraduates in Oxford and

---

[29] Cf. Niklas van Wyle, d. 1479, a prolific translator of Italian humanist literature, author of another translation of the *DCPhil.*, which has not survived. See Worstbrock, *Verfasserlexikon*, vi.1016–35 (1022).

Cambridge in the thirteenth and fourteenth centuries. Secondly, manuscripts of the *De arithmetica* (and to a lesser extent the *De musica*) have significant technical annotation as late as the mid-thirteenth century. Finally, the *De consolatione philosophiae* makes the transition from central scholarly text in the earlier Middle Ages to Everyman's text in the later. Other such patterns will quickly be evident to the ingenious reader.

xi. TOWARDS ANALYSIS

Our intention in compiling *Codices Boethiani* is certainly not to do all the work on Boethius or his commentators, nor to signal that work as somehow 'ours'. Far from it. Our aim is to make clear for others where and what work may be usefully done, and to point them in the direction of interesting texts. To that end, our manuscript descriptions are not exhaustive codicological entries, but rather made for a purpose, which is to attempt to make clear the varieties of Boethius manuscript, their contexts and the extent they have been used. In naming this section 'towards analysis', we aim to provide only a sketch map of the terrain for which this conspectus is the gazetteer. It is designed to aid others to make the complete ordnance survey.

One of the dangers of working with one project or group of texts for any length of time is that one forgets what was unknown in the beginning. This brief overview of which Boethian texts were common and when, and how and with what fellow-travellers they appear, may be obvious to some readers. They must bear with us. Clearly, these remarks are not definitive. We draw our statistics only from the entries in this volume of the conspectus (the UK and Ireland), so that the manuscripts suffer from the specificity of their present location and the accident of their survival. Conversely, this is reasonably large sample and so is a not unreasonable way of considering the history of a family of texts.

This volume of manuscripts in the UK and Ireland contains 247 entries. They date from the ninth to the early sixteenth centuries and are found in all varieties and conditions, from fragments used as limp protective wrappers for other texts (e.g., MS Cambridge, Trinity College, s. n., a tenth-century fragment of the *Cat.*) to showy Italian coffee-table copies made for wealthy private collectors (e.g., MS London, BL, Harley 3302). Some manuscripts contain more than one of Boethius's works. In all, there are 439 separate Boethian items, counting each of the logical texts individually, plus 16 *vitae* and 5 *epitaphs*. However, most of the logical texts occur as constituent parts of logical compendia, the *logica vetus* and *logica nova*, so that generally we have counted a collected volume of logic as one text, rather than as the total number of its constituents. This gives a figure of 296 Boethian texts, and it is this number we used to calculate the percentages given below. The

figures themselves can never be precise: we have had to do some grouping of texts
and judging of types. In particular, the high number of fragmentary logical texts,
some of which may well come from the same original manuscript, may be
skewing the statistics. Our intention is not to give exact counts but rather to make
clear the ratios between numbers of surviving texts in order to give the reader an
idea of popularity and use.

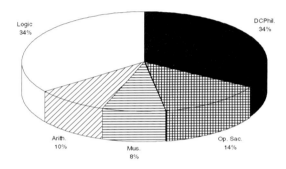

Figure 1 - Frequency of Texts

By far the most common text is the *De consolatione philosophiae*. With 100
surviving manuscripts, it makes up 33.8% of the total, more than twice as common
as any other text. Most come without commentary: only about 25% of the *DCPhil.*
manuscripts have a commentary attached, of which about 60% are Nicholas Trivet,
20% are commentaries by other named authors, such as William Wheteley, and
20% anonymous. Almost all the glossed *DCPhil.* texts date from the fourteenth
century.

The next most common text is the group of five little treatises on the nature of
God, known as the *Opuscula Sacra*. This is not a collective title used very often
in the manuscripts themselves, certainly not in early ones, although they are
sometimes known by the subject of the first treatise, *De trinitate*. There are forty

Op. Sac. manuscripts, making up 13.5% of the total texts catalogued; but the picture is more complicated with them than with the *DCPhil.*, for whereas the *DCPhil.* is almost always given as the whole text, missing parts by mistake or accident but not generally by design, the *Op. Sac.* have a rather more interesting history of transmission. Half (50%) of the *Op. Sac.* texts are partial 'by choice', purposely omitting one or more of the *opuscula*. The most common configuration (20%) leaves out *Op. Sac. IV*, *De fide catholica*. This omission, which appears in no extant manuscript earlier than the twelfth century, reflects an uncertainty about the authenticity of *De fide*, reinforced by its not having been included in the most popular commentary on the *Op. Sac.*, that of Gilbert of Poitiers.[30] Some manuscripts, then, copied only *Op. Sac. I–III, V* to accommodate Gilbert's commentary; others contained all five *Op. Sac.*, leaving *IV* unglossed. Elsewhere, each of the *opuscula* appears individually, *I* and *II* occur together three times, and one manuscript contains *I, II,* and *V*.

The texts of the *De musica* and the *De arithmetica* make up respectively 8.4% (25 texts) and 9.5% (28 texts) of the total number. *Mus.* and *Arith.* occur together, or are bound together in a set, ten times in all. Both were quadrivial texts, and both are heavily geometrical in content. They often *look* alike, since they have the potential for numerous diagrams and tables. A standard set of diagrams and tables went with the texts, but their execution was more varied. They can range from being completely omitted, or being omitted with space left for later insertions, to scrawled additions done almost as afterthoughts (e.g., MS Oxford, Bodleian Library, Bodl. 309), sometimes added in the margins to integrally planned, beautifully coloured and executed productions (e.g., MS Oxford, Bodleian Library, Laud Lat. 54).

The logical texts are divided into Boethius's translations of Aristotle, Cicero and Porphyry, and his original treatises and commentaries, usually appearing in sets containing the *logica vetus* or *logica nova* or both. Copies of any one of these texts individually are rare. Except in cases where a commentary appears with another text of that author (e.g., *1 in Isag.* appears with Isidore's *Etymologies* in MS London, BL, Harley 2713), or in the special case of the *Top. Diff.* (see below), survivals of single books tend to be fragments or incomplete logical sets. The vast majority of fragmentary texts are parts of thirteenth-century *logic* manuscripts, torn apart in the fifteenth and sixteenth centuries, when they were no longer key school texts, to form pastedowns for new printed books. A typical set of the *logica vetus* in these manuscripts consists of Boethius's translations of Porphyry's *Isag.*, Aristotle's *Cat.* (the *Praedicamenta*) and *De Int.* (the *Peri hermenias*), the *Liber sex principiorum*, Boethius's own *Div.*, and *Top. Diff.* The *logica nova* is the

---

[30] N. M. Häring, 'The Commentary of Gilbert of Poitiers on Boethius' *De Hebdomadibus*', *Traditio*, 9, 1953, pp. 177–211.

translations of Aristotle's *Soph. Elench.*, *Topica Aris.*, *Prior Anal.*, and the non-Boethian translation of *Post. Anal.* The *logica vetus* makes up 8.4% of the UK manuscripts, and the *logica nova* another 7.1% (24 and 19 manuscripts respectively). In addition, miscellaneous individual texts of the logical translations make up 13.5% of the total, and one-off copies of the commentaries and original logical treatises 5.7%, bringing the logical texts in their various guises to 34.7% of the UK total. The only single logical text which survives in more than three or four individual copies (not including binding fragments), and which is clearly intended to exist on its own, is the *Top. Diff.*, which appears in eleven manuscripts (3.7% of total). All or part of *Top. Diff.* may be present; *Top. Diff. IV*, which is a handy crib on the difference between dialectic and rhetoric, is often found alongside Cicero, *De inventione* and the *Ad Herennium*, or with Priscian. The UK manuscripts, however, boast the oldest known copy of the *Topica Aris.*, an eleventh-century fragment at St Mary's College, Oscott.

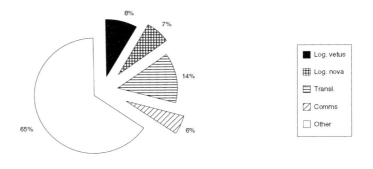

Figure 2 - Logic texts

The surviving texts illustrate a fluctuation of interest over time. The *DCPhil.* has a relatively large number of surviving manuscripts from the ninth to eleventh centuries, reaching a peak in the twelfth century and again, massively, in the fourteenth century: in comparison, the thirteenth century is uninterested in the text. Numbers seem to decline in the fifteenth century, but in fact our figures do not reflect the popularity of vernacular translations of the *DCPhil.* and early printed editions. More than sixty Latin editions of the *DCPhil.* were printed before 1500, as well as vernacular editions in French, Spanish, Catalan, German and English.[31] In fact, the *DCPhil.* gained in readership in the fifteenth century with the growth of humanist ideas and the fashion for Latin classics.

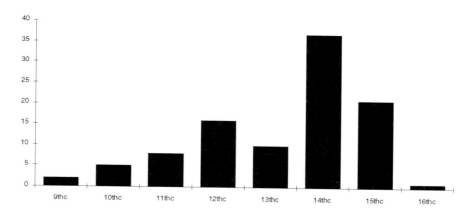

Figure 3 - DCPhil. by date

In contrast, the *Op. Sac.* numbers are concentrated in the twelfth and thirteenth centuries, although two ninth-century manuscripts are extant, and there are *Op. Sac.* survivals right through the period. As popular short expositions of complex theological ideas, the *Op. Sac.* had a steady audience. The nature of God and the basics of the faith were not subject to theological fashion; these works were primers which could be usefully given to the *iuniores*. The *Op. Sac.* texts often came with a Carolingian gloss or, in the twelfth century, the commentary of Gilbert of Poitiers. Of the surviving *Op. Sac.* texts, 25% (10) can be dated to the

---

[31] *Incunable Short-Title Catalogue* (British Library database in course of compilation), s.v. 'Boethius'.

second half of the twelfth century, when Gilbert's attentions gave them a new lease on life. Almost all twelfth- and thirteenth-century *Op. Sac.* manuscripts are glossed or have notes to the text. The *Op. Sac.* were handy, brief and simple texts on a difficult subject. As such, they had a long and relatively stable shelf-life.

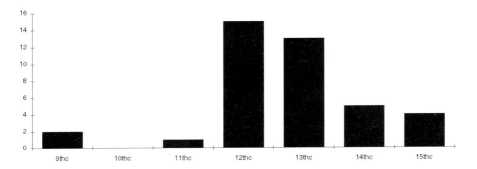

Figure 4 - Op. Sac. by date

Although manuscripts of the *Arith.* and *Mus.* have come down from the whole of our period, it is very clear from the survivals that these works flourished in the twelfth century as teaching texts in the arts. Sixteen manuscripts of the *Arith.* and fourteen of the *Mus.* are extant in UK collections from twelfth century—more than half the total surviving number of each. Numbers drop sharply subsequently. It is not usual for the *Arith.* and *Mus.* to show much sign of use. The earliest texts, such as MS Cambridge, Corpus Christi College, 352 (*Arith.*, s. ix) and MS London, BL, Arundel 77 (*Mus.*, s. xi) have been substantially worked over, but this is not common. Of the two, *Mus.* is more likely to be glossed and noted than *Arith.*

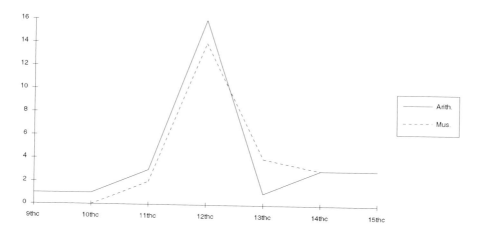

Figure 5 - Arith. and Mus. by date

In comparison to these twelfth-century texts, the *logica* show us Boethius in the thirteenth century, for almost all the survivals of both the *logica vetus* and *logica nova* date from then. Again, these are texts with a working context, subject to the fluctuations of scholastic interest. The *logica* texts generally show much evidence of use. Often the individual treatises have explanatory diagrams and various finding tools; and they may also bear the notes of later readers, as well as pointing hands, *nota* signs and so forth. This is Boethius at his most practical.

Appearing as they do with the *Liber sex principiorum* and the *Prior Anal.* (amongst others), the *logica* texts remind us that although all of the major Boethius works may appear by themselves in manuscripts, they are often found in company with others. Discovering the identity of these fellow-travellers and noting their consistency has been an interesting sideline of the conspectus. A typical set of either *logica vetus* or *nova* leaves little room for other items, but very occasionally there may be space for Priscian or, in an added volume, more Aristotle.

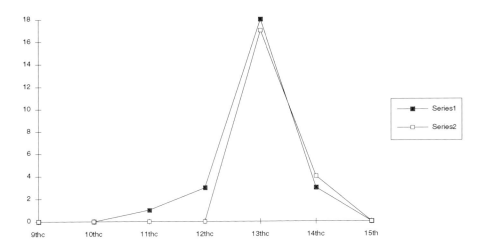

Figure 6 - Logic by date

The *Arith.* and *Mus.* often travel together, but both have other, fairly regular stable-mates. For the *Arith.,* this is likely to be calendar material, computational texts such as Bede or the Ps-Boethian *Geometria*—all texts that need diagrams, and close companions in the quadrivium. Two *Arith.* manuscripts travel with Cicero, *De inventione* and the *Ad Herennium*—an example of trivium and quadrivium merged into one. For the *Mus.*, there is a slightly wider variety. Other musical texts, like Guy of Arezzo's *Micrologus*, are possible, as well as hymns or poetry, such as Horace. With its complicated tonal diagrams, *Mus.* can be found with astronomical, geometrical and Arabic material and, occasionally, the *logica vetus.* However, both *Arith.* and *Mus.* are works long enough to take up a volume to themselves, and most often travel alone.

Since they are so short, the *Op. Sac.* have a large number of fellow-travellers. Only 15% of *Op. Sac.* are *not* found with other texts, and these are overwhelmingly volumes from the twelfth century with Gilbert's commentary. The remaining 85% come with a surprisingly stable set of companions—surprising, because at first sight these volumes can appear to be a miscellaneous hotchpotch reflecting unruly interests. The *Op. Sac.* are sometimes tacked onto the *DCPhil.,* but their other contexts are naturally Trinitarian and theological. They most often appear alongside Augustine's *De trinitate* and *De doctrina Christiana*, and they are commonly with texts of Anselm, (the *Monologion*, *Proslogion* and *Cur Deus homo*); they also live beside Athanasius on the Trinity or John Damascene's *De fide orthodoxa*. Since they were regularly known in the Middle Ages as Boethius, *De trinitate*, they were sometimes copied along with a text known as Boethius, *De unitate*, now credited to Gundissalinus. This pattern remains true until the fourteenth century, when a slight variation emerges. Although three of the six fourteenth-century *Op. Sac.* are set in a theological context (Augustine, Anselm and John Damascene), the other three are found with the *Arith.*, with Aristotle and with Avicenna. Two of the four fifteenth-century copies are in miscellaneous collections, one is with Cicero and the last is alongside Grosseteste, geometry and science. By the fifteenth century, then, interest in the *Op. Sac.* seems to have become antiquarian. They no longer fit into a teaching context. This decline in interest is borne out when we look at the *Op. Sac.* manuscripts for glossing and signs of use.

The *DCPhil.*, although large enough to travel on its own, is found in company in rather more than half its manuscripts. The occurrences are hard to quantify because a *DCPhil.* text may well appear bound together with a later text of Trivet or some other suitable companion, so that what was once a discrete copy has become a fellow-traveller. The *DCPhil.* quite frequently appears with other Boethius texts, especially the *Op. Sac.*, the Ps.-Boethian, *De disciplina scolarium* and the various *vitae* and *epitaphs*. Otherwise it has two common types of friend, according to considerations of form or subject. The *DCPhil.* was admired for its poetry and structure as well as its sentiments, so one set of companions is of straightforwardly poetical manuscripts, such as Gualterus Anglicus's versified Aesop, Walter of Châtillon's *Alexandreis* or the *Disticha Catonis*. The second group of stablemates is Martianus Capella's *De nuptiis*, Prudentius's *Psychomachia* or Fulgentius's *Mythologiae*, where content was more the guide to selection. To some, Boethius was a Roman author to be admired for latinity and style; to others, he was a model of Christian stoicism. These additional texts point up Boethius's shifting place in both antique and Christian camps.

Taken overall, the most common accompanying author by far in our UK manuscripts is Augustine (in eighteen manuscripts). He appears more than twice as often as his nearest rivals, Anselm, Cicero and the *Ad Herennium*. Generally, though, it is rare for any other author to crop up in even five manuscripts, including Lupus, *De metris*.

As so many manuscripts of *DCPhil.* are still extant in UK collections, we may briefly consider the various forms in which the text appears. As we have seen, the *DCPhil.* boasts manuscripts from the ninth to the sixteenth centuries. We have two definite ninth-century manuscripts of the text, one complete and the other a fragment. MS London, BL, Harley 3095, which also contains the *Op. Sac.* and one of the *vitae*, is a simple but fine copy of the text, with wide margins ruled for glossing, which has been extensively supplied for both texts; the gloss is connected to the text by very typical 'Greek' (i.e., Ps.-Greek, weights and measures signs etc.) and Latin letters. The *DCPhil.* text has *tituli* and colophons to every book; the metres are identified with scansion marks; the text has been given rhetorical labels; and the dialogues have been marked as **B** (Boethius) and **Ph** (Philosophy). MS Oxford, Bodleian Library, Digby 174 contains a bifolium with part of bk V.

In all, we have ten *DCPhil.* texts from the ninth and tenth centuries and five from the eleventh. (We note here that the distinctions between manuscripts of the ninth, tenth and even eleventh centuries are often blurred, and cataloguers are inclined to date later rather than earlier, for reasons of prudence, rather than accuracy, it would seem.) Most of these early *DCPhil.* texts are simple, although one or two have fine initials, such as MS Cambridge, Trinity College, O. 3. 7, which has particularly striking black and yellow Celtic initials. MS Oxford, Bodleian Library, Auct F. 1. 15, has a few very finely drawn intials and also a very typical layout of the metres in double columns, as a space-saving device, and an interlinear gloss. A plain but handsome manuscript possibly from Cologne, MS London, BL, Harley 2685, is unusually written in two columns, also with glosses.

In the twelfth century the number of *DCPhil.* texts jumps to sixteen manuscripts (predominantly from the first half of the century) and falls in the thirteenth century to ten copies, but thereafter leaps to thirty-seven extant manuscripts in the fourteenth century, the heyday of the text. Of these thirty-seven, ten contain the Nicholas Trivet commentary. Finally, we have twenty-one fifteenth-century manuscripts and one from the sixteenth.

The twelfth and thirteenth century texts divide equally between glossed or noted texts and entirely plain versions. Most of the twelfth-century volumes have some decoration, and where we have been able to establish provenance the books appear to be monastic. The thirteenth-century copies are rather plainer: they are hard to categorize as any clear 'type'.

The *DCPhil.* in the fourteenth century was generally a showy book. Even the red and blue Paris school type of texts are often to be found with additional borders and initials. A typical fourteenth-century Boethius without Trivet is a quarto volume with wide clean margins (e.g., MS Oxford, Bodleian Library, Canon. Class. Lat. 182), plainly written in an Italian rotunda hand, often with Boethian portrait and half-border to begin (e.g., MSS Glasgow, Hunter 374; London, BL, Harley 2517) and painted initials touched with gold. There are rarely signs of use. Often these manuscripts appear to have been employed as surety for loans: several have Hebrew on the flyleaves which, as far as we have been able to discover, are pledge notes (e.g., MSS Holkham Hall 402; Oxford, Bodleian Library, Canon. Class. Lat. 138). Manuscripts with the Trivet commentary can be just as smart (as the legal style manuscript, MS Oxford, Bodleian Library, Rawl. G. 187 attests), although the fourteenth century has its own version of the private study text, like MS Oxford, Bodleian Library, D'Orville 154, with its three-column metres to save space.

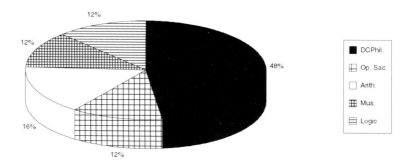

Figure 7 - Harley MSS

About half the fifteenth-century manuscripts are made of paper. They tend to be plain books, simply decorated. A number are pocket-sized, and they have obviously been used and valued by their owners. MSS Oxford, Bodleian Library, D'Orville 153 and Hamilton 46 have inserted commentary (in German in the Hamilton manuscript) on separate sheets. There is a homemade flavour to a number of these books, in marked contrast to the flashy continental collector's items.

With any sample of manuscripts surviving in any one geographical area, it is clearly difficult to draw conclusions about where such texts were commonly made. We have, however, assigned provenances to 162 of our 228 manuscripts (71%), and 82 of these are English, with 7 coming from St Augustine's and Christ Church, Canterbury. Thirty-three manuscripts are Italian, reflecting the large number of fourteenth- and fifteenth-century illuminated *DCPhil.* texts written for gentlemen owners and their collections. These are well-represented in the Bodleian *Canonici* collection. Although the fine group of twenty-three Boethius manuscripts in the Harleian collection in the British Library has twelve *DCPhil.*s, they are spread across English, French, German and Italian provenances. The composition of the Harleian collection, however, represents in microcosm the spread of texts and dates of the conspectus as a whole.

The twenty-three manuscripts here assigned French provenances include a large proportion of the earlier books (although catalogues tend to be caught in the circular argument of assigning ninth to eleventh-century manuscripts N. E. French provenances because they all *look* alike). A large proportion of manuscripts with non-English provenances come from private collections. Manuscripts in Oxford and Cambridge colleges and cathedral libraries are much more heavily weighted to English productions. A few points stand out. The cathedral libraries (Canterbury, Durham, Hereford, Lambeth, Worcester, York: Lichfield is excluded because the work is a pastedown fragment) contain thirteen Boethius manuscripts. Fully ten of these are *logica* texts, from the twelfth and thirteenth centuries. The exceptions are an *Arith.* and *Mus.* text from Lambeth (s. xii 1/2), the York *Op. Sac.* and the Hereford *DCPhil.*, out of place in fact because it is a fifteenth-century manuscript given in the mid-fifteenth century by one of Hereford's two major benefactors. The cathedral libraries' holdings demonstrate trivial and quadrivial teaching in cathedral schools. Like a modern teaching library, Durham has multiple copies: four *logica nova*. All the cathedral books have UK provenances.

If we compare the holdings of the Oxford and Cambridge colleges (excluding pastedown fragments), we can see interesting differences. Oxford Colleges have twenty-five manuscripts containing thirty Boethian texts; Cambridge Colleges have thirty-one manuscripts with thirty-three texts. Of the total fifty-six manuscripts, only six have been assigned non-UK provenances. Many of the fifty come, as one might expect given early college associations, from cathedral towns or as survivals from monastic libraries, 'bought up' at the Dissolution and passed on to colleges.

The Oxford colleges hold equal numbers of *DCPhil.* and *Mus.* manuscripts (nine each), with five *Arith.*, four *Op. Sac.* and three *logica*. The manuscripts are primarily twelfth century, influenced mostly by the *Arith.* and *Mus.* texts, picked up easily later by collectors. The *DCPhil.* and *Op. Sac.* texts tend to be later in date.

The Cambridge story is different. Here, the outstanding single text is the *Op. Sac.* (ten out of thirty-three texts), with seven *DCPhil.*, four *Arith.*, two *Mus.* and ten *logica*. There are manuscripts from right across the period, with a weighting to the thirteenth century. Neither is this predominance of the *Op. Sac.* caused by bias from one college. Every college with Boethian manuscripts, except Trinity, has a copy of *Op. Sac.* The sample is skewed, rather, by the splendid holdings of the medieval library of Gonville and Caius College. Of its ten Boethian manuscripts (containing eleven texts; excluding one *DCPhil.* purchased in 1904), seven are *logica vetus* and *logica nova*, most from the thirteenth century, with two each of *DCPhil.* and *Op. Sac.* Both *DCPhil.*s are fourteenth-century copies. This proliferation of *Op. Sac.* in Cambridge colleges must reflect a difference in curriculum and teaching at the two universities.

In this short consideration of the UK Boethius manuscripts, we have purposefully not sought to draw profound conclusions or to close doors. The aim of our conspectus is to begin research, not to end it. We offer it hopefully, as a useful tool for scholars to come.

Catalogue

ABERDEEN

King's College (f. 1494/95) and the Protestant Marischal College (f. 1593) were united in 1860 as the University of Aberdeen.

M. R. James, *A Catalogue of the Medieval Manuscripts in the University Library, Aberdeen*, Cambridge, 1932.

1. MS Aberdeen, University Library 148
DCPhil. I–II

1509 +

Parchment; ii + 47 + i fols; page 160x115mm; text 98x72mm; 23 lines; one scribe. Original binding of stamped leather on wood; original clasps. A luxury schoolbook.

CONTENTS	Fols 1^r–6^r *Disticha Catonis*; 6^v dates of the kings of England William I – Henry VIII; 7^r–44^r *DCPhil. I–II* (fols 26^r–27^r in reverse order; spaces of 10–12 lines left at end of each prose and metre); 44^v–45^v copybook dicta.
GLOSS	None.
DECORATION	Major initials gold or grey/white letter against a background of blue or gold (see fols 1^r, 7^r, 23^r). Within the initial daisy, thistle, rose, strawberry fruit and flower, pansy. Minor initials gold, blue or red.
PROVENANCE	? Flemish. Early owners: A. Warmyngton (s. xvi: fol. ii^r), Nicholas Charles (1607: fol. ii^v) and R. Gordon (1697: fol. ii^v). Given to Marischal College, Aberdeen, 1738 (fol. ii^v).

BIBLIOGRAPHY James, *Aberdeen*, pp. 48–49.

2. MS Aberdeen, University Library 263
DCPhil.

S. XV

Paper; i (modern) + 267 + i (modern) fols; 2 booklets, each separately foliated [fols 1–104 (Boethius) + 3 blank + 1–160 (Aristotle)]; page 285x210mm; text 200x120mm; 2 cols; 50 lines; one scribe, William Wallace, for *DCPhil.*, carefully written. Scribal colophon, fol. 104^v: 'Expl. sentenciarii ven. Boecii super de cons. phil. et disc. scol. compendiose et artificialiter collecti sec. ord. alphabeti. Jam scripsit totum pro cristo da sibi potum. Qui scripsit scriptum caput eius sit benedictum. Wil^{us} Wallace.' Bk nos as running headers. Rebound, but with original boards covered with parchment; clasp gone.

CONTENTS A: fols 1ra–92rb ***DCPhil.*** with intercalated commentary; 93ra–96vb tables to *DCPhil.*; 96vb–103rb *Sententiae*; 103va–4vb *Sententiae* from *De disciplina scolarium*; 105–8 blank. B: fols 1^r–160^r Aristotle, *Ethics* with commentary.

GLOSS See contents. No other glosses, but a few headings written in margin.

DECORATION Plain blue and red initials; *C(armina)* blue with a little infilling and scrolling in red (fol. 1^r).

PROVENANCE King's College, Aberdeen. 'Iste liber pertinet Iohanni Vaus: studenti alme universitatis (Aberdon)', fol. 1^r. At end: 'Ex libris collegii Aberdonensis ex dono magistri Johannis Vaus regentis gramaticorum.'

BIBLIOGRAPHY James, *Aberdeen*, p. 92; Ker, *MLGB*, p. 2.

CAMBRIDGE

UNIVERSITY LIBRARY (CUL)

The earliest catalogue (1473) records a collection that was dispersed and altered in the sixteenth century. For the foundations of the present collection see John Caius's catalogue (1574), ed. J. Venn and E. S. Roberts, *The Works of John Caius, M.D.*, Cambridge, 1912, section 5, *Historiae Cantebrigiensis Academiae ab urbe condita*, London, 1574, pp. 68–71, MSS in CUL, and 115–16, M. R. James's identification of these MSS, and Thomas James's *Ecloga Oxonio-Cantabrigiensis*, London, 1600, pp. 53–69; the latter was reprinted by Bernard in 1697. The manuscripts of John Moore, bishop of Ely (d. 1714), were given to the library by George I in 1715.

Bernard, *CMA*, I.iii.2181–2439; C. Hardwick, etc., *A Catalogue of the Manuscripts preserved in the Library of the University of Cambridge*, 6 vols, Cambridge, 1856–67 [= CUL Cat.]; Ker, *MLGB*, pp. 24–25; J. C. T. Oates, *Cambridge University Library: A History from the Beginning to the Copyright Act of Queen Anne*, Cambridge, 1986; D. McKitterick, *Cambridge University Library, A History*. II: *The Eighteenth and Nineteenth Centuries*, Cambridge, 1986.

3. MS Cambridge, University Library, Dd. 6. 6
DCPhil., Op. Sac., Vita VI, Epitaphs   s. xii 2/3

Parchment; i (modern) + ii + 89 + i (modern) fols (fol. 88 missing); page 205x138mm; text 155x66mm; 31 lines; one neat, small hand. End papers: s. xv psalter with Hebrew ?caution note (fols 87, 89). *Titulus* (fol. 62^r); colophon (fol. 71^r).

CONTENTS   Fol. 1^v s. xv contents-list; 2^r–61^v *DCPhil.*; 62^r–67^r *Op. Sac. I*; 67$^{r–v}$ note on synonyms; 67^v *Vita VI*; 68^r *Epitaphs I and II* (lines 1–2 only); 68^r–86^v *Op. Sac. II–V*.

GLOSS   None.

DECORATION   Fine three–quarter page miniature (red, blue, green, black, brown, gold) of Philosophy visiting Boethius, with three departing Muses blowing horns to right (fol. 2^v). Major initials red, blue, yellow, green; competent but stereotyped (e.g., 32^v, 40^v). Minor initials and capitals, green, red, blue, ochre (single colour and combination).

PROVENANCE   English or Northern French.

BIBLIOGRAPHY   CUL Cat., i.291–92; Saxl and Meier, III.i.418; P. Courcelle, *Histoire littéraire des grandes invasions germaniques*, 3rd edn, Paris, 1964, pl. 41a; Troncarelli, *Boethiana*, no. 71; Troncarelli, 'Opuscula', p. 18.

4. MS Cambridge, University Library, Ff. 4. 37
Op. Sac. I   s. xiii

Parchment; 205 + i fols (fol. 3 missing); page 275x187mm; text 2 cols, each
192x52mm; 50 lines; same or very similar scribe throughout. Library binding
of s. xvii. Running headers, often in red. Entire MS is indexed with Arabic
numerals down the centre of each page; columns are numbered in Arabic
numerals along the top margin.
A useful reference volume.

CONTENTS   Fol. 2^r s. xvii contents list; 4^r–14^r 3–col. subject-index to
                  columns of book; 14^v table of kindred and affinity; 16va s. xvi
                  contents-list, by hand that occasionally annotates texts; 16vb s.
                  xiv list of commentators on individual books of Bible. Four
                  names added to Apocalypse commentators: Robertus abbas,
                  Joachim abbas, Berengarius, Cantuariensis (s. xiv); 17ra–40ra
                  Augustine, *Retractationes*; 40ra–109vb ten opuscula by
                  Augustine, or attributed to him; 110vb–12vb *Op. Sac. I*, missing
                  prologue. Begins at c. 1, 'Christianae religionis reuerenciam';
                  113ra–35vb Augustine, three minor works, one spurious;
                  137ra–205va *Remediarium conuersorum*, attrib. Peter of Blois.

GLOSS   None.

DECORATION   Blue or red initials with contrasting penwork; blue and red
                  paraph signs; rubrication.

PROVENANCE   English or Northern French.

BIBLIOGRAPHY   1574 catalogue; Bernard, *CMA*, I.iii.2191; CUL Cat., ii.467–70.

5. MS Cambridge, University Library, Gg. 5. 35
DCPhil.   s. xi

Parchment; ii (modern) + iii [foliated 0, i, ii, ii*, iii] + 446 + 2 (paper) + i
(modern) fols (includes one leaf, present but separated); page 223x152mm; text
190x112mm; 31 lines; similar scribes throughout, until last quire; *DCPhil.*
written in open hand with insular features. Early foliation with Arabic
numerals. *Tituli* to every book of *DCPhil.* in red. Rebound in 1974.

A school anthology of forty-four, mainly theological, treatises which include the 'Cambridge Songs' (fols 432^r–441^v). Boethius was once a separate MS.

CONTENTS Fol. iii^v contents-list (s. xii) with pagination (s. xiv); 1^r–53^r Juvencus, glossed; 53^r–84^v Sedulius, *Carmen paschale*; 85^v–126^r Arator, *Historia apostolica*; 126^v–46^r Tiro Prosper, *Epigrammata super dicta S. Augustini*; 146^r–48^r idem, *Exortatio ad uxorem*; 148^r–164^r Prudentius, *Psychomachia*; 164^r–67^r idem, *Tituli de historiis veteris et novi testamenti* (in verse); 167^r–69^v Lactantius, *Libellus de Fenice Paradisi habitatrice*; 170–209^v **DCPhil**; 209^v–62^r Rabanus, *De laude sancte crucis*; 263^r–76^r a treatise on music, in prose; 280^r–446^v 32 further items mostly hymns and liturgical verses, including Aldhelm, Abbo of St Germain, Alcuin and Bede; 447^v–48^r table of contents (s. xix).

GLOSS Extensive contemporary marginal and interlinear annotation to *DCPhil.*, with reference-signs (symbols and Greek letters).

DECORATION *DCPhil.* has plain red initials, and red headings to metres and proses. Elsewhere simple red capitals. Fine initial in red, pink, and yellow, portraying an abstract pattern with animals' heads (fol. 1^r). Fols 211^r–25^r figures and diagrams including Christ in red robe, a kneeling person praying, the symbols of the Evangelists. All various colours (red, orange, green, yellow, brown, blue) in boxes over rustic capital texts, or as acrostics and hidden-word games.

PROVENANCE St Augustine's, Canterbury (fol. iii^v).

BIBLIOGRAPHY CUL Cat., iii.201–5; Ker, *Anglo-Saxon*, no. 16, with extensive bibliography; Ker, *MLGB*, p. 40; Bolton, pp. 54–55; A. G. Rigg and G. R. Wieland, 'A Canterbury Classbook of the Mid-Eleventh Century (the "Cambridge Songs" Manuscript)', *Anglo-Saxon England*, 4, 1975, pp. 113–130; M. T. Gibson, M. Lapidge and C. Page, 'Neumed Boethian *metra* from Canterbury: A Newly-Recovered Leaf of MS Cambridge University Library, Gg. 5. 35 (the "Cambridge Songs" Manuscript)', *Anglo-Saxon England*, 12, 1983, pp. 141–52; Troncarelli, *Boethiana*, no. 72; Robinson, *Cambridge*, no. 44; Minnis, *Chaucer*, p. 94.

6. MS Cambridge, University Library, Ii. 3. 12
Arith., Mus.   s. xii 1/2

Parchment; ii (modern) + 137 + ii (modern) fols; page 291x198mm; text
220x132mm; 31–32 lines, ruled in pencil; two MSS in similar hands. *Tituli* in
red.
The last bifolium is a catalogue of Christ Church, Canterbury (s. xii 3/4), in
which this MS cannot be identified. Cf. MSS Cambridge, Trinity College, R.
15. 22 and New Zealand, Wellington, Alexander Turnbull Library 140.
A MS in mediocre script, with a few outstanding initials.

CONTENTS   Fols 1^v–60^r ***Arith.***; 62^v–133^v ***Mus.***; 135^v–37^r Christ Church
                Canterbury catalogue (*CBMLC*, VI).

GLOSS   None.

DECORATION   Indifferent line drawing of Boethius and Symmachus (fol. 1^r),
                having a common ancestry with MS Bamberg Staatsbibl. HJ
                IV. 12 (s. ix: belonged to Charles the Bald; Koehler, pl. 90a);
                excellent full-page coloured line drawing of Boethius and
                Pythagoras (above, with musical instruments) and Plato and
                Nicomachus (below, with books), fol. 61^v; major initial with
                Christ (R) and Ecclesia (L), holding *agnus dei*, hand of God
                above, sun (L), moon (R) and naked devil trodden underfoot
                below (fol. 62^v). Major initials, e.g., 1^v, 4^v, 25^v, 65^v (angel with
                Host), 79^r, 93^v, 106^v, 127^v (last 4 drawn but not coloured).
                Minor initials in red, purple or green. Excellent diagrams
                throughout, including amazing divisions of *essentia* (fol. 22^v).

PROVENANCE   Christ Church, Canterbury: *ex libris* 'Musica Boecii de claustro
                ecclesie Xti cantuar' (fols 2^r and 62^r: s. xiv). Note
                misidentification of *Arith.* at fol. 2^r.

BIBLIOGRAPHY   CUL Cat., iii.418–19; W. Koehler, *Die Karolingischen Minia-*
                turen I: die Schule von Tours, Berlin, 1930, pl. 90a; C. R.
                Dodwell, *The Canterbury School of Illumination 1066–1200*,
                Cambridge, 1954, p. 35; Ker, *MLGB*, p. 30; Kauffmann, no.
                41; Bower, no. 18.

7. MS Cambridge, University Library, Ii. 3. 21
DCPhil.

s. xiv 2/2

Parchment; ii (modern) + 299 + ii (modern) fols (each vol. foliated separately: 180+119; fol. 1 of B excised); page 320x222mm. Running headers in red.
A: text 230x95mm; 21 lines; ruled for gloss; one scribe.
B: text 2 cols, each 240x67mm; 42 lines; one scribe.
The *DCPhil.* (fols 9–180) once existed on its own.

CONTENTS | A: fols 1ʳ–8ᵛ subject index ('tabula') to *DCPhil.*; 9ʳ–180ᵛ *DCPhil.*, with cursive Latin marginal gloss; Chaucer's English translation intercalated in cursive in the text. A sketchy Latin gloss to this version, bks I–III.
B: fols 2ʳ–10ʳᵃ Prefaces I and II to William of Aragon's Commentary on *DCPhil.*; 10ʳᵃ–119ᵛᵃ William of Aragon, Commentary on *DCPhil.*; 119ᵛ colophon preserving the name of an earlier scribe: Johannes Theutonicus *a.* 1306 (Minnis).

GLOSS | A: extensive excerpts from Trivet's commentary, in the scribe's hand.
B: William of Aragon, Commentary on *DCPhil.*: continuous, with lemmata.

DECORATION | A: opening three-quarter border with gold, blue, pink, brown (fol. 9ʳ), the main initial *C(armina)* excised. Ugly blue initials with red flourishing and infilling. Red paraph signs marking the marginal glosses.
B: good initials at the beginning of each book. Blue initials with red flourishing and infilling. Red and blue paraph signs; rubrication; lemmata underlined in red.

PROVENANCE | A: English; see Chaucer's translation, and style of border (fol. 9ʳ).
B: probably English.

BIBLIOGRAPHY | Bernard, *CMA*, I.iii.2256; CUL Cat., iii.424–25; Kottler, Ca; Minnis in Gibson, chap. 13; Minnis, *Chaucer*, passim.

8. MS Cambridge, University Library, Ii. 6. 6
Top. Diff. IV   s. xii 2/2

Parchment; ii (modern) + 91 + ii (modern) fols; early foliation in Arabic
numerals; page 193x123mm; text 138x67mm; 34 lines; one minute hand
except fols 45^v–46^v.
Note Greek and Anglo-Saxon in s. xvii hand at the foot of fol. 1^r.
A very attractive small volume.

CONTENTS   Fols 1^r–41^v Cicero, *De inventione*; 41^v–46^v *Top. Diff. IV*;
                   47^r–88^r Ps.-Cicero, *Ad Herennium*.

GLOSS   None.

DECORATION   Remarkable major initials in red, gold, silver: fols 2^r, 19^v (both
                   abstract), 41^v cockatrice, 47^r, 62^r (both abstract), 70^r (dragon).
                   Other minor initials red, blue, green with simple penwork
                   flourishing. Major initial added in same style, pale blue and
                   red (fol. 1^r).

PROVENANCE   French. 'Ex bibliotheca Nicotiana'. 100' (fol. 1^r); contents-list
                   in hand of J. B. Hautin (s. xvii 2/2), a number of whose books
                   passed to John Moore, bp. of Ely (d. 1714) and so to the
                   University Library.

BIBLIOGRAPHY   CUL Cat., iii.502; D. McKitterick, *Cambridge University
                   Library*, Cambridge, 1986, II, pp. 139–40.

9. MS Cambridge, University Library, Kk. 3. 21
DCPhil.   c. 1000

Parchment; i (modern) + 104 + i (modern) fols; page 300x235mm; text
205x120mm; 22 lines; drypoint ruled for glosses; same or similar scribe for
text and gloss. Alphabetical reference-signs in column between text and gloss.
Metres in good rustic capitals, with metres identified.
Rhetorical labels in red: e.g., fol. 24^r APOSTROPHAM, PROPOSITIO, ASSUMPTIO.
Brief summaries of subject-matter at bottom of page throughout MS (s. xiv).
Tituli to every book of *DCPhil.*, in red.
Virtually a facsimile of MS Cambridge, Trinity College, O. 3. 7.

CONTENTS   Fols 1ʳ–103ʳ ***DCPhil.***, glossed; 103ᵛ schema of *Assumpta est Maria*; 104ᵛ neumes, Anglo-Saxon notes, names of winds in Anglo-Saxon.

GLOSS   Extensive annotation throughout *DCPhil.*: broadly comparable to 'the reviser of Remigius' (Bolton). Glosses connected to the text by Roman letters with a few Greek letters (all capitals).

DECORATION   Plain gold initials, e.g., fols 1ʳ, 15ᵛ, 34ᵛ. Red (rather oxidized) and brown capitals. First letter of all metres in red.

PROVENANCE   Abingdon. 'byrnstan beoffansunu ælfnoδ ælrices sunu aethrocanlea' (fol. 104ᵛ).

BIBLIOGRAPHY   CUL Cat., iii.630; Bishop, *English Caroline*, p. 15; Ker, *Anglo-Saxon*, no. 24; Ker, *MLGB*, p. 2; Courcelle, p. 15; Bolton, pp. 55, 61; Troncarelli, *Boethiana*, no. 73; Minnis, *Chaucer*, p. 94.

10. MS Cambridge, University Library, Kk. 4. 11
Op. Sac. I–II, V   s. xiv 1/4

Parchment; ii (modern) + 285 + ii (modern) fols (fols 1, 239ʳ–74ᵛ missing); page 338x210mm; text 2 cols, each 260x62mm; 58 lines; one rather grand black-letter script throughout. *Titulus* for *Op. Sac. V*; space left for *tituli* to *I–II*. Red chapter headings; red running headers.
Standard theological context for *Op. Sac.* in later Middle Ages. An excellent MS with superb illuminations.

CONTENTS   Fols 2ᵛ–3ʳ analytical list of Augustine's *Retractationes*; 4ᵛ contents-list; 5ʳᵃ–226ᵛᵃ Augustine, 23 works, including *Retractationes* (fols 143ᵛᵃ–64ʳᵃ), *Enchiridion* (fols 164ʳᵃ–81ʳᵃ), *De doctrina christiana* (fols 181ʳᵃ–213ᵛᵇ), some spurious; 227ʳᵃ–34ʳᵇ ***Op. Sac. I–II, V*** (*Op. Sac. I, II* run together as if one text; *V* starts with illuminated initial and ends on fol. 234ʳᵇ: 'bonorum omnium causa perscripsit. ipsi honor et gloria in secula seculorum. amen'); 234ʳ–85ʳ 10 short treatises which include sermons by Augustine, theological treatises by Prosper of Aquitaine and Augustine, and a fragment on music.

GLOSS   None.

DECORATION   Three-quarter borders (with initials excised) with men and
                    animals, gold with pink, blue, green (fols 4ᵛ, 5ʳ, 53ʳ). Other
                    initials small but relatively ambitious, e.g., fol. 46ᵛ, 47ᵛ, 69ʳ.
                    Elsewhere blue initials with red flourishing.

PROVENANCE   Norwich Cathedral; Alexander 'de Sproutstone', monk of the
                    cathedral priory, who studied at Oxford 1309–10 (fol. 4ᵛ).

BIBLIOGRAPHY   Bernard, *CMA*, I.iii.2340; CUL Cat., iii.649–54; Emden,
                    BRUO, p. 1747; Ker, *MLGB*, p. 137.

11. MS Cambridge, University Library, Kk. 5. 32
Arith.   s. xii 1/2

Parchment; i (modern) + 76 + i (modern) fols (fols 73–75 lost); page
250x167mm.
A: text 195x115mm; 32 lines; one scribe for *Arith.*.
B: text 195x120mm; one scribe.
Titulus in red (fol. 1ʳ)

CONTENTS   A: fols 1ʳ–43ᵛ *Arith.*; 44ʳ notes on the elements; verses, *inc.*
                    'Vir mulier iacuere thoro simul atque puella'; 44ᵛ–48ʳ
                    calendrial material in a later s. xii hand.
                    B: fols 49ᵛ–60ᵛ Calendar and computistical tables (s. xi); 60ᵛ
                    Anglo-Saxon text (Ker); 61ʳ–72ᵛ Easter tables (s. xii); 76ʳ⁻ᵛ
                    computistica (s. xii: another hand).

GLOSS   Fols 3ᵛ–4ʳ only.

DECORATION   A: *I(n dandis)* (fol. 1ʳ) green and ochre abstract; *I(nter)* (fol.
                    2ʳ) red, yellow, green abstract; otherwise plentiful plain single-
                    colour initials red, blue, yellow, green throughout A.
                    Rubrication to each chapter. Floral elaboration of two initials
                    (fol. 13ᵛ). Diagrams brown, red, green.
                    B: none. Tables in brown, red, green.

PROVENANCE   Glastonbury.

BIBLIOGRAPHY CUL Cat., iii.701–2; Wormald, I, pp. 71–83; Ker, *Anglo-Sax-on*, no. 26 (section B); Ker, *MLGB*, p. 90.

12. MS Cambridge, University Library, Mm. 2. 18
DCPhil.

s. xiv 2/2

Parchment; i + 344 fols (several are missing, including fols 275, 330–31 of *DCPhil.*; list inside back cover); page 365x248mm; text 2 cols, each 277x80mm; 63 lines; one scribe. Brown running headers.
A grand folio compendium of texts.

CONTENTS   Fol. i^v s. xiv contents-list; 1ra–49vb Jober, *De astrologia*; 49vb–82vb texts on arithmetic, algebra and measurement, mainly translated from Arabic; 82^{va-vb} list of works in fols 1ra–82vb; 83ra–103^r Solinus, *De mirabilibus mundi*; 103^r–15^v *Ethicus philosophus*; 115vb–31vb Frontinus, *Strategemata*; 131vb–33vb Clement of Lanthony, patristic *sententiae*; 133vb–45va Macrobius, *Saturnalia* (excerpts); 145va–47vb Gerald of Wales, *De mirabilibus*; 147vb–48ra *De vita S. Zozime*; 148ra–49va Martial, *Epigrams*; 149va–65rb John of Salisbury, *Metalogicon* (excerpts); 165rb–69ra *Entheticus* (abridged); 169ra–220ra Ovid, *Metamorphoses* prose summary; 220ra–24va commentary on Ovid, *Epp.*; 224va–68rb Valerius Maximus, *Facta et dicta*; 268va–344vb *DCPhil.*, with Trivet's commentary.

GLOSS   Trivet. Almost no sign of use.

DECORATION   Half-borders (blue, pink, red, white, gold) beginning most treatises. Blue initials with red penwork; red and blue paraph signs. Space left for diagrams in *DCPhil.*, not supplied.

PROVENANCE   English? 'Iste liber est fratris Galfridi de Wyghtone' (fol. i^v); bought for 8s by Thomas Knyvett (s. xvii 1/2: fols i^r, 344^v) whose library was dispersed 1693+, partly to John Moore, bp. Ely, thence passing via George I to the University Library.

BIBLIOGRAPHY Bernard, *CMA*, I.iii.2281; Kottler, Mm; D. J. McKitterick, *The Library of Sir Thos Knyvett of Ashwellthorpe c. 1539–1618*, Cambridge, 1978; Minnis, *Chaucer*, p. 35.

13. MS Cambridge, University Library, Add. 1867
Logica vetus   s. xiii–xiv

Parchment; i + 45 fols; page 213x163mm; text 120x90mm; 26–27 lines; same or similar Italian bookhands. Running headers in red. Binding: white skin on boards (probably original) now covered in s. xix^{in} Italian marbled paper.

CONTENTS   Fols i^r–1^v grammatical notes; 2^r–8^v *Isag.*; 8^v–20^r *Cat.*; 20^r–27^v *De Int.*; 27^v–34^r *Liber sex principiorum*; 34^r–43^r *Div.*; 43^v–44^v logical notes and questions; 45^r–back pastedown Virgil, *Aeneid*, ii.182–284.

GLOSS   Extensive users' annotation.

DECORATION   Red and blue initials with mauve and red flourishing; red and blue paraph signs.

PROVENANCE   Italian (script and grammatical fragment). Acquired from W. Bragge of Sheffield, 1876.

BIBLIOGRAPHY *AL*, 1912; CUL typescript catalogue.

14. MS Cambridge, University Library, Add. 2992
DCPhil.   s. xii 2/2

Parchment; 57 fols; page 194x125mm; text 160x62mm; 39 lines; one scribe. Types of metre identified in red; a little Greek.

CONTENTS   Fols 4^r–54^v *DCPhil.* I–V.pr.vi.95, 'eve[nire]'.

GLOSS   Extensive and systematic throughout in one or two hands. Further users' glosses in cursive s. xii and later, some in Old High German.

DECORATION   Red initials with plain brown ink flourishing. Red paraph signs; red headings to proses and metres; rubrication.

PROVENANCE   German.

BIBLIOGRAPHY Bergmann, no. 90.

15. MS Cambridge, University Library, Add. 3038
DCPhil.
                                                              s. xii

Parchment; 62 fols; page 240x185mm.
A (s. xiv): text 165x90mm; 16 & 32 lines; one scribe.
B (s. xii): text 180x100mm; 33 lines; one, possibly two, scribes.
C (s. xii): text 180x95mm; 33 lines; one hand similar to B.
Binding: s. xiv/xv, white leather on boards, outer wrapper of skin, originally red. Five bands across spine; double strap and pin fastening (straps gone) on back; label on back with horn cover: BOECIUS DE CONSOLAC'/ ITEM AC-CENTUARIUM.
Excellent evidence of how *DCPhil.* used in s. xiv.

CONTENTS   A: fols 1ʳ–26ᵛ *Accentuarius, inc.* 'Cum primus metrice incho-assem scribere'.
                B: fols 27ʳ–57ᵛ ***DCPhil.***, *inc.* imperf., II.pr.iv.89, 'non sinit esse' to V.pr.vi.172 'esse non possunt'. Omission fols 51ᵛ–52ʳ = IV.pr.vii.40 – V.pr.i.51.
                C: fols 58ʳ–62ᵛ Martianus Capella, *De nuptiis* I.26.

GLOSS   A: a little gloss throughout.
                B: none.
                C: none.

DECORATION   A: clumsy red and blue initials with penwork.
                B: ***H****(ec)* blue, red, green, brown, rather finely drawn dragon, beginning of bk IV (fol. 42ᵛ); minor initials red (oxidized), blue or green, some lightly flourished. Rubrication.
                C: two red initials touched with brown (fol. 58ʳ)

PROVENANCE   English. Reference to 'magister H. de Bollech Arche' (fol. 62ᵛ: s. xiv). Brent Eleigh parish church, Suffolk (no. 2, fol. 1ʳ). Brent library was founded c. 1700 by Henry, son of Richard Colman, of Trinity College, Cambridge. This MS acquired by the University Library in 1891.

BIBLIOGRAPHY N. R. Ker, *The Parochial Libraries of the Church of England,*

London, 1959, pp. 70–71; Leonardi, no. 35; J. A. Fitch, 'Suffolk Parochial Libraries', *Proc. Suffolk Institute of Archaeology*, 30, 1967, pp. 44–87.

16. MS Cambridge, University Library, Add. 7114
DCPhil.
S. XV

Paper; iii (modern) + 77 + iv (modern) fols; page 290x205mm; text 185x123mm; 17 lines; one cursive scribe. *Titulus* to bk I added in top margin, fol. 1^r. Proses and metres marked in the margin.

CONTENTS	Fols 1^r–77^v *DCPhil.*
GLOSS	Scattered notes to bks I–III (fols 1–38).
DECORATION	None; space left for initials which have not been added.
PROVENANCE	German. Sir T. Clifford Allbut, Regius professor of Physic (d. 1925); whence (still bound in boards) to H. F. Stewart (d. 1948), Fellow of Trinity College, Cambridge, and editor of Boethius, by whom the MS was bequeathed to the University Library.
BIBLIOGRAPHY	None.

17. MS Cambridge, University Library, Add. 7115
DCPhil.
1424

Paper; i + 51 fols; page 295x220mm; text 195x125mm; 21–30 lines; panel ruled for gloss; one German scribe. Colophon, 'Explicit Boetius de consolatu philosophico Anno 1424. Decolacionis sancti Johannis Baptiste in Brema' (fol. 49^r).

CONTENTS	Fols 1^r–49^r *DCPhil.*; 49^v table of virtues and vices; 51^r scribbled music with a few German words.
GLOSS	Extensive contemporary marginal and interlinear annotation

throughout, chiefly by one user.

DECORATION   Red or brown initials. Internal capitals touched with red; all proses and metres marked in red (fols 1–10 only).

PROVENANCE   Bremen (see colophon). L. Tross of Hamm (s. xix); Phillipps 4737; H. F. Stewart (see Add. 7114) bequeathed the MS to the University in 1948.

BIBLIOGRAPHY Robinson, no. 115, pl. 209.

CAMBRIDGE COLLEGES

CORPUS CHRISTI COLLEGE, f. 1352

Few manuscripts survive from the pre-Reformation library. [Leland noticed a MS of *Op. Sac.*, given by Thomas Markaunt in 1439: James I, p. xii.] The major bequest is that of Archbishop Parker (d. 1575). It reflects his interest in English history and his access to the monastic and indeed the cathedral libraries of England. Manuscripts from other sources are numbered 201–49 in M. R. James's catalogue.

Bernard, *CMA*, I.iii.1277–1662; M. R. James, *A Descriptive Catalogue of the Manuscripts in the Library of Corpus Christi College, Cambridge*, 2 vols, Cambridge, 1912; Ker, *MLGB*, pp. 25–26; B. Dickins, 'The Making of the Parker Library', *Transactions of the Cambridge Bibliographical Society*, 6, 1972, pp. 19–34.

18. MS Cambridge, Corpus Christi College, 83
DCPhil.
s. xiv

Parchment; flyleaves i–ii (beg.), iii–iv (end); page now 370x240mm (slightly cut down); text 2 cols, each 295x95–115mm; 31 text lines; c. 80 commentary lines; one professional scribe; gloss surrounds each col. on three sides. Greek given in Latin transliteration. Red and blue roman nos as running headers. Host book is a fine copy of Peter Riga's *Aurora*. Note that fols i^r, ii^v and iv^v

are pasted down and cannot be read.

Style of a civil law book. Once a 'sumptuous' copy (James) for a professional man.

CONTENTS   Fol. iv *DCPhil.* I.pr.ii.1 to end of pr.ii; iir I.pr.iv.94 'potest? Atque' to I.pr.iv.132 'in senatum'; iiir–v I.pr.i.1 'Hec dum' to end of pr.i; ivr I.m.v.7 'Condat stellas' to I.pr.v.19 'mereatur. At'.

GLOSS   Cf. Trivet. No other notes.

DECORATION   Pretty initials in blue, pink, ochre, orange, white, light brown. Red and blue paraph signs.

PROVENANCE   ?French.

BIBLIOGRAPHY James, *Corpus*, i.167–69.

19. MS Cambridge, Corpus Christi College, 206
Isag., Op. Sac.   s. ix

Parchment; ii (modern) + 131 + ii (modern); page 300x230mm; drypoint ruling. Probably two separate MSS, though very similar.

A: text 220x130mm; 26 lines; one scribe.

B: text 200x110mm; 23 lines; three or four very typical s. ix Carolingian hands with marked insular features. Greek looks securely copied (e.g., fol. 90v), with Latin interlinear transliteration/gloss to most of the words. *Tituli* and colophons to *Op. Sac.* I, V. Rebound 1953.

An honest, useful book.

CONTENTS   A: fols 1r–23r Martianus Capella *De arte dialectica* (= *De nuptiis* bk 4) with marginal and interlinear gloss, fols 1–2.
              B: fol. 24r Alcuin (ed. E. Dümmler, *MGH: Poetae aevi Carolini*, I. 295, 10 lines only); 24r–39v Ps.-Augustine, *Categoriae decem*, with extensive marginal notes; *expl.* imperf. 'Eodem modo accipienda sunt' (p. 154, line 22); 40r–48v Ps.-Apuleius, *Peri hermenias*, lightly glossed; *inc.* imperf. 'obnoxia quem vocat Sergius'; 49r–60r *Isag.* with very few glosses and marginal notes; 60r–71r *Glosae de Isagogis, inc.* 'Fidi

interpretis quod fidus solet interpres'; 71^v a stray page of text, *inc*. 'Neque enim est commune'; 72^r–101^r ***Op. Sac. I–V***, with marginal and interlinear glosses, sometimes connected to text by symbols; 101^r–19^v Letter of Charlemagne to Alcuin (ed. E. Dümmler, *MGH: Epistolae*, IV, pp. 228–30); 120^r–31^v Augustine, *Dialectica*, with very occasional glosses.

GLOSS   See contents. Gloss related to text by very typical symbols and 'Greek' letters.

DECORATION   ***H****(ec)* is a glorious creation of intertwined beasts, leaves, scrolling, in green, red, purple-brown. Red (slightly oxidised), purple-brown, green headings and capitals (fol. 1^r). Lovely knotted, simple, self-coloured ***Q****(uia)* (fol. 101^r). Otherwise simple self-colour initials and capitals. Beginning of *Op. Sac.* has *titulus* in self-colour rustic capitals, occupying whole page. Very primitive map (fol. 38^r); marginal diagrams.

PROVENANCE   NE France. Probably from Daniel Rogers (see MS 214).

BIBLIOGRAPHY   James, *Corpus*, i.495–98; *AL*, 2036; Leonardi, no. 29; Troncarelli, 'Opuscula', p. 16; Burnett, *Glosses*, pp. 79n, 99–100.

20. MS Cambridge, Corpus Christi College, 214
DCPhil.
         s. xi

Fragmentary leaves, very badly eaten by rodents, stuck to paper for protection and bound as a paper book.
Parchment; 123 surviving fols; page c. 240x170mm; text c. 190x110mm; originally 18 lines; drypoint ruled for commentary; two fine hands. Gloss linked to text by Roman and Greek letters, very nicely done. Originally *tituli* in red and green.
Once a very fine copy, beautifully produced in fine hands.

CONTENTS   Fols 1^r–122^r ***DCPhil.*** with many gaps where leaves are missing, but the *expl.* is perfect.

GLOSS   Extensive and unusual:
         Bks I–II pr.v (fol. 25^v): extensive Latin marginal and

interlinear gloss.

Bk II: gloss only at m.v–viii, with Anglo-Saxon letters giving word order of Latin.

Bk III pr.i–pr.ix (fol. 53ʳ, first word): Anglo-Saxon interlinear gloss/ translation; Anglo-Saxon letters giving word order.

Fols 53ʳ–122ʳ: Anglo-Saxon letters giving word order of Latin. The different types of gloss appear in different quires, rather than depending on content.

DECORATION   Plain initials in red or green beginning each section. Headings in red (partly oxidized).

PROVENANCE   English. Given by Daniel Rogers, MA (Oxon.) 1561.

BIBLIOGRAPHY   James, *Corpus*, i.511–12; T. A. M. Bishop 'Notes on Cambridge Manuscripts' in *Transactions of the Cambridge Bibliographic Society*, 2, 1954–58, p. 187; Ker, *Anglo-Saxon*, no. 51; Ker, *MLBG*, p. 39; Bolton, p. 58; W. C. Hale, 'An Edition and Codicological Study of CCCC 214', *Diss. Abstracts*, 39, 1979, no. 6142; Troncarelli, *Tradizioni*, pp. 3, 49; Troncarelli, *Boethiana*, no. 69.

21. MS Cambridge, Corpus Christi College, 352
Arith.   s. ix–x

Parchment; ii (modern) + 80 + ii (modern) fols; page 300x220mm; text 220x120mm; 22 lines; ruled for gloss in drypoint; one lovely insular hand for text; gloss in the text hand and a Norman hand. Rebound 1949. *Tituli* in red to both books. Colophon to bk I (book II ends imperf.). Gloss connected to text with symbols and Greek letters.
A carefully-made book.

CONTENTS   Fol. 1ʳ quatrefoil diagrams of latitude and longitude (repeated on fol. 14ʳ); 2ʳ–80ᵛ *Arith.*, glossed; *expl.* imperf., II, c. 54, 170/1 'aequaliter vel quotlibet' (i.e., missing last leaf).

GLOSS   Extensive marginal and interlinear gloss added in a Norman hand s. xi–xii.

DECORATION Orange-red (some oxidation) chapter headings; orange-red, green, or self-colour simple initials. Simple orange-red and brown diagrams and tables in text and margin, some with slight ornamentation.

PROVENANCE St Augustine's, Canterbury (fol. 1^r: s. xiv).

BIBLIOGRAPHY Bernard, *CMA*, I.iii.1576; James, *ALCD*, p. 303, no. 1008; James, *Corpus*, ii.185–6; Bishop, *English Caroline*, no. 4; idem, 'Notes on Cambridge Manuscripts', *Transactions of the Cambridge Bibliographic Society*, 2, 1954–58, p. 330; Ker, *MLGB*, p. 41.

EMMANUEL COLLEGE, f. 1584.

The first substantial evidence is provided by Bernard in 1697.

Bernard, *CMA*, I.iii.1–137; M. R. James, *The Western Manuscripts in the Library of Emmanuel College*, Cambridge, 1904.

22. MS Cambridge, Emmanuel College, 28 (I 2 7)
Op. Sac. I–III, V

s. xii^{ex}/xiii^{in}

Parchment; ii (modern) + 72 + ii (modern) fols (some water damage); page 235x165mm; text 2 cols; inner col. is text, 180x37mm; outer col. is gloss, 180x66mm; text, 20 lines (to fol. 40^v) then 31–36 lines; gloss 39 lines; ruled for gloss, but text and gloss not well-fitted to one another; one hand, or very similar scribes. Red bk nos as running headers. Volume virtually in two parts, dividing after fol. 40^v (e.g., after quire 5).
The volume has a monastic look.

CONTENTS Fols 1^r–71^v *Op. Sac. I–III, V*.

GLOSS Gilbert of Poitiers. A few extra marginal notes and corrections throughout.

DECORATION   Simple red and blue, rather monastic initials and capitals, some with slight flourishing. **L**(*ibros*) red and brown with slight acanthus flourishing (fol. 1^r). After fol. 30^r decoration almost stops. Space left for decoration, not supplied.

PROVENANCE   Chichester: 'Boicius de Trinitate glosatus Walteri decani' (fol. 1^r: s. xiv). Master Walter de Segrave, BCL (d. 1349).

BIBLIOGRAPHY   Bernard, *CMA*, I.iii.94; James, *Emmanuel*, p. 27; Emden, *BRUO*, p. 1664; Ker, *MLGB*, p. 50.

THE FITZWILLIAM MUSEUM, f. 1816.

The core of the collection is 130 manuscripts acquired and presented by Viscount Fitzwilliam in 1816. With subsequent additions it was catalogued by M. R. James in 1895; the more recent accessions, if illuminated, were catalogued by Wormald and Giles in 1982. The bequest of Frank McClean (d. 1904), an Ulster engineer and a fine amateur astronomer, was catalogued by James in 1912.

M. R. James, *A Descriptive Catalogue of the Manuscripts in the Fitzwilliam Museum*, Cambridge, 1895; idem, *A Descriptive Catalogue of the McClean Collection of Manuscripts in the Fitzwilliam Museum*, Cambridge, 1912; F. Wormald and P. M. Giles, *A Descriptive Catalogue of the Additional Illuminated Manuscripts in the Fitzwilliam Museum acquired between 1895 and 1979*, Cambridge, 1982.

23. MS Cambridge, Fitzwilliam Museum, 252
Logica vetus et nova   s. xiii; s. xvi

Parchment and paper; i (modern) + 86 + i (modern) fols; page 336x238mm. A (s. xiii, parchment): text 2 cols, each 220x70mm; 54 lines; ruled in pencil; one nice neat hand.
B (s. xiii, parchment): fols 37^r–47^r text 208x130mm; 43 lines; one hand. Fols 47^v–56^v text 2 cols, each 220x70mm; 53–57 lines; same scribe, except for fol. 53^r, where s. xiv hand finishes text of *Prior Anal.* on this page. Fols 53^v–54^v

blank.

C (s. xvi, paper): text 2 cols, 215x65mm each; 44 lines; one good cursive hand.

Catchwords. Oak binding with leather spine; two clasps, missing; label on exterior back cover 'Textus aristotelis'. Re-sewn and repaired, 1989.

A fine folio collection of logic.

CONTENTS   A: fols 1ra–8vb *Post. Anal.*, *expl.* 'et sanitas et salus. Maxime autem in quibus', continued fol. 55^r; 9ra–11rb **Isag.**; 11va–15vb **Cat.**; 15vb–18rb **De Int.**; 18va–20vb *Liber sex principiorum*; 21ra–36vb **Topica Aris.**, *expl.* imperf. 'non accidentie ex hiis que posita sunt ponunt autem' VIII.1, 291/3 (156b39).
B: fols 37ra–53rb **Prior Anal. I–II**, *expl.* 'quod singulare [est]' (67a3); 55$^{ra–rb}$ *Post. Anal.* cont'd, *expl.* 'ad omnem rem'; 55va–56vb **Soph. Elench.**, *expl.* 'uel quod inter haec' (166b12), adding meaningless phrase, *expl.* 'fluens latum est folium omnis'.
C: fols 57ra–86^r **in Cat. I–III**, *expl.* imperf. 'perficiatur passibiles vero qualitates' (*PL*, 64:250A).

GLOSS   *Isag.* a few users' notes; *Cat.* glossed *ad in.*; *De Int.* some annotation; *Topica Aris.* glossed *ad in. Post. Anal.* is the most used text, but nowhere are there signs of extensive use.

DECORATION   Rough Italian decoration to A and B, with miniatures (usually of doctor with book, and sham Arabic writing) or decorative initials and half-borders at the beginning of each treatise except *Prior Anal.* where space is left. Palette: yellow (pretending to be gold), blue, green, orange, pink.
A: typical red and blue initials with alternate pen flourishing; red and blue paraph signs. Pen diagram of tree of Porphyry (fol. 9^v).
B: large pen-drawn initial in red and blue (fol. 55^v); small initial, blue with red penwork (fol. 37^r). No other decoration, but space left.
C: no decoration, but space left.

PROVENANCE   Italian. Libri sale, Sotheby's, 28 March 1859; Phillipps 16237.

BIBLIOGRAPHY *AL*, 1906; Wormald and Giles, pp. 176–77, 199.

24. MS Cambridge, Fitzwilliam Museum, 345
Logica nova   c. 1270

Parchment; 128 + ii fols; page 245x178mm; text 135x80mm; 19–21 lines; one scribe. Once chained.

CONTENTS   Fols 1^r–96^v ***Topica Aris.***; 97^r–128^v ***Soph. Elench.***; i^r–ii^v miscellaneous notes.

GLOSS   *Topica* some marginal gloss; fols 1^r–2^v have extensive interlinear reader's notes, s. xiii^{ex}.
                Soph. Elench. s. xiii^{ex} reader's notes, fols 97^r–99^r; intermittent thereafter.

DECORATION   Historiated initials with gold: Aristotle with pupils (1^r, 97^r). Minor initials with gold (23^v, 30^v, 42^v, 58^r, 77^v, 83^r with silk guard, 112^v). Red and blue capitals with contrasting penwork.

PROVENANCE   French.

BIBLIOGRAPHY   *AL*, 1910; Wormald and Giles, p. 338.

25. MS Cambridge, Fitzwilliam Museum, McClean 165
Top. Diff. I–IV, Cat.   s. xi/xii

Parchment; i (modern) + 140 fols; page 235x156mm.
A (s. xii): text 205x128mm; c. 48 lines; various hands. Red chapter headings.
B (s. xi/xii; s. xii): text c. 190 x c. 130mm, very variable; c. 34 lines.

CONTENTS   A: fols 1^r–88^v Mathematics and astronomy (incl. Adelard of Bath).
                B: fols 89^r–102^r Logic: anon. comm. on *Isag.* (*inc.* 'Cum res omnes quae digne expetuntur propter aliquam trium causarum quas docet Tullius in genere deliberatiuo sint expetendae.– iste quidem liber'; *expl.* 'Sunt quidem alia. sed hec sufficiunt' ; 102^r–16^v anon. comm. on *Cat.*, *inc.* 'Subtilis indagator rerum Aristoteles de decem generibus quae pro excellentis continentiae causa predicamenta uocauit acturus prologomena quaedam id est predicenda in suo premisit tractatu'; *expl.* 'de

qualitate multa interposuisse de relatiuis ut fecimus a partibus. Habitudines enim et dispositiones'; 117^r–34^v *Top. Diff. I–IV*, *expl.* imperf. 'quod gestum est negotio' (*PL*, 64:1213D); 135^v–39^r (s. xii) *Cat.*, *expl.* imperf. 'Dubitare autem de singulis non erit inutile' (63/16). Followed by short notes of eclipses calculated for Marseilles and seen at St Trond, 1289, 1290, 1292.

GLOSS   None.

DECORATION   A: quite ambitious red, green, ochre main initials matching throughout. Simple red and green capitals. Nice tables in red, green, brown.
B: almost none. *C(um)*, decorated black and brown (fol. 89^r). Elsewhere a few simple red initials. Space left for initials, not supplied.

PROVENANCE   A: St Trond (Belgium), s. xiii 4/4; notices of eclipses 'apud sanctum Trudonem' 1285–88 (fol. 66^r).
B: French.

BIBLIOGRAPHY   James, *Fitzwilliam: McClean*, pp. 316–19; *AL*, 258; Leonardi, no. 3; Burnett, *Adelard*, no. 42; Burnett, *Glosses*, pp. 87n, 95, 103, 111.

26. MS Cambridge, Fitzwilliam Museum, McClean 169
Op. Sac. I–II, V, IV, III
                                                           S. XV

Parchment; iii + 283 fols; page 184x121mm; text 130x80mm; c. 50 lines. One scribe, Robert Emylton of Durham, throughout, writing in a distinctive small cursive; he signs many texts (e.g., fols 66^v, 75^v, 280^v). Medieval binding of white leather on wood; two clasps, back fastening; repaired 1986. *Tituli* to I, V; colophons to I–V. Some running headers.
A nice solid copy of these texts.

CONTENTS   Fol. ii^v Emylton's list of contents; 1^r–66^v Ps.-Boethius, *De disciplina scolarium* with Trivet's commentary; 67^r–75^v *Op. Sac. I–II, V*; 75^v–84^r Ps.-Clement, *De fide*, with commentary; 85^r–164^r Plato, *Timaeus*, with Chalcidius's commentary;

164^v–67^v *Op. Sac. IV, III*; 168^r–78^v Hermes Trismegistus; 179^r–228^r Cicero, *De questionibus Tusculanis*; 228^v–34^r Apuleius, *De deo Socratis*; 234^v–39^v Isaac, *De diffinicionibus*; 240^r–45^v Alfarabi, *De diuisione scientiarum*; 246^r–51^r Grosseteste, *De ortu philosophorum*; 251^v–53^v *Prophecia Sibille*; 254^r–56^v Bradwardine, *De memoria artificiali*; 256^v–59^v *Practica geometrie Campani*; 260^r–62^r *De praxi geometrorum*; 262^v–63^v *Propositiones philosophorum magistrales de deo*; 264^r–65^r part of a chronicle; 266^r–80^v Fulgentius, *Mythologiae*.

GLOSS   None.

DECORATION   Pink, blue and gold abstract three-quarter border (fol. 1^r); blue initials with red penwork flourishing: unpretentious and competent. Lemmata underlined in red. Some neatly drawn diagrams.

PROVENANCE   Durham; Phillipps, 3547.

BIBLIOGRAPHY   James, *Fitzwilliam, McClean*, pp. 323–27; Ker, *MLGB*, p. 61.

GONVILLE AND CAIUS COLLEGE, f. 1349.

M. R. James reckoned that well over 300 manuscripts survived *in situ* from the medieval library. John Caius himself added no medieval material of note, but there was a major bequest in 1659 from William Moore, Fellow of Caius and University Librarian. The Caius library is rich in school texts of the later thirteenth and fourteenth centuries: here is Boethius in use.

Bernard, *CMA*, I.iii.691–1276 (1065–1211, bp. Moore); M. R. James, *A Descriptive Catalogue of the Manuscripts in the Library of Gonville and Caius College*, 2 vols, Cambridge, 1907.

27. MS Cambridge, Gonville and Caius College, 199 (105)
***Logica vetus, Soph. Elench*.**   s. xiii 2/3

Parchment; i (modern) + 224 + i (modern) pages; page 196x147mm; text

107x60mm; 20–24 lines ruled for an ample gloss; early panel ruling; similar scribes throughout. Bound in boards, with bevelled edges; leather renewed. Rebound 1909. The 'fragment of a medical MS (xiii)' which James refers to has now been lifted and is loose in the front of the volume.
A homogeneous manuscript.

CONTENTS   P. i medical fragment; 1–18 *Isag.*, glossed; 18–49 *Cat.*, glossed; 49–69 *De Int.*, glossed; 69–91 *Div.* with a few notes only; 91–106 *Liber sex principiorum*, glossed; 107–55 *Top. Diff.*, with a few glosses (*lacuna* at end of III); 157–220 *Soph. Elench.*, glossed; 221–24 notes on *Isag.* etc. in a later cursive hand.

GLOSS   See contents.

DECORATION   Blue and red ink initials with flourishing and infilling; red and blue simple capitals; red paraph signs. Pencil drawing of a man in a hat (p. 45, lower margin). Marginal tree diagrams.

PROVENANCE   Unknown.

BIBLIOGRAPHY   Bernard, *CMA*, I.iii.1022; James, *Gonville and Caius*, p. 228; *AL*, 224.

28. MS Cambridge, Gonville and Caius College, 309 (707)
Op. Sac., DCPhil., Vitae   s. xii 1/2; s. xiv^ex

Parchment; ii + 172 + i fols; page 292x176mm.
A (s. xii 1/2): text 210x88mm; 37 lines, ruled with a stylus for gloss; one good scribe.
B (s. xiv^ex): text 220x130mm; 49 lines; one heavy scribe.
Final flyleaf: folio Bible, s. xii: Exodus.
Gloss related to text by symbols and Greek letters, as in the Carolingian vols. Rubrics identify the metres throughout *DCPhil. Tituli* in red; colophons to I, V. Binding rebacked, 1914.
A fine monastic small folio.

CONTENTS   A: fols 1^r–27^v *Op. Sac. I–V*, glossed; 28^v–86^v *DCPhil.*, glos-

sed; 87^v–88^v schemata of ages of man, planets, elements.
B: fols 89^r–170^v William of Aragon, commentary on
DCPhil.; 171^r **Vitae I–II**; 171^r–72^v Lupus, *De metris.*

GLOSS   A: systematic marginal and interlinear gloss by various
                 contemporary scribes. Some additional s. xiv notes. For *Op.
                 Sac.* cf. MS Cambridge, King's College, 3.

DECORATION   A: good, simple monastic initials in red, green, blue, ochre.
                 Schemata (fols 87^v–88^v) are finely done in colours.
                 B: heavy-handed red and blue initials with thick pen-
                 work; red paraph signs.

PROVENANCE   A: Gloucester. B.T. (fol. 1^r: s. xiv or later).

BIBLIOGRAPHY   Bernard, *CMA*, I.iii.763; James, *Gonville and Caius*, pp.
                 354–55; Cappuyns, 'Opuscula Sacra', pp. **237-72**; Ker, *MLGB*,
                 p. 92; Courcelle, p. 414; Bolton, p. 60; Minnis, in Gibson,
                 chap. 13, p. 314, note 15; Minnis, *Chaucer*, p. 94.

29. MS Cambridge, Gonville and Caius College, 458 (396)
Logica nova   s. xiii/xiv

Parchment; ii + 186 + ii fols; page 294x210mm.
A: text 150x77mm; 28 lines.
B: text 130x66mm; 29 lines.
C: text 145x88mm; 27 lines.
Several hands. Rebound, 1913.
A working book, covered in successive generations of annotations, some (in
B) in a minute and fine hand.

CONTENTS   A: fols 1^r–33^v **Prior Anal.**, glossed, *inc.* imperf. 'necessitate
                 alie non in esse ipsum', I.17, 40/15 (37a22).
                 B: fols 34^r–63^r *Post. Anal.*, glossed.
                 C: fols 63^r–72^r Aristotle, *Ethica noua*, glossed; 72^v–89^v
                 idem, *Ethica uetus*, lightly glossed; 90^{r-v} questions on
                 Post. Anal.; 91^r–114^v **Soph. Elench.**, glossed; 115^r–85^r
                 Topica Aris., glossed.

GLOSS   See contents.

DECORATION   Red and blue initials with penwork flourishing at the beginning of texts. Diagrams in red and blue.

PROVENANCE   Bayham (Sussex) O. Premonst. (fol. 185ʳ: s. xiv^in, a detached leaf). 'Liber fratris Gilberti de Stanton' (fol. 100ᵛ: s. xiv). Flyleaf: 'Ex dono Pulham' and contents list (s. xv).

BIBLIOGRAPHY Bernard, *CMA*, I.iii.1012; James, *Gonville and Caius*, pp. 532–33; *AL*, 229; Ker, *MLGB*, p. 8; Burnett, *Glosses*, p. 143n.

30. MS Cambridge, Gonville and Caius College, 465 (572)
Logica vetus   s. xiii^ex

Parchment; ii (modern) + i + 90 + ii (modern) fols (many are half-sheets or are cut and damaged); page 270x190mm; text 135x80mm; 19 lines, ruled for gloss with panels in inner and outer margins, the outer margin normally ruled as a double panel; two scribes. Scholars' names, fols 43ᵛ–49ᵛ.
Useful elementary textbook of home-made type with massively wide margins.

CONTENTS   Fol. iiiʳ John de Sacro Bosco, two fragments; 1ʳ–15ᵛ *Isag.*, glossed; 15ᵛ–37ᵛ *Cat.*, glossed; 38ʳ–52ᵛ *De Int.*, glossed; 53ʳ–66ʳ *Liber sex principiorum*, glossed; 66ʳ–81ʳ *Div.*, glossed; 81ʳ–90ᵛ *Top. Diff. I–II*, slightly glossed, *expl.* imperf. 'est sapientie amor huic' (*PL*, 64:1187D).

GLOSS   See contents; extensive but not really heavy annotation throughout. Very little to *Top. Diff.*

DECORATION   *C(um)* red, white, green and gold initial, blue background (fol. 1ʳ); otherwise major initials crudely supplied by the scribe, sometimes (fol. 10ʳ) touched by red. Brown and red capitals and initials, supplied by scribe. Red paraph signs (including those linking glosses to text). Marginal drawing of church (fol. 90ᵛ).

PROVENANCE   Unknown.

BIBLIOGRAPHY Bernard, *CMA*, I.iii.1020; James, *Gonville and Caius*, pp.
538–40; *AL*, 230; M. B. Hackett, *The Original Statutes of
Cambridge University*, Cambridge, 1970: matricula, pp. 167
and nn, 348.

31. MS Cambridge, Gonville and Caius College, 466 (573)
Logica vetus et nova   s. xiii

Parchment; i (modern) + 177 + ii + i (modern) fols; page 266x190mm; four
vols bound together (A & D of identical manufacture).
A: text 143x70mm; 39 lines.
B: text 140x80mm; 24 lines; triple panel ruled for gloss.
C: text 135x77mm; 31 lines; double panel ruled for gloss.
D: text 143x70mm; 39 lines.
A variety of competent small s. xiii bookhands. Fols ii–iii (end flyleaves) are
from a lovely s. xi service book. The first pastedown is paper leaf (s. xv) with
portions of a statute prescribing the books to be read by Masters of Arts.
Erasure of a caution note (?), fol. 177^v.

CONTENTS   A: fols 1^r–5^r *Isag.*, glossed; 5^v–15^r *Cat.*, glossed; 15^v–21^r *De
Int.*, lightly glossed; 21^r–26^r *Liber sex principiorum*, glossed;
26^r–32^v *Div.*, glossed; 32^v–53^r *Top. Diff.*, glossed.
B: fols 54^r–108^v *Prior Anal.*, glossed.
C: fols 109^r–35^v *Post. Anal.*, glossed.
D: fols 136^r–50^r *Soph. Elench.*, heavily glossed;
151^r–77^v *Topica Aris. I–VI*, lightly glossed, *expl.* imperf. 'nam qui die utitur et sole utitur…talia' VI.4,
261/15.

GLOSS   See contents. Much successive working over. Many marginal
tree diagrams.

DECORATION   A: good blue, red, and white painted initials, some with gold.
Two initials (fols 1^r, 5^v) added, in an odd palette, by someone
wanting a grand style, but uncertain how to achieve it.
B: nice initial **P**, red, blue, white, green, gold (fol.
54^r); otherwise competent red and blue initials with
penwork; red and blue paraph signs.
C: initial **O**, as in B. A few blue paraph signs.

D: red and blue intials with penwork; red and blue
paraph signs.

PROVENANCE   Magister Henry de Langham, fellow of Michaelhouse
(1324–32) (fol. ii^v). 'Hunc librum contulit magister Johannes
Halle, sacre theologie professor ac rector de Garblysham,
Norwycensis dyocesis, hospicio sancte Marie de Cantebrygia
ad usum ibidem studencium' (fol. 176^v: s. xv).

BIBLIOGRAPHY   Perhaps Bernard, *CMA*, I.iii.1016; James, *Gonville and Caius*,
pp. 540–41; *AL*, 231; M. B. Hackett, *The Original Statutes of
Cambridge University*, Cambridge, 1970, pp. 297–99; Emden,
BRUC, p. 350.

32. MS Cambridge, Gonville and Caius College, 468 (575)
Logica vetus et nova
s. xiii

Parchment; ii (modern) + iv + 438 + ii (modern) pages; page 250x190mm.
A: text 150x90mm; 26 lines; one hand.
B: text 135x90mm; 23–26 lines; at least three hands. Red and blue running
headers.
Double panels, glossed throughout; ample margins, as MSS 465–466.
A very typical-looking production of the mid-s. xiii.

CONTENTS   A: pp. 1–20 *Isag.*, glossed; 20–54 *Cat.*, glossed; 56–75 *De Int.*,
lightly glossed; 76–91 *Liber sex principiorum*, glossed; 92–112
Div., glossed.
B: pp. 113–53 *Soph. Elench.*, glossed; 153–275
Topica Aris., partly glossed (glosses rare in bks
IV–VII); 277–366 *Prior Anal.*, glossed; 369–432 *Post.
Anal.*, glossed.

GLOSS   See contents. Much used by successive generations. Pointing
hands and a few diagrams.

DECORATION   A: red and blue ink initials with rough penwork flourishing
and infilling at beginning of each treatise. Some smaller red
and blue capitals; mostly simple red capitals; red paraph signs.
B: red and blue initials with delicate infilling and

scrolling. Red and blue paraph signs. Pencil
drawings of two men conversing, and seated
scribe, p. 432.

PROVENANCE   'Iste liber est in custodia fratris Wateri de Boxsted ... Accom-
modatus est fratri Roberto de Donmowe' (probably
Franciscans; p. ii^v: s. xiv). 'Iste liber est de communitate aule
Annunciationis beate Marie Cantabrigie' (p. 432). *Ex dono*
Walter Elveden (p. 432).

BIBLIOGRAPHY   Perhaps Bernard, *CMA*, I.iii.1016; James, *Gonville and Caius*,
p. 543; *AL*, 232; Emden, *BRUC*, pp. 210–11.

33. MS Cambridge, Gonville and Caius College, 469 (576)
Topica Aris., Soph. Elench.   s. xiii 2/2

Parchment; ii (modern) + 114 + ii (modern) fols; page 252x180mm; text
122x71mm; 24 lines; double panel ruling; one neat scribe.
A professionally-produced school textbook.

CONTENTS   Fols 1^r–12^v *Post. Anal.*, *inc.* imperf. 'quoniam nullum accidens
recipiunt' (29/10; lacuna between I and II); 13^r–97^v *Topica
Aris.*; 98^r two columns of notes in a minute hand; 99^r–114^v
Soph. Elench., *expl.* imperf. 'nam propter hoc saepe fit
elenchus' (176a35/36).

GLOSS   Extensive throughout. Marginal tree diagrams. Later hand has
added crude running headers.

DECORATION   Red and blue with penwork flourishing in major and minor
initials. Red and blue paraph signs.

PROVENANCE   Probably French.

BIBLIOGRAPHY   Bernard, *CMA*, I.iii.1021; *AL*, 233; James, *Gonville and Caius*,
p. 544; Burnett, *Glosses*, pp. 168, 171.

34. MS Cambridge, Gonville and Caius College, 484 (480)
DCPhil.

s. xiv

Parchment; i + 92 + ii fols; page 370x225mm; text 2 cols, each 295x75mm; 57 lines; hand changes at fol. 75^r. Medieval wooden binding, stripped of leather covering; two clasps (lost); repaired 1913. *Titulus* fol. 75ra; colophon fol. 92ra. Proses and metres marked in *DCPhil.*
One coherent volume, judging by the initials.

CONTENTS   Fols 1ra–74vb Nicholas Trivet's commentary on *DCPhil.*, with lemmata; 75ra–92ra *DCPhil.*

GLOSS   Trivet. Very few signs of use.

DECORATION   Dark blue initials with red penwork flourishing and infilling. Lemmata underlined in red.

PROVENANCE   Unknown.

BIBLIOGRAPHY   Bernard, *CMA*, I.iii.1007; James, *Gonville and Caius*, pp. 554–55; Minnis, *Chaucer*, p. 35.

35. MS Cambridge, Gonville and Caius College, 494 (263)
Logica vetus et nova

s. xiii 1/2

Parchment; ii + 216 + ii fols; page 350x215mm; text 175x88mm; 32 lines, with panels ruled for gloss; similiar scribes throughout. Running titles in pencil in upper margin. Much-repaired medieval binding of white leather on wood, with two clasps (missing); chain mark on front and fol. i^r. Binding repaired, 1911. Pastedowns are part of a folio printed legal text.
A fine library copy of *logica vetus et nova*.

CONTENTS   Fol. ii^v contents-list (s. xv); 1^r–8^r *Isag.*, glossed; 8^r–21^r *Cat.*, glossed; 21^r–29^v *De Int.*, glossed; 29^v–39^r *Div.*, glossed; 39^v–63^v, 70^r *Top. Diff.*, glossed; 64^r–69^v *Liber sex principiorum*, glossed; 70^v–117^r *Topica Aris.*, glossed; 117^r–33^r *Soph. Elench.*, glossed; 133^v–72^v *Prior Anal.*, with lacuna bks I/II, lightly glossed; 172^v–97^r *Post. Anal.*, glossed; 198^r–216^v Aristotle, *Ethics* II–V, I, little to no gloss.

GLOSS See contents. Successive generations have added glosses after the principal marginal and interlinear one. Marginal tree diagrams.

DECORATION Good quality initials (now mostly excised), which had silk covers (stitching remains fol. 1). fol. 1^r *C(um)* has master demonstrating tree of Porphyry to pupils. No other initials survive complete. Good three-quarter borders (blue, red, brown, pink, green, with gold) with dragons (e.g., fol. 64^r). Internal books have competent red and blue ink initials with penwork flourishing, rather darker than the norm. Red and blue paraph signs. Some ink-drawn grotesques, fols 124–33, and tiny animal and human faces.

PROVENANCE English (script). *Ex dono* 'domini Petri Blome' (fol. ii^v: s. xv). Notes of purchase in 1276 and 1349 (fol. 197^r).

BIBLIOGRAPHY Bernard, *CMA*, I.iii.1011; James, *Gonville and Caius*, pp. 565–66; *AL*, 236.

36. MS Cambridge, Gonville and Caius College, 497 (266)
Op. Sac. s. xiii/xiv

Parchment; ii (modern) + 71 + ii (modern) fols; page 330x235mm; text 2 cols, each 228x70mm; 46 lines; same or similar hands throughout. Binding: s. xix. *Tituli* in red. Red and blue running headers; red chapter headings. A homogeneous manuscript, little sign of use.

CONTENTS Fols 1ra–46ra Avicenna, *De anima* (5 books); 46ra–47ra Gundissalinus, *De unitate et uno*; 48ra–52vb Avicenna, *De primis et secundis substantiis*; 53ra–57va Alexander of Aphrodisias, four treatises; 58ra–66vb *Op. Sac. I–V*; 67ra–71va *De materia et forma* (five treatises).

GLOSS None.

DECORATION Red and blue initials with penwork; red and blue paraph signs.

PROVENANCE Unknown.

BIBLIOGRAPHY   Bernard, *CMA*, I.iii.996; James, *Gonville and Caius*, pp. 568–70.

37. MS Cambridge, Gonville and Caius College, 720 (747)
DCPhil.

s. xiv

Parchment; i (modern) + 48 + i (modern) fols (somewhat mouse-eaten); page 222x150mm; text 146x95mm; 26 lines; one hand throughout.

CONTENTS   Fols 1ʳ–48ʳ *DCPhil.* Omits II.m.iv.3 – pr.vii.68 '[qui]dam' and V.pr.ii.16 'potestas. Hu[manas]' – pr.iii.68 'quod sentire'; III.m.ix followed by three fols of commentary (fols 23ᵛ–25ᵛ).

GLOSS   A scattering of user's glosses throughout.

DECORATION   Normally plain red or blue initials; red splash on first letter of each line of verse; a few red and blue paraph signs. Rather nice diagram, fol. 23ʳ.

PROVENANCE   Italian (James). Purchased in 1904.

BIBLIOGRAPHY James, *Gonville and Caius*, p. 691.

JESUS COLLEGE, f. 1496.

In the late seventeenth century Thomas Man, Fellow of Jesus and vicar of Northallerton (Yorks), gave over fifty manuscripts, chiefly from the old monastic libraries of northern England.

Bernard, *CMA*, I.iii.2160–66; M. R. James, *A Descriptive Catalogue of the Manuscripts in the Library of Jesus College, Cambridge*, London, 1895.

38. MS Cambridge, Jesus College, Q. D. 7 (48)
DCPhil.   s. xiii 1/2–s. xv

Parchment; v + 354 + v fols; page 175x125mm.
A (s. xiii/s. xv): text 140x70mm; 27 lines; at least five hands of s. xiii 1/2 to s.
xv.
B (s. xv): text 132x80mm; 30 lines; one hand, or similar hands.
Colophons fols 66ʳ, 86ʳ. Replacement folios (s. xv) at *DCPhil.* III.m.vi.5 to
m.viii.2 and V.pr.iii.72 to end. Fols 28ʳ–56ʳ were once part of a completely
different copy. The *DCPhil.* text has been cobbled together, in order to provide
a text to precede the Trivet commentary. Late medieval binding of white
leather on wood, with two clasps (lost).
A small, fat, unwieldy volume.

CONTENTS	A: fols 1ʳ–66ʳ *DCPhil.* B: fols 71ʳ–86ʳ 'tabula' to *DCPhil.*; 91ʳ–354ᵛ Nicholas Trivet, commentary on *DCPhil.*
GLOSS	Frequent annotation in scribe's hand and some later notes and drawings. Occasional diagrams in commentary.
DECORATION	*C(armina)* green and red abstract initial (fol. 1ʳ); otherwise plain red initials throughout *DCPhil.* Lovely opening initials and full borders to 'tabula' (fol. 71ʳ) and each book of the Trivet (fols 91ʳ, 149ʳ, 188ʳ, 254ᵛ, 316ʳ), gold, blue, green, pink, orange. Blue and red paraph signs; lemmata underlined in red.
PROVENANCE	Durham. Presented by Thomas Man, 21 January 1685.
BIBLIOGRAPHY	James, *Jesus*, p. 78; Ker *MLGB*, p. 61; Minnis, *Chaucer*, pp. 35–55.

39. MS Cambridge, Jesus College, Q. G. 16 (64)
Op. Sac.   s. xii

Parchment; 119 + i fols; page 193x124mm; text 160x86mm; 40 lines, ruled
with a stylus; one high-quality small hand. Bound in a folio of canon law (s.
xiv, 2 cols, glossed), tied with two leather thongs. Parchment tags (s. xvii) at
the beginning of each text. *Titulus* fol. 2ʳ.

CONTENTS Fol. 2^v contents-list in red (s. xii), giving texts in the same order as now; 2^r, 3^r–15^r *Op. Sac. I–V*; 16^r–118^v Anselm, seven treatises, incl. *Monologion* and *Proslogion*.

GLOSS *Op. Sac.* I–III and V *ad in.*

DECORATION Plain initials in red or green at the beginning of each treatise.

PROVENANCE Durham. Presented by Thomas Man in 1685 (fol. 2^v).

BIBLIOGRAPHY James, *Jesus*, pp. 99–100; Ker, *MLGB*, p. 62.

KING'S COLLEGE, f. 1496.

A good contemporary catalogue survives of the medieval library (James, pp. 72–83), but the manuscripts are all lost. The collection now consists of miscellaneous donations by Fellows and others of the mid-sixteenth century onwards.

Bernard, *CMA*, I.iii.2167–73; M. R. James, *A Descriptive Catalogue of the Manuscripts other than Oriental in the Library of King's College*, Cambridge, 1895; Ker, *MLGB*, p. 26.

40. MS Cambridge, King's College, 3
Op. Sac.
s. xii 1/4

Parchment; iv (modern) + i (printed title page, 1575) + 208 + iv (modern) fols (fols 1–4 missing); page 330x234mm. MS in four sections, foliated separately.
A (s. xii 1/4: 126 fols): text 2 cols, each 260x80mm; one hand.
B (s. xii 1/4: 32 fols): text 2 cols, each 260x80mm; one or two similar hands.
C (s. xii 2/3: 18 fols): text 2 cols, each 260x76mm.
D (s. xii 1/4: 32 fols): text 250x123mm; 24 lines; panel ruled for gloss in pencil; one big early s. xii hand.
Similar scripts, throughout, except for C (fols 7–18). Between both B & C, and C & D is another title page of 1575; each is foliated as fol. 1. Rebound, 1981. *Titulus* in red, fol. 1^r.

CONTENTS   A: fols 1–4 missing; 5va–126rb Augustine, *De trinitate*,
                   beginning with relevant section from *Retractationes*; 126^{rb-vb}
                   prayer.
                   B: fols 1ra–31vb Augustine, *De natura et origine anime
                   ad Renatum*.
                   C: fols $1a^{ra}$–18rb Augustine, *Dialectica*.
                   D: fols $1a^{r}$–32^{v} **Op. Sac. I–V.**

GLOSS   Systematic marginal and interlinear Carolingian gloss to *Op.
                   Sac. I–V*. Gloss related to text by alphabet a–x.

DECORATION   D: simple initials in red, green, and combinations. Comparable
                   initials in A and B (s. xii 1/4). The two initials in C are later:
                   s. xii 2/3.

PROVENANCE   ? Bury St Edmunds. Given to King's in 1576 by Richard Day,
                   Fellow. A title-page noting his gift is inserted at the beginning
                   of each section.

BIBLIOGRAPHY James, *King's*, pp. 5–8; Ker, *MLGB*, p. 17.

PEMBROKE COLLEGE, f. 1343.

A good part of the medieval library survives, mainly school texts. In 1599
however William Smart, a local official in Ipswich (Suffolk), gave Pembroke c.
150 manuscripts from the monastic library of Bury St Edmunds. This donation
greatly enhanced the biblical and patristic holdings.

Bernard, *CMA*, I.iii.1930–2159; M. R. James, *A Descriptive Catalogue of the
Manuscripts in the Library of Pembroke College, Cambridge*, Cambridge,
1905.

41. MS Cambridge, Pembroke College, 84
Op. Sac.   s. xi^{ex}/xii^{in}

Parchment; iii (modern) + i + 39 + i + iii (modern) fols; page 242x162mm.
A (s. xi^{ex}/xii^{in}): text 182x105mm; 25 lines ruled in pencil; one hand

throughout.

B (s. xii 1/2): text 205x110mm; 36 lines; different smaller hand, last folio by a third hand. *Tituli* for *Op. Sac.* I–III, V.

CONTENTS	A: 1^r–31^v ***Op. Sac. I–V***.

CONTENTS

A: 1^r–31^v ***Op. Sac. I–V***.

B: 32^r–39^r Scholia on Boethius, *DCPhil.* (III.m.ix), *inc.* 'O admirantis est non uocantis'; *expl.* 'regimen non iugum uocatur qui omnibus uolentibus principatur'; 39^v Definitions, *inc.* 'Quot sunt species qualitatis IIII'; *expl.* 'et pictus homo et uerus homo'.

GLOSS

A: pencil annotation; some marginal and interlinear gloss for *Op. Sac.* (especially I and V).

B: no gloss except for frequent *nota* signs; corrected.

DECORATION

A: simple red initials.

B: none.

PROVENANCE

Bury St Edmunds (*ex libris* fol. i^v: s. xiii). Press mark, B. 319.

BIBLIOGRAPHY

Bernard, *CMA*, I.iii.2143; James, *Pembroke*, pp. 74–75; Ker, *MLBG*, p. 18.

42. MS Cambridge, Pembroke College, 155
DCPhil.

S. XV

Parchment; iii (modern) + 259 + i + iii (modern) fols; page 350x223mm; text 2 cols, each 228x65mm; one scribe. Catchwords; broad margins, ruled for gloss; no sign of use and no *tituli*.

A well-made folio, two–column book in which text and commentary are intercalated.

CONTENTS

Fols 1^r–86^r Ps.-Boethius, *De disciplina scolarium*; 86^v–259^r ***DCPhil.***, with William Wheteley's intercalated commentary, *inc.* 'Philosophie servias ut tibi contingat vera libertas. Ista proposicio scripta est a Seneca.'

GLOSS

Wheteley; otherwise virtually none.

DECORATION   Initials of books in red and blue with red infilling and
                  elaborate flourishing along the page; red and blue paraph
                  signs; rubricated in yellow; beginning of each text in blue and
                  red flourishing.

PROVENANCE   'Iste liber constat M. Thome Westhagh prec. xliii^s. iiii^d' (fol. i^r,
                  endleaf).

BIBLIOGRAPHY James, *Pembroke*, p. 152.

43. MS Cambridge, Pembroke College, 193
Logica vetus et nova   s. xiii^{ex}

Parchment; iii (modern) + 236 + iii (modern) fols; page 345x232mm; text
165x98mm; 28 lines; one scribe.
A well-made academic book with spacious margins for notes.

CONTENTS   Fols 1^r–8^v *Isag.*; 9^r–22^r *Cat.*; 23^r–31^v *De Int.*; 32^r–39^r *Liber sex
                  principiorum*; 39^r–49^r *Div.*; 49^v–78^v *Top. Diff.*; 79^r–98^v *Soph.
                  Elench.*; 99^r–164^v *Topica Aris.*; 165^r–215^r *Prior Anal.*;
                  216^r–36^r *Post. Anal.*

GLOSS   Heavy marginal and interlinear gloss by one main
                  contemporary hand neatly written; several other later
                  annotators. Gloss connected to text with yellow rubrication and
                  underlined key words; later pencil-annotations by at least two
                  hands.

DECORATION   Excellent initials with gold and elaborate flourishing along the
                  page using a pattern of animals and human faces (mostly
                  excised), e.g., initial includes man chopping wood with an axe
                  on a golden background and flourishing down the page (fol.
                  39^r); rubbed initial of two people in bed (fol. 216^r). Pencil
                  sketch of a bearded man kneeling with scroll saying 'tu es
                  asinus' (fol. 223^r). Blue paraph signs; blue capitals with red
                  flourishing.

PROVENANCE   'Iste liber constat aule Valenc. marie', i.e., Pembroke (fol.
                  236^v, twice).

BIBLIOGRAPHY Bernard, *CMA*, I.iii.1999; James, *Pembroke*, pp. 180–81; *AL*, 221; Burnett, *Glosses*, p. 132.

44. MS Cambridge, Pembroke College, 269
Arith.

s. xii 3/3

Parchment; 49 + i fols; page 200x130mm; text 140x80mm; 33 lines; one scribe throughout in a very good hand. Binding: leather over boards with two clasps missing and a staplemark in second cover.
A little-used book.

CONTENTS   1ᵛ–49ᵛ ***Arith.*** (numbers of sections added in the margins). After the usual text (fol. 49ᵛ) is an additional passage, *inc.* 'Cum liberalis experiencia boecii disputavit subtiliter'; *expl.* 'speciebus inequalitatis contigit'. Followed, in a s. xiv hand, by 'Expl[icit] Arithmetica Boecii. Amen.'

GLOSS   Some marginal additions of the scribe; few interlinear contemporary annotations.

DECORATION   Blue, green, red initials with minor flourishing in an alternate colour; the first word is marked with green; neat diagrams; a serpent-like S in red, green, blue at the beginning of book ii (fol. 21ᵛ).

PROVENANCE   'Arismetica boecii empta a quodam ffratre praedicatore. Liber aule Valence marie Cantabrig. [vulgariter nuncupatur pen-brokhall]' (fol. 1ʳ: s. xiv).

BIBLIOGRAPHY Bernard, *CMA*, I.iii.1994; James, *Pembroke*, pp. 246–47.

PETERHOUSE, f. 1284.

Characterized by M. R. James as 'the best specimen we have in Cambridge of a mediaeval College library', the Peterhouse manuscripts were listed in detail in 1418. Further donations are recorded throughout the fifteenth century, and nothing thereafter.

Bernard, *CMA*, I.iii.1663–1930; M. R. James, *A Descriptive Catalogue of the Manuscripts in the Library of Peterhouse*, Cambridge, 1899.

45. MS Cambridge, Peterhouse, 245
Op. Sac. I–II, III, V   s. xiii^ex

Parchment; ii + 150 fols; page 255x173mm; text 2 cols, each 198x56mm; 39 lines. Binding is parchment on cardboard (s. xvii). *Titulus*, fol. 5va.
A good small folio, with a typical textual milieu for *Op. Sac.* in the later Middle Ages.

CONTENTS   Fol. ii^v s. xv contents-list; 1ra–2ra *Op. Sac. III*; 2ra–5va commentary on *Op. Sac. III*, *inc.* 'Precurre prior in domum tuam et illic lude et age concepciones tuas' (Ecclesiasticus 32.15); *expl.* 'Et in hoc terminatur expositio libri'; 5va–9va *Op. Sac. I–II*; 9va–15ra *Op. Sac. V*; 15^r–28^r John Damascene, *Logic*; 28^r–38^r Bede, *De arte metrica*; 38^v–42^r idem, *De schematibus*; 43^r–48^v Anselm, *De grammatico*; 48^v–80^v idem, *De similitudinibus, De beatitudinibus*; 81^r–86^r Augustine, *De uisitatione infirmorum*; 86^r–95^v Jerome, *Ep. ad Eustochium*; 95^v idem, *Quia pondus Dei*; 96^r–105^r Honorius Augustodunensis, *Sigillum sancte Marie*; 105^v–28^r Jerome, four *opuscula*; 128^r–50^v Anselm, prayers.

GLOSS   Some user's notes to *Op. Sac. I* (fols 6va–9ra).

DECORATION   Blue or red initials with contrasting penwork flourishing. Red and blue paraph signs. Space left for *tituli* in *Op. Sac.*, not supplied.

PROVENANCE   Given to Peterhouse by Michael Causton, master of the College and dean of Chichester, d. by July 1396 (fol. ii^v).

BIBLIOGRAPHY   Bernard, *CMA*, I.iii.1743; James, *Peterhouse*, pp. 297–99; Emden, *BRUC*, p. 128.

46. MS Cambridge, Peterhouse, 248
Arith.
                                                                    s. xi

Parchment; i + 92 + i fols (A (fols 1–28) is unfoliated; B (fols 1–64) is
sporadically foliated); page 260x175mm.
A (s. xi): text 220x123mm; 40 lines; one scribe in neat, small hand. No *titulus*,
but book ii is marked in the margin.
B (s. x): text 210x120mm; 41 lines; one scribe. Contemporary title in red at
bottom of fol. 32ʳ.
Pastedown and flyleaf at each end from a s. xiii MS of Roman law. Chain
mark on lower part of end pastedown. Binding: cardboard covered with white
parchment.

CONTENTS   A: fols 1ʳ–27ʳ ***Arith.*.**
               B: 29ᵛ–59ʳ Cicero, *De inventione*; 60ʳ–92ʳ Ps.-Cicero,
               Ad Herennium, followed by a contemporary list of
               capitula.

GLOSS   A: a few ?s. xiii annotations, but hardly any sign of frequent
               use; s. xv notes on Boethius and Cicero on flyleaves.
               B: extensive marginal and interlinear gloss, particularly
               to *Ad Herennium* in various hands from s. xii–xiii;
               pointing hands.

DECORATION   A: rubricated (fols 1–4 only), plain red initials with simple
               flourishing. Diagrams and tables in red and ochre.
               B: good serpentine initials in green and red (fols 1ᵛ,
               32ᵛ). *Ad Herennium* partially rubricated with simple
               red capitals and red rustic titles to sections.

PROVENANCE   'Liber collegii S. Petri Cantebriga' (fol. iiᵛ). In pencil: 'Iste
               liber est Willelmi de Sulle' (fol. 28ʳ). 'arismetica. Musi. re-
               thorica. diale. phisica. calchidius super' (fol. 28ᵛ: s. xiii, rest
               erased).

BIBLIOGRAPHY   Bernard, *CMA*, I.iii.1691; James, *Peterhouse*, pp. 302–3.

47. MS Cambridge, Peterhouse, 275
DCPhil.   s. xiv

Parchment; ii + 196 + iii fols; page 265x190mm; text 190x130mm; 42–43 lines for commentary, 29 for text. One scribe throughout. Pastedowns, canon law (s. xiv). *Titulus*, fol. 3ʳ. Blue and red running headers of bk numbers. Binding: s. xvii.
An ugly, late copy.

CONTENTS   Fols 1ʳ–194ᵛ *DCPhil.* with intercalated commentary of Nicholas Trivet.

GLOSS   Trivet; connected to text by lemmata underlined in red. Some further contemporary glossing (not in the scribe's hand), e.g., I.pr.vi, V.m.iv.

DECORATION   Dark blue capitals with red flourishing. *E(xplanacionem)* a good initial with blue and red infilling and flourishing down the page (fol. 1ʳ). Proses rubricated. Prose and metre nos in margin in red.

PROVENANCE   English.

BIBLIOGRAPHY   Bernard, *CMA*, I.iii.1684; James, *Peterhouse*, p. 348; Kottler, Pe; Minnis, *Chaucer*, p. 35.

ST JOHN'S COLLEGE, f. 1511.

The first and major accession of western manuscripts was the gift of the Earl and Countess of Southampton in 1635. Other, significant, donations followed during the seventeenth and eighteenth centuries.

M. R. James, *A Descriptive Catalogue of the Manuscripts in the Library of St John's College, Cambridge*, Cambridge, 1913.

48. MS Cambridge, St John's College, 17 (A. 17)
Op. Sac. I–III, V

s. xiii

Parchment; iv + 157 + ii fols; page 351x231mm; 2 cols, text 236x64mm each; 44 lines. Two scribes, changing at fols 91–2. *Titulus*, fol. 125vb.
Marginal signs fols 1–91 erroneously attributed to Grosseteste: R. W. Hunt in D. A. Callus, ed., *Robert Grosseteste*, Oxford, 1955, p. 138.

CONTENTS   Fol. iii^v contents list (s. xiv), showing association with St John's, 47 (B. 25); 1ra–91ra Anselm, sixteen works, including *Cur Deus homo, Monologion, Proslogion*; 92ra–121ra Athanasius, *De trinitate et spiritu sancto*; 123ra–34rb **Op. Sac. I–III, V**; 135ra–57vb Rabanus, *De corpore Christi, expl.* imperf. 'Tria hec que sunt in te'.

GLOSS   Subject-headings in margin in a small scholastic cursive.

DECORATION   Blue and red initials with penwork flourishing.

PROVENANCE   Lincoln OFM. William Crashaw, MA, St John's (1572–1626); Thomas Wriothesley, earl of Southampton, 1635.

BIBLIOGRAPHY James, *St John's*, pp. 22–24; Ker, *MLGB*, p. 118; *DNB*, v.36–38 (Crashaw); XXI, pp. 1069–72 (Wriothesley).

SIDNEY SUSSEX COLLEGE, f. 1511.

A miscellaneous collection, due to many donors (often unrecorded) throughout the seventeenth century and later.

Bernard, *CMA*, I.iii.103–6; M. R. James, *A Descriptive Catalogue of the Manuscripts in the Library of Sidney Sussex College, Cambridge*, Cambridge, 1895.

49. MS Cambridge, Sidney Sussex College, 31
Mus.   s. xiii/xiv

Parchment; i (modern) + 154 + i (modern) fols; page 290x190mm; text (for
Mus.) 225x155mm; 60–64 lines; several neat hands in volume. Running
headers in brown. *Mus.* text is all present, but scrambled: I–II as normal; III
begins but runs into end of IV; V runs into rest of IV (binding too tight to
work out the problem). Once were all separate texts, but long ago
homogenized.

CONTENTS   Fols 1ʳ–51ʳ Augustine, *De Genesi ad litteram, inc.* imperf.
                  (begins iv.10); 51ʳ–98ʳ Ambrose, *Hexaëmeron*; 98ᵛ–119ᵛ **Mus.**;
                  119ᵛ–40ᵛ Chalcidius, *In Timaeum, expl.* imperf. 'opinione
                  potius', p. 338 line 15 (ed. J. H. Waszink, *Plato Latinus*,
                  London etc., 1962); 141ʳ–54ᵛ Aristotle, *Metaphysics, inc.*
                  imperf. (first 10 bks only).

GLOSS   A few notes to Augustine and Ambrose, nothing elsewhere.
                  Many diagrams to *Mus.*

DECORATION   *Mus.* has rather rough diagrams and tables in red and brown.
                  Simple red or brown initials. Other treatises have very simple
                  decoration and crude diagrams.

PROVENANCE   Gift of William Pratt, MA, vicar of Bossal, Yorks (d. 1701–2).
                  He gave MSS 30–39.

BIBLIOGRAPHY   James, *Sidney Sussex*, pp. 14–15; *AL*, 240; Bower, no. 16.

50. MS Cambridge, Sidney Sussex College, 94
Op. Sac. I–II   s. xiii

Parchment; iii (modern) + ii + 184 + iii (modern) fols (unfoliated); page
340x235mm; text 2 cols, each 242x72mm; 62 lines; drypoint ruled for gloss;
one neat professional hand. Running headers and chapter headings in red.
Colophon to *Op. Sac. I* (fol. 179ʳ). Blind-stamped, s. xix College binding.
A nice folio professional textbook.

CONTENTS   Fol. iiᵛ s. xv contents list; 1ʳ–121ᵛ Augustine, treatises incl. *De trinitate*, *Confessions*, *De Genesi*; 121ᵛ–23ʳ Sixtus, *Enchiridion*; 123ʳ–24ᵛ Isidore, *Admonitio*; 124ᵛ–27ʳ Hugh 'Farsitus', *De gratia conseruanda*; 127ʳ–29ʳ Hugh of St Victor, *Liber quattuor questionum*; 129ʳ–31ᵛ Seneca, *Letters*; 131ᵛ–32ᵛ Jerome, Commentary on Jeremiah (excerpt); 132ᵛ–44ʳ Athanasius, various treatises; 144ᵛ–77ᵛ Augustine, treatises on marriage and virginity; 178ʳ–79ʳ **Op. Sac. I–II**, glossed, *inc.* imperf. 'motu abstracta' (I.ii.14) to end of *Op. Sac.* II; 179ʳ–84ʳ Bernard of Clairvaux, *De gratia et libero arbitrio*.

GLOSS   Heavily glossed in all four margins, in same hand as text. No other gloss in MS.

DECORATION   Red and blue initials with alternate flourishing; red and blue simple capitals; rubrication.

PROVENANCE   York Franciscans (fol. 1ʳ); gift of Dr Sam Ward, master of Sidney Sussex 1609–1643.

BIBLIOGRAPHY James, *Sidney Sussex*, pp. 75–76; Ker, *MLGB*, p. 218.

TRINITY COLLEGE, f. 1546.

Two early benefactors, Archbishop Whitgift and Dean Nevile (both Masters of Trinity), established the manuscript collection. They drew heavily on the former monastic library of Canterbury cathedral.

Bernard, *CMA*, I.iii.138–690; M. R. James, *The Western Manuscripts in the Library of Trinity College, Cambridge*, 4 vols, Cambridge, 1900–4.

51. MS Cambridge, Trinity College, O. 3. 7 (1179)
DCPhil., Epitaph II
s. x

Parchment; ii (modern) + 52 + ii (modern) fols; page 290x225mm; text 230x135mm; 28 lines; one fine scribe. Metres in rustic capitals throughout. *Tituli*. Gloss related to text by letters of alphabet and Tironian notes in red.

Rhetorical subject-headings in capitals in margin: e.g., LAUS SIMACHI (II.pr.
iv.15: fol. 11ᵛ). Colophon 'Deo gratias' transliterated into Greek, fol 51ʳ.
A very striking volume, beautifully written; unfortunately trimmed in re-
binding.

CONTENTS   Fol. 1ᵛ prolegomena to gloss; 2ʳ–51ʳ *DCPhil.*, glossed; 51ʳ⁻ᵛ
                  theological note as part of *DCPhil.* whose *explicit* comes after
                  it: *inc.* 'Est enim deus pater quo omnia'; *expl.* 'et ideo im-
                  mutabilis'; 51ᵛ–52ᵛ Lupus, *De metris*; 52ᵛ *Epitaph II*.

GLOSS   Systematic Carolingian interlinear and marginal gloss, related
                  to text with reference signs, generally in red.

DECORATION   Full-page drawing of Philosophia, with writing-tablets in R
                  hand and flowering rod in L (fol. 1ʳ). Black ink Celtic initials
                  with bird-heads, red and yellow infill. Lovely palette of russet,
                  ochre, black. Offset red capitals to *metra*. Schema of elements
                  (fol. 24ᵛ).

PROVENANCE   St Augustine's, Canterbury.

BIBLIOGRAPHY   James, *ALCD*, cat. 993; James, *Trinity*, iii.188–89; H. F.
                  Stewart, 'A Commentary by Remigius Autissiodorensis on the
                  De consolatione philosophiae of Boethius', *Journal of
                  Theological Studies*, 17, 1917, pp. 22–42 (MS C); F. Wormald,
                  English Drawings of the Tenth and Eleventh Centuries,
                  London, 1952, pp. 27–29, 63–64, and pl. 3; Ker, *MLGB*, p. 42;
                  Courcelle, p. 405 and pl. 22; Bolton, pp. 51, 60; Troncarelli,
                  Boethiana, no. 70. See pl. 1.

52. MS Cambridge, Trinity College, O. 7. 9 (1337)
Soph. Elench.   s. xii/xiii

Parchment; i (modern) + iii + 182 + i (modern) fols; page c. 170 x c. 110mm.
Four MSS bound together by s. xiii (fol. iiiʳ).
A (s. xii/xiii): text 138x80; 38 lines; one good hand.
B (s. xiii): text 130x70mm; variable no. of lines (minimum 17); several similar
hands.
C (s. xii/xiii): text 128x76mm; 29 lines.

D (s. xii): text 128x80mm; 31 lines.

CONTENTS

Fol. iv^{r–v} table of contents for the sermons.
A: fols 1^r–121^v Peter Comestor, Sermons.
B: fols 122^r–35^r Alexander Nequam, *De utensilibus*
(glossed); 142^v–51^v *Formulae epistolarum*; 151^v–59^v
Proprietates ignis.
C: fols 160^r–75^v **Soph. Elench.**
D: fols 176^r–82^r Theological excerpts.

GLOSS

None for C.

DECORATION

A: red or green header (for number of sermon) and simple red
capitals.
B: none.
C: space left for initials, not supplied.
D: plain red capitals (rather oxidized); red headings to
the excerpts, and rubrication.

PROVENANCE

Buildwas O. Cist. (Shrops.): 'Liber sancte marie de Buldewas
sermones petri manducatoris qui bene vult disponere Liber
elencorum et quedam alia' (fol. iii^v: s. xiii). 'Rogerus de
S…gham' (fol. 173^v: s. xiii).

BIBLIOGRAPHY James, *Trinity*, iii.351–53; *AL*, 243; Ker, *MLGB*, p. 14.

53. MS Cambridge, Trinity College, R. 15. 16 (940)
Arith.

s. xii 1/2

Parchment; i (modern) + i + 63 + i (modern) fols; fols 1–3, 60–63 are the old
flyleaves to the vol.; page 222x135mm; text 153x80mm; 30 lines; small hand.
Tituli in red.
A prettily produced copy.

CONTENTS

Fols 1^v–3^r Discussion of liberal arts, *Ex cerebro Testardi. inc.*
'Arcium liberalium doctrina aut in sermonum proprietate
consummatur'; *expl.* 'et quidam modernorum in eadem claru-
erunt ut alardus Johannes Willelmus. Musicam'; 4^r–59^v **Arith.**;
59^v 'Explicit liber arithmetice Nicomachi translate a Boecius

Se. Incipit secunda pars artis que est practica eiusdem. secundum Grecos Arabos et Indos. Artis numerandi due sunt partes. Altera quam Boe a greca transferens inuentione soli uacans speculationi'; *expl.* 'Nichil autem libri anxiomatum exceptis cara/[cteribus dicimus]'; 60^r–63^v diagram of two checkered boards (for arithmetic ?) and notes.

GLOSS   Occasional annotation *ad in.*

DECORATION   Fine opening initial *I(n dandis)*, fol. 4^r, with gold, red, green; thereafter good quality simple red, blue, green initials, and very pretty diagrams in blue, red, green, brown.

PROVENANCE   English; Franciscans of Coventry (fol. 3^v: s. xiv); 'Boecii de communitate fratrum minorum Couentr' et registratus Boecius A' (fol. 3^v); given to Trinity by John Laughton, canon of Worcester and Lichfield.

BIBLIOGRAPHY   James, *Trinity*, ii.354–45; Ker, *MLGB*, p. 55; C. Burnett, 'Ocreatus' in *Vestigia Mathematica: Studies in Medieval and Early Modern Mathematics in Honour of H. L. L. Busard*, ed. by M. Folkerts and J. P. Hogendijk, Amsterdam, 1993, pp. 69–77 (76–77).

54. MS Cambridge, Trinity College, R. 15. 22 (944)
Mus.   s. xii 1/2

Parchment; ii (modern) + 140 + ii (modern) fols (fols 6–9 missing); page 303x212mm; text 210x155mm; 27 lines for *Mus.*; one scribe for *Mus.*, writing large, clear Christ Church script; another similar hand thereafter. *Titulus* fol. 1^r. Self-coloured running headers, s. xiv. Greek well-done in red with Latin gloss, fols 2^v–3^r. In lay-out, rubrication, and initials *Mus.* is closely related to MS Cambridge, University Library, Ii.3.12. Neumes, fols 123^v–24^r, 'ut queant laxis'.
A spectacular book.

CONTENTS   Fols 1^r–101^v *Mus.*; 102^r–17^r Guy of Arezzo, *Micrologus*, glossed; 121^v–24^r *Opuscula*; 124^{r-v} *De positione sonorum, tonorum et symphoniarum secundum Boetium*; 124^v–26^r Berno of Reichenau, *Prologus in Antiphonarium* (excerpt); 126ᵛ–29ʳ four texts on the measurement of organ pipes; 129ʳ–31ʳ *Scholia in Enchiriaden* (excerpts); 131ʳ⁻ᵛ two texts on the measurement of cymbala; 131ᵛ–34ᵛ Guy of Arezzo, Ep. to Michael; 134ᵛ–36ᵛ texts on the measurement of pipes and the monochord; 136ᵛ–40ʳ six short musical texts.

GLOSS   None.

DECORATION   Author-portrait, with dividers: *O(mnium)*, fol. 1ʳ. Spectacular inhabited initials, in green, purple, red, blue, ochre, and occasional yellow, fols 5ᵛ, 11ᵛ, 28ʳ, 49ʳ, 66ʳ, 92ʳ, 102ʳ (a striking David killing a lion). Rubrics of each chapter red, green, purple rustic capitals. Gorgeous, big diagrams in green, red, ochre, purple.

PROVENANCE   Christ Church, Canterbury, c. 1180: identifying mark EE: 'MUSICA BOETII ET MUSICA GUIDONIS EE' (fol. 1ʳ: s. xii); '*de claustro Cant.*' (fol. 1ʳ: s. xiv); 'this ys John hills bok wrytte the second day of April 1564' (fol. 140ᵛ); given by George Willmer, fellow-commoner of Trinity (d. 1626).

BIBLIOGRAPHY   Bernard, *CMA*, I.iii.384; James, *Trinity*, ii.361–63; James, *ALCD*, pp. xxxiii, 8 no. 39, 35 no. 438; C. R. Dodwell, *The Canterbury School of Illumination 1066–1200*, Cambridge, 1954, pp. 32, 38; Ker, *MLGB*, p. 33; Bower, no. 17; *Registrum Anglie*, 58.4.

55. MS Cambridge, Trinity College, s. n.
Cat.   s. ix–x

Parchment; a single page 150x270mm; insular features to Caroline hand. Used as a book wrapper; ties still partially intact.
Once a fine large volume.

CONTENTS   Fol. 1ʳ two and a half lines of *Cat.*, *inc.* 'habere uxorem'; *expl.* 'sunt annumerati' (last lines of c. 15); 1ᵛ *Categoriae decem*, *expl.* 'paulatim oratio' (*AL*, i.5, 133/16).

GLOSS   None for *Cat.*, but *Categoriae decem* glossed.

DECORATION   None for *Cat. Categoriae decem* has orange-red heading; drawing of bishop's head in margin. Headings in good rustic capitals.

PROVENANCE   N. E. France.

BIBLIOGRAPHY   Schenkl, II.2, p. 70; *AL*, 2040.

CANTERBURY

LIBRARY OF THE DEAN AND CHAPTER

The libraries of all the religious houses in Canterbury *except* the cathedral were dispersed at the Reformation. Over the next half century most of the cathedral collection was conveyed to London, Cambridge and elsewhere. Eventually the cathedral acquired further manuscripts, not of Canterbury provenance, and some Canterbury books returned to their native city.

C. E. Woodruff, *A Catalogue of the Manuscript Books in the Library of Christ Church, Canterbury*, Canterbury, 1911; Ker, *MLGB*, pp. 29–48; Ker, *MMBL*, ii.265–330.

56. MS Canterbury Cathedral, Lit. D 5 (49)
Logica vetus s. xiii^{ex}

Parchment; 158 fols; page 254x191mm; text 120x72mm; 26 lines; one scribe (fols 3–85); ruled for gloss. Red and blue titles as running headers.
A handbook of elementary grammar, logic and (lost) ethics.

CONTENTS   Fols 3^r–11^r *Isag.*; 11^r–26^r *Cat.*; 26^v–35^r *De Int.*; 35^r–43^r *Liber sex principiorum*; 43^r–53^v *Div.*; 54^r–85^r *Top. Diff.*; 85va–88vb Nicholas of Amiens, *De articulis fidei* (Glorieux, *Théologie*, 107a); 89^r–146^r Priscian, *Institutiones* xvii–xviii (Passalacqua, no. 96); 146^v–51^v idem, *De accentibus* (*GL*, iii.519–28);

152^v–53^v *Regule versificandi*; 154^r–58^v Donatus, *Ars maior*, from 'De barbarismo' to end (*GL*, iv.392–402); 158^v 'Incipit primus liber etycorum' (title only).

GLOSS   Extensive user's gloss, fols 3–85.

DECORATION   Blue and red initials with penwork flourishing.

PROVENANCE   English. John of London (s. xiv 1/3) gave the book to St Augustine's, Canterbury (fols 2^v, 3^r).

BIBLIOGRAPHY   James, *ALCD*, p. 350, no. 1286; *AL*, 264; Ker, *MLGB*, p. 42; A. B. Emden, *Donors of Books to St Augustine's Abbey, Canterbury*, Oxford, 1968, pp. 11–12; Ker, *MMBL*, ii.277.

DURHAM

LIBRARY OF THE DEAN AND CHAPTER, f. 995.

Durham is the only English cathedral to have retained its library (and archives) *in situ* until the present day. All the manuscripts described below belonged to the medieval monastic community.

Bernard, *CMA*, II.i.66–602; T. Rud, *Codicum manuscriptorum ecclesiae cathedralis Dunelmensis catalogus classicus, completed 1727*, Durham etc., 1825; R. A. B. Mynors, *Durham Cathedral Manuscripts to the End of the Twelfth Century*, Oxford, 1939; Ker, *MLGB*, pp. 60–76; Ker, *MMBL*, ii.483–511.

57. MS Durham Cathedral, A. II. 11
in Cat.
                                                        s. xii mid

Four consecutive folios from the middle of a single quire of *in Cat.* now form the two last fols (143–144) of the first volume of a three-vol. s. xiii commentary in French on the Psalter (MSS Durham Cathedral, A. II. 11–13). Parchment; page (trimmed) c. 245x165mm; text 2 cols, each c. 240x70mm; 74

lines extant; at least two scribes with small, spiky hands.
Originally an undistinguished text for private use.

CONTENTS *in Cat.*, *PL*, 64:177A–214A (some lines missing at upper and lower margins).

GLOSS None.

DECORATION None. Space for initial, not supplied.

PROVENANCE Durham Cathedral. 'Robert of Hilton' in vol. 2 of the three-volume set.

BIBLIOGRAPHY Rud, pp. 16–17; *AL*, 1943; Ker, *MLGB*, p. 63.

58. MS Durham Cathedral, C. I. 16
Logica vetus et nova   s. xiv^{in}

Parchment; i (modern) + 251 + i + i (modern) fols; page 360x250mm; text 2 cols, each 240x55mm; 31 lines; double-frame ruled in pencil; one scribe. Durham Cathedral binding with clasps. Scribal colophons, e.g., fol. 217va, 'Scriptor scripsisset plus si scripto reperisset. Amen.' Running titles. A noble folio, consistently produced, and sporadically used in s. xiv.

CONTENTS Fols 2ra–8va *Isag.*; 9ra–20rb *Cat.*; 20va–28vb *De Int.*; 29ra–35vb *Liber sex principiorum*; 36ra–45vb *Div.*; 46ra–75vb *Top. Diff.*; 76ra–97vb *Soph. Elench.*; 98ra–170vb *Topica Aris.*; 171ra–217va *Prior Anal.*; 217vb gloss (inner and outer cols.); 218ra–51vb *Post. Anal.*, *expl.* 'utique erit scientie principium principiis'.

GLOSS Ruled for ample gloss, only partly utilized. Miscellaneous user's glosses throughout (s. xiv). The only systematically commented texts are *Soph. Elench.* and *Post Anal.* Text has been corrected; nota signs, small faces, and diagrams.

DECORATION First page of text (fol. 2^r) bordered in red and blue scrollwork; blue initial touched with gold, with red infilling and scrolling; red, blue and gold primitive dragon at bottom right. Some blue initials, touched with gold, with red infilling, and partial borders at beginning of each treatise. Blue and red initials with scrolling and red or blue paraph signs throughout.

PROVENANCE   Durham Cathedral: *Liber sancti Cuthberti de Dunelmo* (fol. 2^r: s. xiv).

BIBLIOGRAPHY Rud, p. 262; *AL*, 268; Ker, *MLGB*, p. 69.

59. MS Durham Cathedral, C. IV. 16
Logica nova   s. xiii 2/3

Parchment; i (modern) + 304 + i (modern) fols; page 265x185mm.
A: text 140x75mm; 29 lines; double-panel ruling fols 1^r–126^v; triple-panel ruling, fols 127^r–66^v; one scribe.
B: text 2 cols, each 182x58mm; *c.* 59 lines for gloss; one hand throughout, with one primary glossing hand.
Durham Cathedral binding, 2 clasps. B is a smarter book than A. Running headers in red and blue; pointing hands, drawings, etc.
A good school workbook, well-used, carefully kept up.

CONTENTS   A: fols 1^r–16^v *Soph. Elench.*; 17^v–72^v *Topica Aris.*; 74^r–131^r *Prior Anal.*; 132^r–66^v *Post. Anal.*
              B: fols 168^r–304^r Aristotle, *Physics* with Averroes's commentary.

GLOSS   A: extensive glossing in ruled marginal space, mostly by one hand.
              B: one primary glossing hand; a few extraneous comments.

DECORATION   A & B: red and blue initials with infilling and scrolling; red and blue paraph signs.

PROVENANCE   Probably English; Durham Cathedral.

BIBLIOGRAPHY Rud, p. 301; *AL*, 276; Ker, *MLGB*, p. 71.

60. MS Durham Cathedral, C. IV. 17
Logica nova   s. xiii 2/3

Parchment; i (modern) + 239 + i + i (modern) fols; page 290x200mm; text 130x80mm; 24 lines; double-panel ruled for gloss; one scribe. Catchwords. Durham Cathedral binding, two clasps. Red running headers with title and book nos; red chapter nos in margin.

CONTENTS	Fol. 3^r scrawled s. xv contents-list; 3^r–34^r *Soph. Elench.*; 34^r–129^r *Topica Aris.*; 129^v–98^v *Prior Anal.*; 199^r–239^r *Post. Anal.*
GLOSS	Fairly continuous but not heavy marginal and interlinear glossing in late s. xiii hand, with some s. xvi notes.
DECORATION	Red and blue initials and paraph signs, etc. up to fol. 15^r, then only red. Space left for some initials, not supplied.
PROVENANCE	Durham Cathedral. *Ex dono* Uthred of Boldon, 'Liber sancti cuthberti de Dunolmo ex procuracione uthredi monachi eiusdem' (fol. 2^v: s. xiv).
BIBLIOGRAPHY	Rud, pp. 301–2; *DNB*, xx.17–18; *AL*, 277; Ker, *MLGB*, p. 71.

61. MS Durham Cathedral, C. IV. 19
Logica nova   s. xiii 2/3

Parchment; iii (modern) + i + 200 + iii (modern) fols; page 275x190mm; text 115x80mm; 21 lines; double panel ruled for gloss.
A university book with wide margins; very used and battered, in a bad state of repair.

CONTENTS	Fol. 1^r s. xiii contents-list; 1^r–29^v *Soph. Elench.*; 30^r–108^v *Topica Aris.*; 109^r–62^v *Prior Anal.*; 163^r–200^v *Post. Anal.*
GLOSS	Constant marginal and interlinear gloss in at least two major hands; some s. xv and s. xvi notes in pencil.
DECORATION	Jolly historiated red and blue initial *D(e)* of tonsured, red-haired Aristotle (?) in green robe with red stockings and black

shoes, sitting on red stool with green cushion, teaching clerical students in brown; purple-brown background (1ʳ). **D**(*e responsione*) Jesus and three men, one of whom is in bed (15ʳ); wonderful ink drawing of knight's head (23ᵛ, margin). **P**(*ropositum*), a miniature of the annunciation: Gabriel (with scroll) in dark blue and Mary in green (30ʳ). Red and blue capitals and initials with alternate flourishing; red and blue paraph signs; funny faces, drawings, pointing hands etc.

PROVENANCE   Durham Cathedral (fol. 1ʳ).

BIBLIOGRAPHY Rud, p. 303; *AL*, 279; Ker, *MLGB*, p. 71.

UNIVERSITY LIBRARY, f. 1832.

The core collection is that established in 1669 by John Cosin, bishop of Durham, for the use of the diocesan clergy. Bishop Cosin's Library became a unit within the University Library in 1937.

Rud's catalogue of the Cosin manuscripts—which, like his cathedral catalogue, long remained in manuscript—was published by James Raine in *Catalogi veteres librorum ecclesiae cathedralis Dunelm.*, Surtees Society, Durham, 1838, pp. 136–91; Ker, *MMBL*, ii.513–21.

62. MS Durham University, Cosin V. ii. 11
DCPhil.
                                                                            s. xiv

Parchment; i (modern) + i + 136 + i + i (modern) fols; page 265x182mm.
A: text 195x125mm; 47–53 lines; probably two hands, varying in size. Running titles.
B: text 170x105mm; 35–36 lines; one neat scribe.
'Nomen scriptoris benedicat deus omnibus horis', fol. 130ʳ. Binding: s. xvii with s. xix spine and clasp replacement.
A coherent and homogeneous MS.

CONTENTS   A: fols 1ʳ–130ᵛ *DCPhil.*, with Trivet's commentary.

B: fols 131^r–36^v Ps.-Boethius, *De disciplina scolarium* (incomplete; # 25 of O. Weijers edition, p. 112 line 2 to p. 134 line 11).

GLOSS   A: Trivet. A few corrections and notes in s. xv hand; no further gloss. *DCPhil.* metres in left-hand column with Trivet's commentary in right-hand column.

DECORATION   A: one ambitious initial, with gold (paint), purple, blue, green, red, white with foliated flourishing (fol. 1^r). Blue initials with red flourishing and infilling, with some unusual human heads in the penwork. Circular spaces for diagrams left blank, fols 94^v–95^r. A few red grotesques, e.g., fol. 82^r. Fols 1^r–10^v, 126^r red underlining, rubrication etc, elsewhere in brown; fols 35^r–41^v initials not supplied.
B: blue initials with red infilling and scrolling (as A); blue paraph signs.

PROVENANCE   English. Geo. Davenport, 1664.

BIBLIOGRAPHY   A. Piper and I. Doyle, provisional typescript catalogue of the Cosin MSS.

EDINBURGH

NATIONAL LIBRARY OF SCOTLAND, f. 1925.

By 1700, the Society of Advocates in Edinburgh had a considerable library, recently augmented by the collection of James Balfour of Kinnaird and Denmilne (d. 1657), Lyon King-of-Arms to Charles I. In 1925 all the non-legal manuscripts of the Advocates' Library passed to the National Library of Scotland (Ker, *MMBL*, ii.526; *Encouragement*, chap. 10). Manuscripts acquired subsequently are described in seven published volumes (1–9500) and a continuing typescript.

National Library of Scotland: Catalogue of Manuscripts acquired since 1925, Edinburgh, 1938– ; *Summary Catalogue of the Advocates' Manuscripts,*

Edinburgh, 1971; Ker, *MMBL*, ii.526–30; P. Cadell and A. Matheson, *For the Encouragment of Learning: Scotland's National Library 1689–1989*, Edinburgh, 1989.

63. MS Edinburgh, National Library of Scotland, Advocates 18. 5. 14
DCPhil., Vita

s. xv 1/2

Paper; ii (parchment) + iii (paper) + 108 + ii (parchment) fols; page 217x141mm; text 138x75mm; 21 lines ruled to allow user's annotations; one scribe, writing a clumsy but clear humanistic hand. Tooled leather binding on wood, two clasps (lost), s. xvi. Red and blue roman numerals as running headers.

CONTENTS   Fols 1ʳ–105ᵛ *DCPhil.*; 106ʳ–7ʳ a late *Vita*, *inc.* 'Ad sciendum de vita et morte Boetii. Notandum quod'; *expl.* 'eius corpus requiescit nunc in ecclesia papiensi'.

GLOSS   Sporadic user's annotation throughout, mainly in English.

DECORATION   At the beginning of each book penwork initials in red and blue, with green, purple, and red delicate infilling; competent red and blue rubrication throughout. Red and blue paraph signs.

PROVENANCE   A continental MS; in Edinburgh by *c.* 1600, owned by Robert Abircrumby, MA 1598 (fol. viᵛ), Thomas Drummond (fol. viᵛ), and John Hamilton (fol. iᵛ), who probably all studied at Edinburgh University, and Alexander Yule (*ex libris* fol. 108ᵛ), editor of George Buchanan. In the library of the Society of Advocates after the mid-s. xviii, in whose collection it passed to the National Library in 1925.

BIBLIOGRAPHY *Summary Catalogue*, nos 1297, 1564.

64. MS Edinburgh, National Library of Scotland, Advocates 18. 5. 18
Op. Sac. I–III, V   s. xiii[ex]

Parchment; xiv (modern) + 238 + xvi (modern) fols; page 200x160mm; 21
lines, written below the top line; text 145x80mm; several hands. Titles in red
in text. Binding: plain Denmilne leather on cardboard, with two clasps; sewing
stiffener is early s. xiii law text.

CONTENTS   Fol. 1[v] almost contemporary table of contents, as now; 2[r]–37[r]
                 Op. Sac. I–III, V; 38[r]–93[v] Augustine, *De cognitione verae
                 vitae, De decem cordis, De trinitate* (sermon); 93[v]–118[r] Ps.-
                 Anselm, *De excellentia uirginis Marie*; 118[r]–41[v] idem, *De
                 conceptione sancte Marie*; 141[v]–64[v] Augustine, *De penitentia*;
                 164[v]–203[v] idem, *De spiritu et anima*; 204[r–v] Gregory of Tours,
                 Gesta Francorum, i.21–24; 204[v]–5[r] Augustine, sermon;
                 205[r]–28[r] *Gesta Salvatoris*; 228[r]–38[v] *Conflictus civium Babi-
                 lonie et Iherusalem.*

GLOSS   A few pencil corrections in the margin.

DECORATION   Blue, red, and green initials with penwork flourishes at the
                 beginning of all items except fols 55[r], 79[r], 93[v], 118[v] where the
                 main initials are in gold leaf against blue and light purple.

PROVENANCE   Rochester Cathedral priory: *Radu[l]fi de Eylesburi monachi*
                 (fol. 2[r]). Acquired in 1629 by James Balfour of Kinnaird (fol.
                 1[r]) and Denmilne (cypher on fol. 238[v]), in whose collection it
                 passed to the Society of Advocates and thence (1925) to the
                 National Library of Scotland.

BIBLIOGRAPHY *Summary Catalogue*, nos 1277, 1800; Ker, *MLGB*, p. 161;
                 Encouragement, chap. 6 (Denmilne).

65. MS Edinburgh, National Library of Scotland, Advocates 18. 6. 3
DCPhil.   1443/44

Paper; iv (modern) + 230 + ii (modern) fols (a number of pages glued to
modern sheets for conservation); page 205x140mm; text 155x100mm; 30 lines;
one cursive scribe, Michael Miniclardus of Dieppe (scribal colophons giving

dates, fols 139^v, 221^v, 228^r); Greek poor, e.g., fol. 39^v. *Titulus* fol. 1^r. Modern binding. Very small running headers until bk III.
A low-quality, cheap, personal book.

CONTENTS   Fols 1^r–5^v Trivet's prologue; 5^v–221^v **DCPhil.**, with Trivet's commentary; 222^r–28^r anonymous *Exhortatio*; 228^v–30^v sheets of notes in a later hand.

GLOSS   Trivet. Reader marks include *Nota bene* signs.

DECORATION   Not much decoration except rubrication of lemmata and red paraph signs; some drawings of faces, dogs etc. done by the scribe. Red chain line fillers. First initial **E***(xplanationem)* (fol. 1^r) in red with elaborate infilling and scrolls; smaller versions of this occur at the beginning of books and sections. Bad diagram (fol. 43^r) of phases of the moon; space for diagrams not added fol. 49^r, 115^r, 116^v.

PROVENANCE   *Ex dono* Gulielmi Mansfeldio Comitis, 3rd earl of Mansfield, 1820 (fol. iii^r).

BIBLIOGRAPHY   *Summary Catalogue*, nos 1320, 1563.

66. MS Edinburgh, National Library of Scotland, 9247
DCPhil.
s. xii 2/3

Parchment; i (modern) + 59 + i (modern) fols; the fourth quire (fols 24–31) is inverted; page 115x80mm; text 100x55mm; 21 lines; one good scribe, except for fol. 39. Plain Victorian binding. In IV.pr.ii (fols 55^r–58^r) the dialogue is marked **B**(oethius) and **Ph**(ilosophy) in red.
Pocket *DCPhil.*

CONTENTS   Fols 1^r–59^v **DCPhil.**, I.pr.iv.89 – IV.m.iii.32. Pages missing at II.pr.vii.60 (fol. 23^v) and III.m.ix.1 (fol. 39^v).

GLOSS   Some careful contemporary annotations fols 1^r–22^v, but most notes badly cropped by the binder.

DECORATION   Major initials red or blue, with slight flourishing in contrasting colour; alternating red and blue initials to each line in the metres. Drawing of crowned figure in margin, fol. 11^r.

PROVENANCE English.

BIBLIOGRAPHY Ker, *MMBL*, ii.528; *National Library* (1989), VII, pp. 128–29.

ETON

ETON COLLEGE LIBRARY, f. 1443.

Sir Henry Savile (1596–1622), concurrently warden of Merton College, Oxford, was one of the great provosts of Eton. He established a systematic collection of printed books: classics and patristics, scholastic and modern theology, history. In his time books and manuscripts were rebound, including MSS 120 and 129 discussed below.

Bernard, *CMA*, II.i.1799–1924; M. R. James, *A Descriptive Catalogue of the Manuscripts in the Library of Eton College*, Cambridge, 1895, [193 MSS], entirely redone by Ker, *MMBL*, ii.628–798 [280 MSS]; Ker, *MLGB*, pp. 79–80.

67. MS Eton College, 120
Op. Sac.   s. xiv mid

Parchment; i (modern) + ii + 333 + ii (modern) fols; page 336x218mm; text 2 cols, each 278x80mm; 66–67 lines; several contemporary scribes, but volume planned as a unit. Chain-mark on front cover. Williamson binding, s. xvii. Red titles and running headers. *Titulus*, fol. 212ra.
A well-written book which does not seem to have been extensively used.

CONTENTS   Fol. iii^r almost contemporary contents-list; 1^r–211^v twenty-six theological treatises by Augustine or attributed to him, and twenty-three treatises by Anselm or attributed to him (including *Monologion, Proslogion, Cur Deus homo*); 212ra–18ra *Op. Sac. I–V*; 218$^{ra–vb}$ Gundissalinus, *De unitate et uno*; 218vb–333^r Hugh of St Victor, *De archa Noe* and a further nineteen,

mainly theological, items by John Chrysostom, John Damascene, Ps.-Dionysius and Bernard of Clairvaux.

GLOSS   Virtually none; very few annotations including a pointing
                 finger.

DECORATION   Fair blue initials with red penwork flourishing.

PROVENANCE   Written in England. Launde (Leics.), Can. Reg. John de Burgo,
                 prior of Launde in 1306; 'Liber fratris [six lines erased] anno
                 gratie m°ccc° octavo decimo' (fol. iii^r). Given to Eton by John
                 Bonour, a former member (d. 1467): donation note, fol. ii^v.
                 Price mark, 'viii marke', fol. 333^r.

BIBLIOGRAPHY   Bernard, *CMA*, II.i.1823; James, *Eton*, pp. 52–53; Emden,
                 BRUO, p. 219; Ker, *MLGB*, p. 112; Ker, *MMBL*, ii.721–39.

68. MS Eton College, 129
Op. Sac. III
                                                                        s. xiv

Parchment; ii + 217 (actually 218) + iii fols; page 270x185mm.
A (s. xiii): text 185x115mm; 33 lines; one scribe in pointed hand.
B (s. xiv): 175x112mm; 31 lines; one Italian scribe.
C (s. xiv): 172x113mm; 32 lines; one Italian hand (not that of B).
Williamson binding, s. xvii. Colophons, fols 153^r, 217^v.
A well-made book.

CONTENTS   A: fols 1^r–67^v Aristotle, *Ethics*.
                 B: fols 68^r–150^v Aristotle, *Politics*; 150^v–52^v Ps.-Aris-
                 totle, *De bona fortuna, inc.* imperf. '[Ha]bitum autem';
                 expl. 'Quoniam autem segregare volumus potentiam
                 ipsarum et de virtute articulati tractandum ea que ex
                 hiis quam vocamus kalokanganthiam et cetera';
                 153^r–54^r *Op. Sac. III*.
                 C: fols 155^r–206^v Aristotle, *Rhetoric*; 206^v–17^v idem,
                 Poetics, bk I.

GLOSS   No annotations for Boethius; *Ethics* annotated by at least two
                 annotators; few annotations for Aristotle's texts in B and C.

DECORATION   A: splendid decorated initial O(mnia), fol. 1^r, in gold, blue,
pink; rubricated; red and blue initials with penwork flourish-
ing; red and blue and paraph signs.
B: splendid historiated initial Q(uoniam), fol. 68^r:
Aristotle bearded with book and red–brown gown on
blue background. Red and blue initials with blue and
red flourishing; red and blue paraph signs and running
headers (but not for *Op. Sac.*).
C: splendid initial in gold, blue, brownish red R(he-
torica), fol. 155^r: two men teaching, with book and
scroll. Border with bearded man and angel with trum-
pet; abstract flourishing in grey, white, blue, brownish
red and gold. Initial to bk III Q(uoniam), fol. 193^v, has
bearded man with book, speaking.

PROVENANCE   Italian. B & C at Eton by 1609.

BIBLIOGRAPHY Bernard, *CMA*, II.i.1811; James, *Eton*, pp. 59–60; *AL*, 282;
Ker, *MMBL*, ii.748–49.

GLASGOW

GLASGOW UNIVERSITY LIBRARY

No manuscripts survive from the medieval library. Those acquired in the late
seventeenth and the eighteenth centuries were dramatically augmented in 1807
by the collection of Dr William Hunter: see Ker's Edwards Lecture, below.
Later acquisitions (if not in named collections) have the shelf-mark 'Gen.'

J. Young and P. H. Aitken, *A Catalogue of the Manuscripts in the Library of
the Hunterian Museum in the University of Glasgow*, Glasgow, 1908; Ker,
MMBL, ii.871–933; N. R. Ker, *William Hunter as a Collector of Medieval
Manuscripts*, Edwards Lecture on Palaeography 1, Glasgow, 1983.

69. MS Glasgow, Hunter 272 (U. 5. 12)
DCPhil.

s. xi/xii

Parchment; iii (modern) + 40 + iii (modern) fols; page 231x138mm; text 166x85mm; 33–34 lines; one principal scribe throughout, beautiful hand; ruled with stylus; Hunterian binding (s. xix$^{in.}$). *Titulus* in poor display capitals in red, green, brown ink (fol. 1^r).
Well-used and useful.

CONTENTS   Fols 1^r–40^r *DCPhil.*; 40^{r-v} fragment of commentary on III.m.ix in another s. xii hand, *inc.* '*Tu numeris elementa ligas*: id est numerabilibus qualitatibus. ignis est siccus et calidus'.

GLOSS   Quite extensive s. xii marginal gloss in several hands (not the scribe's), *inc.* 'In miseri persona Boetius miseriam suam deplorat, et proponit unde tractaturus sit cum dicit, Ego cogor inire mestos modos'; *expl.* 'reges adhuc illos qui hodie sunt et cetera sic.' Some later annotation by a reader who has marked the beginning of each book; also pointing hands, pencil notations, notas etc. Reference signs are gallows paragraph marks.

DECORATION   Splendid and unusual major initials different from one another at the beginning of each book. Knot patterns with lion breathing out foliage (fol. 7^v). Minor initials opening a prose or metre in red, blue, ochre, green, purple; single colour capitals offset on each line of most of the metres. Diagrams fols 31^v–32^r (IV.pr.vi).

PROVENANCE   ? S. France. ? Italy. Bought by William Hunter from Archibald Dodd, 27 July 1775.

BIBLIOGRAPHY   Young and Aitken, pp. 220–21; Ker, *William Hunter*, pp. 10, 21; N. Thorp, *The Glory of the Page: Medieval and Renaissance illuminated Manuscripts from Glasgow University Library*, Glasgow, 1987, no. 4, p. 53, with plate; Troncarelli, *Boethiana*, no. 74.

70. MS Glasgow, Hunter 279 (U. 5. 19)
DCPhil.   c. 1120–1140

Parchment; ix (modern) + i + 66 + iv (modern) fols; page 240x175mm; 2 cols;
Boethius text col. 175x75mm; commentary text col. 175x45mm; 32 lines;
ruled with stylus and pencil; one scribe. Hunterian binding (s. xix[in.]); rebound
1954. Once bound with MSS Hunter 278 and 280 (see s. xii/xiii contents list,
fol. 1[v]: 'In hoc volumine continentur Tullius de Amicicia cum glosis [Hunter
278], Boecius de consolacione philosophie [Hunter 279], Martianus [Hunter
280]'). Parchment repaired with added pieces where initials have been cut out.
Hebrew on flyleaf (fol. 1[v]).
A scruffy little book.

CONTENTS   Fols 1[r]–65[r] *DCPhil.*, *inc.* imperf. I.pr.i.28 'luminibus. quis
                inquit has scenicas'; 65[r]–66[v] misc. philosophical and theologi-
                cal notes (s. xii/xiii).

GLOSS   Extensive marginalia, mostly in one, contemporary hand.
                Linked to text by brown gallows signs. Some evidence of later
                (s. xiv/xv) pencil notas and pointing hands.

DECORATION   Mutilated. Splendid illuminated initials, of which only the
                opening to bk V survives (fol. 54[v]) in brown, orange and red
                ink. Originally contained a portrait of Boethius (fol. 31[r]).
                Simple minor initials red or red and yellow. Fol. 45[v]: part of a
                lovely ink picture of Ulysses reaching safety as his crew are
                turned into animals (see Kauffmann and Thorp for pictures).

PROVENANCE   Unknown. Was in Scotland by mid s. xii, possibly produced at
                Durham. Bought by William Hunter from Gregory Sharpe, 8
                April 1771.

BIBLIOGRAPHY   Young and Aitken, p. 225; Beaumont, in Gibson, pp. 296–97,
                pl. ix; Bolton, in Gibson, p. 429; Ker, *William Hunter*, p. 15;
                C. M. Kauffmann, in *English Romanesque Art 1066–1200*, ed.
                G. Zarnecki, et al., London, 1984, p. 102; N. Thorp, *The Glory
                of the Page: Medieval and Renaissance Illuminated Manu-
                scripts from Glasgow University Library*, Glasgow, 1987, no.
                13, p. 61; Troncarelli, *Boethiana*, no. 75.

71. MS Glasgow, Hunter, 292 (U. 6. 10)
Prior Anal.   s. xiii 1/4

Parchment; iii (modern) + 51 + iii (modern) fols; page 217x143mm; 37 lines; one scribe (except fols 18–21: an intercalated small quarternion, s. xii 1/2).

CONTENTS   Fols 1ʳ–17ᵛ *Prior Anal. I*; 18ʳ–21ᵛ Latin-French word-list; 22ʳ–32ʳ *Prior Anal. II*; 32ᵛ fragment of notes or commentary (cropped margins); 33ʳ–44ᵛ *Post. Anal. I*; 44ᵛ–51ʳ *Post. Anal. II*.

GLOSS   Extensive users' gloss in various hands throughout, especially fols 33 ff.

DECORATION   Major initials red and blue with penwork flourishing (fols 1ʳ, 33ʳ, 44ᵛ); frequent minor initials and paraph signs red and/or blue, with flourishing.

PROVENANCE   French (script). Jean Charpentier, dean and canon of Abbeville (fol. 1ʳ: s. xvi). Bought by William Hunter from Robert and Andrew Foulis, booksellers in Glasgow, in 1771.

BIBLIOGRAPHY   P. Meyer, *Documents manuscrits*, Paris, 1871, pp. 120–26 (the French word-list); Young and Aitken, pp. 234–35; *AL*, 283; Ker, *William Hunter*, pp. 10, 21; *AL*, iii.1–2, siglum Gw.

72. MS Glasgow, Hunter 374 (V. 1. 11)
DCPhil.   1385

Parchment; iii + 110 + ii fols; page 345x250mm; Boethius text 170x120mm; text and commentary 260x195mm; 23 lines for main text, 43–62 for the commentary; ruled for commentary; one scribe 'frater Amadeus' (fols 1ʳ, 3ʳ). Beautiful Italian hand, so even as to look printed; central text with surrounding commentary. Water damage in bk III. Greek is either omitted or bungled; where present it is in gold (e.g., fol. 93ᵛ).
A display MS; not much sign of use.

CONTENTS   Fols iiiᵛ–1ʳ elaborate alphabets and prayers; 1ᵛ–3ᵛ Trivet's prologues; 4ʳ–99ᵛ *DCPhil.*, with Trivet's commentary; *expl.*

imperf. 'sed imaginaria ratione iudicandi', V.pr.iv.115.

GLOSS   Trivet.

DECORATION   Very ambitious Bolognese illumination, signed and dated. Boethius teaching and visited by seven arts (fol. 4^r); splendidly decorated initials for each book with leaf, flower and bird motifs. The many gold letters in a very good condition are surrounded by blue cross-hatching. The commentary has red and blue initials and scrolling and infill; red and blue paraph signs in text. Large letters are in blue, grey, orange, beige, white, green and mud gold. Nicely-drawn diagrams.

PROVENANCE   Italian: Bologna. 'Istud opus est Gregorii de Janua (Genoa) mccclxxxv' (fol. 1^r). Pieter Burmann sale, Leiden, 27 September 1779.

BIBLIOGRAPHY Young and Aitken, pp. 300–1; P. Courcelle, 'Étude critique sur les commentaires de la "Consolation" de Boèce', *Archives d'histoire doctrinal et littéraire du Moyen Âge*, 12, 1939, pp. 133–34; idem, *Histoire littéraire des grandes invasions germaniques*, 3rd edn, Paris, 1964, App. viii + pl. 44b; B. Wolpe, '*Florilegium alphabeticum*: Alphabets in Medieval Manuscripts', in *Calligraphy and Palaeography. Essays presented to Alfred Fairbank*, ed. A. S. Osley, London, 1965, pp. 69–74; Courcelle, pl. 18.1; Ker, *William Hunter*, pp. 9–10, 17; N. Thorp, *The Glory of the Page: Medieval and Renaissance Illuminated Manuscripts from Glasgow University Library*, Glasgow, 1987, no. 71, p. 131.

73. MS Glasgow, Gen. 337
DCPhil.

s. xv 2/2

Parchment; 56 fols (Ker's flyleaf now gone); page 215x150mm; text 145x95mm; 25 lines ruled in pencil; one scribe (humanistic cursive). Red roman bk nos as running headers. Catchwords. *Titulus*, fol. 1^r; colophon, fol. 56^v.

CONTENTS   Fols 1^r–56^r *DCPhil.*

GLOSS   Stylized nota signs in the margin, otherwise none.

DECORATION   Major initials blue with extensive red and white infilling and scrolling at beginning of each book. Some smaller blue initials with red scrolling and red initials with yellow scrolling. Small red and rubricated initials; red gallows paraph signs.

PROVENANCE   ? Spanish.

BIBLIOGRAPHY Ker, *MMBL*, ii.911–12.

HEREFORD

HEREFORD CATHEDRAL LIBRARY

The medieval chapter library survived the Reformation *in situ*, being augmented by manuscripts from other collections in the west of England, notably Cirencester.

Bernard, *CMA*, II.i.1593–1798; A. T. Bannister, *A Descriptive Catalogue of the Manuscripts in the Hereford Cathedral Library*, Hereford, 1927; Ker, *MLGB*, pp. 96–99; R. A. B. Mynors and R. M. Thomson, *Catalogue of the Manuscripts of Hereford Cathedral Library*, Woodbridge, 1993.

74. MS Hereford Cathedral, P. III. 6
DCPhil.
                                            s. xv^{in}

Parchment; i (modern) + 244 + i (modern) fols; page 200x150mm; text 160x105mm; 30–36 lines; 2 cols to fol. 56^v, long lines thereafter; one hand, except for fols 61^r–62^v, 78^r in a secretary hand which corrects and annotates elsewhere. Most of the Boethius text is written on inserted additional leaves. Catchwords. Rebound, 1961; trimmed by binder.
A chained book with chain still in place.

CONTENTS   Fols 1^r–54^v Commentary on Aristotle, *Rhetorica*; 54^v–56^r 'Incipit tabula super libros rethoricorum Aristotelis'; 56$^{r–v}$ note on rhetoric; 57^r–241^r ***DCPhil.*** with Trivet's commentary, intercalated; (fols 69^v, 71^v, most of 74^v, 241^v–4^v blank).

GLOSS   See contents.

DECORATION   *DCPhil.*: 3/4 border, flourished in red, blue and violet, fol. 57^r. Plain blue initials; circular diagrams in ink of text, e.g., fols 67^v, 72^v, 86^r, 88^v.

PROVENANCE   'Ex dono M. Oweyni lloyd legum doctoris', canon and prebendary of Hereford, d. by Oct. 1478 (fol. 2^r: see Mynors and Thomson, pp. xxiii–xxiv). 'Liber M. Pe… Wal… [pro]…x…vi d.' (erased, fol. 244^v: s. xv). 'Blake' (fol. 66^v: s. xvi).

BIBLIOGRAPHY   Mynors and Thomson, p. 86; Emden, *BRUO*, pp. 1153–54 (Lloyd).

HOLKHAM HALL, NORFOLK

LIBRARY OF THE EARLS OF LEICESTER

The collection of over 700 manuscripts was largely inherited or acquired by Thomas Coke (1698–1759), the builder of Holkham Hall. They were listed by William Roscoe and Frederic Maddan in the 1820s; and that list was eventually published by Seymour de Ricci in 1932. Twenty years later many of the finest manuscripts were set against death duties, 153 passing to the Bodleian Library and 21 to the British Museum (Hassall, p. 42). The three described below are still at Holkham.

S. de Ricci, *A Handlist of Manuscripts in the Library of the Earl of Leicester at Holkham Hall*, Oxford, 1932; J. E. Graham, 'The Cataloguing of the Holkham Manuscripts', *Transactions of the Cambridge Bibliographical Society*, 4.2, 1965, pp. 128–54; W. O. Hassall, *The Holkham Library: Illuminations and Illustrations in the Manuscript Library of the Earl of Leicester*, Oxford, 1970.

75. MS Holkham Hall, 402
DCPhil.
                                                                          late s. xiv

Parchment; iii (modern) + ii + 113 + iii (modern) fols (actually 112 as foliation misses 72); page 345x230mm; text 190x120mm; 20 lines for text, c. 78
for gloss; panel ruled for gloss in pencil; one big, round, loose hand for text.
Gloss on all four sides of central text. Leaf signatures (horizontal lines, one to
five, in blue, red, or brown ink) at bottom right hand corner for most quires.
Binding: s. xix, Holkham. Hebrew pledge note, fol. iv^r. Red roman nos as
running headers.

CONTENTS   Fols iv^v–v^v prologue to Trivet; 1^r–113^v *DCPhil.,* with Trivet's
                  commentary.

GLOSS   Extensive, systematic marginal and interlinear gloss in at least
                  three contemporary hands. A few later notes.

DECORATION   Showy but ugly initials at beginning of each book of *DCPhil.*
                  (gold, pink, blue, red, green). Minor initials and capitals in
                  blue with red, or red with purple flourishing. Red and blue
                  paraph signs and brown gallows signs mark the paragraphs of
                  gloss in the margin.

PROVENANCE   Italian. Belonged in 1440 to Giovanni Marcanova, a Venetian
                  doctor in Padua (c. 1418–67); *ex libris* in red (fol. v^v; cf MS
                  London, BL, Harley 3234), and his donation note in red (fol.
                  113^v). Given to the monastery of S. Giovanni di Verdara, in
                  Padua, in 1467; thence to Thomas Coke in 1717.

BIBLIOGRAPHY   De Ricci, p. 35; P. Sambin, 'La formazione quattrocentesca
                  della biblioteca di S. Giovanni di Verdara in Padova' in *Atti
                  dell'Istituto Veneto di scienze, lettere ed arti*, 114, 1955–56,
                  pp. 263–80; Hassall, p. 38; C. E. Wright, *Fontes Harleiani*,
                  London, 1972, p. 233 and pl. VIIIa (Harley 3234).

76. MS Holkham Hall, 403
DCPhil.
                                                                            s. xv

Parchment; iii (modern) + 25 + iii (modern) fols; page 260x190mm; text

203x140mm; 38 lines; one Italian hand. Greek either incomprehensible or translated. Catchwords. Binding: s. xix, Holkham.
A striking, attractive book.

CONTENTS   Fols 1ʳ–25ᵛ *DCPhil.*, *expl.* imperf. V.pr.vi.79 'omnia suo'.
                Lacuna from III.pr.ix.31 'ex parte videatur' (fol. 16ᵛ) to
                IV.pr.iv.116 'pati]antur iniuriam' (fol. 17ʳ).

GLOSS   None. A s. xvii hand has added marginal notes on contents,
                fols 18ʳ, 21ʳ, 25ʳ.

DECORATION   Striking, painted historiated initials, sadly affected by damp, at
                beginning of each bk of *DCPhil.* in orange-red, blue-green,
                pale blue, purple, gold (mostly rubbed away). Boethius in hat
                and gown with three-quarter border; pious pelican feeding
                young; shield for owner's crest, not supplied (fol. 1ʳ). Woman
                in red dress and blue and white headdress (fol. 6ʳ); young
                woman in red and blue dress with blue headdress (fol. 12ᵛ);
                Christ in blue and purple robe (fol. 21ʳ). Elsewhere capitals
                blue with red flourishing, red with purple flourishing. A few
                pen-drawn faces and animals.

PROVENANCE   Milan (de Ricci). Mr Witherstone (? s. xix: fol. iᵛ).

BIBLIOGRAPHY   De Ricci, p. 35; Hassall, p. 38.

77. MS Holkham Hall, 404
in Topica Cic.   s. xiv 1/2

Parchment; ii (modern) + 86 + ii (modern) fols; page 270x200mm; text
190x127mm; 33 lines; two or three scribes. Catchwords. Red chapter headings.
Binding: s. xix, Holkham.

CONTENTS   Fol. 1ʳ prologue to commentary, *inc.* 'Argumentum artis rhe-
                torice. Incipientes quamcumque rem scribere'; 1ʳ–86ʳ *in Topica
                Cic.*

GLOSS   A few marginal annotations (often summaries of subject mat-
                ter) in the first text hand throughout. Ink is rubbed away in

places but there are few signs of use.

DECORATION   Major initial *I(ncipientes)* of gold with purple, blue, green, silver in floral pattern (fol. 1^r). Otherwise blue initials with red flourishing, red with purple. A few red and blue paraph signs.

PROVENANCE   ? Italian.

BIBLIOGRAPHY De Ricci, p. 35.

LICHFIELD

CATHEDRAL LIBRARY, f. 669

Virtually nothing survives of the medieval library. While some manuscripts were listed in the seventeenth and eighteenth centuries, the first complete catalogue to be published is Ker, 1983.

Ker, *MMBL*, iii.112–26.

* 78. MS Lichfield Cathedral, 1a
in Cat., De Int.
     s. x 2/2

Two complete leaves and part of a third leaf used, presumably, as medieval binding to the Lichfield Gospels (MS 1; ?s. viii mid; pp. 241-44). Parchment; text 212x140mm; 34 lines; pp. 241–42 one good scribe; pp. 243–44 two scribes.
The insular Gospel book came to Lichfield in the later tenth century, immediately from Wales. The Boethian flyleaves, which are not insular, were incorporated in a binding of (we may conjecture) the twelfth century or later, in Lichfield.

CONTENTS   Pp. 241–42 *in Cat.* (frag.), from 'perpenserit' to 'in qualitatibus posse' (*PL*, 64:249, line 77–251, line 12). Pp. 243–44 are two conjoint leaves of a bifolium laid sideways, one leaf complete, the other cut down the middle. The complete leaf is an abbreviation of *in Cat.* from 'convertuntur' to 'spetiesque contineat quando' (*PL*, 64: 287, line 14–294 end). The half leaf is most of chaps 10–11 of **De Int.** (*AL*, II.i, 23/3 – 29/5).

GLOSS   Unknown.

DECORATION   Unknown.

PROVENANCE   ? France.

BIBLIOGRAPHY   Bernard, *CMA*, II.i.1387; Ker, *MLGB*, p. 115; J. J. G. Alexander, *Insular Manuscripts 6th to the 9th Century*, London, 1978, no. 21; Ker, *MMBL*, iii.113–14.

LINCOLN

LIBRARY OF THE DEAN AND CHAPTER, f. 1072

Although c. 100 manuscripts survive from the medieval library, these include no Boethius; nor do they reflect the notable scholars and scholarly activity in Lincoln in the late twelfth and thirteenth centuries. The fragments below may or may not be native to Lincoln.

Ker, *MLGB*, pp. 115–18; R. M. Thomson, *Catalogue of the Manuscripts of Lincoln Cathedral Chapter Library*, Woodbridge, 1989 (without these fragments).

79. MS Lincoln, Cathedral Library, Fragm. 48
Prior Anal.

Parchment; 1 fol.; page 160x120mm (heavily cut down and folded); text 74mm wide; 23 lines surviving on each side; ruled for gloss; one scribe.

CONTENTS   ***Prior Anal.***: 'solus insit' to 'ad minorem' (84/7 – 85/22); 'non enim suscipit' to before 'esse autem' (86/10 – 87/23).

GLOSS   Contemporary marginal and interlinear gloss.

DECORATION   Red and blue paraph signs.

PROVENANCE   Unknown.

BIBLIOGRAPHY *AL*, 1950.

80. Lincoln, Cathedral Library, Aa. 6. 5
Cat.
                                                                s. xiii^ex

Parchment; 1 fol. cut in half to make front and back pastedowns to A. Talaeus, Paris, 1553; page (front) 155x122mm (back) 155x99mm; text 65mm wide; (front) 17 & 18 lines (back) 7 & 7 lines; ruled for double gloss; one scribe. Marginal tree diagram.

CONTENTS   *Cat.* cc. 10–12: 'cum uero' to 'ut sanita[ti' (74/12–28);
                 'contraria est' to 'languere' (75/1–8); 'contrarium est'' to
                 'existentibus' (75/8–25); 'sit reliquum' to 'prius' (75/27–76/5).

GLOSS   Considerable contemporary marginal and interlinear gloss.

DECORATION   Red initial with blue flourishing.

PROVENANCE   Arthur Gregory.

BIBLIOGRAPHY Ker, *Pastedowns*, no. 864b; *AL*, 1951.

LONDON

THE BRITISH LIBRARY

The British Museum, f. 1753. From 1973, *The British Library.*

Established by Act of Parliament in 1753, in which year the Harley and Sloane collections were purchased. For the present collection see M. A. E. Nickson,

The British Library: Guide to the Catalogues and Indexes of the Department of Manuscripts, 2nd edn, London, 1982, and *Index of Manuscripts in the British Library*, 10 vols, Cambridge, 1984, I, Introduction (not paginated).

ADDITIONAL MANUSCRIPTS

Manuscripts acquired 1756–1955 are catalogued by the year of accession (BL, *Cat. Add.*). Manuscripts acquired after 1955 are listed in a series of 'Rough Registers' (1974–): see *Index of Manuscripts* (above). See also EGERTON (below).

81. MS London, BL, Add. 10093
DCPhil.   s. xiv

Parchment; i + 66 + i fols.
A (s. xiv): page 170x120mm; text 120x77mm; 29 lines; several similar scribes.
B (s. xiii): page 170x120mm; text 126x85mm; one scribe.
Flyleaf (fol. 66: s. xii) fragment of canon of Mass.
Ideal school text.

CONTENTS   A: fols 1ʳ–6ᵛ *Disticha Catonis*; 7ʳ–17ᵛ two grammatical trea-
                tises, *inc.* 'In presenti opusculo rudium utilitati uolens in-
                tendere'; *expl.* 'tibi sunt communia lector' (15ʳ); *inc.* 'Notaque
                vi sunt adverbia localia' (15ᵛ); *expl.* 'uel apud montem pen-
                sulanum uel prope'; 18ʳ–40ᵛ Ps.-Prosper of Aquitaine, *Car-
                mina*, with *accessus*; 41ʳ–56ʳ *DCPhil*. I–III.pr.i.l0.
                B: fols 57ʳ–65ᵛ Galterus Anglicus, *Aesop* (Hervieux, i.
                566).

GLOSS   A few users' notes and pointing fingers.

DECORATION   Line-drawing of Cato (fol. 6ᵛ) and *Justitia* with sword and
                scales (fol. 56ᵛ). Small painted initials in blue, red and ochre in
                A.

PROVENANCE   'Colle<gium> Agen<ense>' (fol. 1ʳ), a Jesuit college, dép. Lot
                et Garonne. Acquired from Heber in 1836.

BIBLIOGRAPHY BL, *Cat. Add.* (1836), p. 10.

82. MS London, BL, Add. 14792
DCPhil.

s. xiv^{ex}/xv^{in}

Parchment; iii + 89 + iii fols; flyleaves i–vi foliated 1–3, 88–90 (s. xiii); page 280x195mm: text 176x90mm; 24 lines; one scribe for the text; gloss added in a minute and elegant contemporary cursive.

CONTENTS Fol. 1^v notes in Italian; 2^{r-v} heavily-glossed quadrivial text, as fol. 89^{r-v}; 3^r–87^r *DCPhil.* I–V.pr.iv.56; 87^v–88^v *probationes pennae* (verses and aphorisms, s. xv); 89^{r-v} as fol. 2^{r-v}.

GLOSS Gloss, *inc.* 'Volens igitur Boetius agere de phylosophica consolatione duo facit. Nam primo ostendit se talem qui indigeat consolatione et inducit personam consolationem afferentem ibi prosa prima "Hec dum mecum"' (fol. 3^r); *expl.* 'habent liberos "exitus" et non "necessarios" et hoc probat "Nam"' (79^v: V.pr.iv.55–56). Cf. William of Conches.

DECORATION Initials in red, blue and pale purple with elaborate penwork infill beginning each book.

PROVENANCE N. E. Italy. *Ex libris* (fol. 3^r, bottom centre: s. xv^{ex}) 'magistri Eustachii Lippi', written across a shield (on the left, green; on the right, red, white and gold horizontal bars). 'Nicholaii' (erasure fol. 2^v: s. xv^{in}). 'Ioannes de possa pulto' (fols 87^v–88^r: s. xv).

BIBLIOGRAPHY BL, *Cat. Add.* (1844), p. 6; Kottler, D.

83. MS London, BL, Add. 15407
Op. Sac. I–III, V

s. xiii 2/2

Parchment; ii + 252 + iii fols; page 259x179mm; text 2 cols, each 185x59mm; 49 lines; several similar scribes.

CONTENTS Fols 1ra–26vb Anselm, *Similitudines*; 27ra–43vb idem, *Mono-*

logion; 43vb–46ra idem, *Proslogion*; 46ra–81rb idem, seven opuscula; 81rb *Prophetia sibille hispanice* (added s. xiii–xiv); 82ra–88va ***Op. Sac. I–III, V***; 88va–93va Ps.-Anselm, *De sacramento altaris*: *inc.* 'Henrico electo ex militibus suis'; *expl.* 'animam nostram efficit'; 93va–100va Anselm, *De concordia prescientie et liberi arbitrii*; 100va–19vb idem, *Cur Deus homo*; 119vb–59vb John Damascene, *De fide orthodoxa*; 160ra–92rb Richard of St Victor, *De trinitate*; 192rb–202ra Isidore, *De ordine creaturarum*; 202ra–52vb Richard of St Victor, *De contemplatione*.

GLOSS   None.

DECORATION   Red and blue penwork initials: minor products of the workshop responsible for the principal manuscripts of Vincent of Beauvais (Stones; cf. BL, Egerton 628 below).

PROVENANCE   *Liber S. Marie de Camberone* (*ex libris* fols 1^r, 54^r, 82^r, 122^r, 155^r etc.): St Mary, Cambron, a Cistercian house in the diocese of Cambrai.

BIBLIOGRAPHY   BL, *Cat. Add.* (1845), pp. 2–3; A. Stones, *The Minnesota Vincent of Beauvais Manuscript and Cistercian Thirteenth Century Book Decoration*, Minneapolis, 1977.

84. MS London, BL, Add. 15601
DCPhil.   s. x^ex/xi^in

Parchment; v (modern) + 108 + v (modern) fols.
A: page 248x145mm; text 220x115mm; 32–34 lines; similar hands.
B: page 247x145mm; text 215x105mm; 36 lines; an idiosyncratic scribe, fols. 75^r–101^v, with distinctive ligatures and abbreviations.
Titulus to bk I in poor display script (fol. 16^v). Metres written as prose. Bk nos as running headers for *DCPhil.*.

CONTENTS   A: fols 1^r–16^v Continuous commentary on *DCPhil.* I–III.m.ix.22, *inc.* 'Unde hodie…purgantes carminare dicimus'; *expl.* 'humorem ab aqua'; 16^v–59^r ***DCPhil.***; 59^r–60^v Lupus, *De metris* with brief addition; 60^v–70^r Persius, *Satires* (glossed interlinearly); 70^r–74^v commentary on Persius (*CTC*,

iii.201–312, tradition B).
B: fols 75^r–88^r Plato, *Timaeus* (Waszink A3, with some annotation); 88^r–101va Prudentius, *Psychomachia*, *Peristephanon* III and VI and *Cathemerinon* III–VI; 101va Gennadius, *De scriptoribus ecclesiasticis* 13 (on Prudentius); 102ra rules of quantity, versified, *inc.* '<Om>ne per exemplum soliti cognoscere rerum'; 102va–108rb *Ilias latina* (Walther 9580).

GLOSS

Some interlinear notes to *DCPhil.* (e.g., I.m.v.i: fol. 21^{r-v}).

DECORATION

Ink-drawn initials with interlace, backed with orange-red and (rarely) yellow, e.g., fols 17^r, 75^r, 88^v. Red dotting of capitals for *DCPhil.*

PROVENANCE

Convent of the Celestines, Avignon: 'Iste liber est monasterii fratrum Celestinorum Auimonum ex hereditate magistri Iohannis Unsqueti' (fol. 108rb: s. xiv). Mottley Collection, Paris; Thos Rodd 1845 (fol. v^r).

BIBLIOGRAPHY

BL, *Cat. Add.* (1845), pp. 30–31; Gibson, *Timaeus*; Troncarelli, *Boethiana*, no. 83; Minnis, *Chaucer*, p. 195n.

85. MS London, BL, Add. 17298
DCPhil.

s. xiv

Parchment; i + 104 + i fols; page 294x202mm; text 156x98mm; 29 lines; one scribe.

CONTENTS

Fols 1^r–36^v Horace, *Ars poetica* and *Epistles II*; 37^r–104^r *DCPhil.*

GLOSS

Some annotation fols 37^r–38^v; rare thereafter.

DECORATION

Good initials in red, blue, pale purple, green, gold, with white penwork; minor initials red or blue with penwork flourishes; single letters within text often touched with yellow. Cf. MS Add. 19585.

PROVENANCE

Monastery of Monte Oliveto d'Accona, near Siena

(*ex libris*: fol. 1^r, s. xv).

BIBLIOGRAPHY BL, *Cat. Add.* (1868), p. 3; Kottler, M.

86. MS London, BL, Add. 17406
DCPhil.   s. xiv

Parchment; iv + 71 + iii fols; page 287x202mm; text 180x117mm; 22 lines;
two main scribes, changing at fols 31^v–32^r.

CONTENTS   Fols 1^r–71^v *DCPhil.*, lacking III.m.ii.26 – pr.iii.32 (fols 33–34)
                and III.pr.xi.121 – IV.pr.iii.62 (fols 47–48).

GLOSS   Extensive users' notes throughout.

DECORATION   *C(armina)*, Boethius teaching (fol. 1^r: poor); otherwise (fols
                1^v–29^r) red or blue with penwork flourishing. The only major
                initial is red and blue, with grille-work (II.pr.i: fol. 13^v). Ini-
                tials from fol. 32^r onwards not added.

PROVENANCE   English or French.

BIBLIOGRAPHY BL, *Cat. Add.* (1868), p. 14; Kottler, E.

87. MS London, BL, Add. 18342
Logica vetus   s. xii 2/2

Parchment; ii + 82 + ii fols.
A (c. 1200): page 190x142mm; text 166x115mm; 24–25 lines, written below
top line; similar hands throughout.
B (s. xii 2/2): page 189x142mm; text 140x72mm; 36 lines, written in several
small hands below top line. Fols 49^r–56^v one scribe; 56^v continued in new and
later hand, which runs to end, with catchwords.

CONTENTS   A: fols 1^r–44^v Sermons with *exempla*; 44^v–45^r Old High Ger-
                man note on Ten Commandments, added later; 45^r–48^v devo-
                tional texts.
                B: fols 49^r–55^v *Isag.*; 56^r–68^r *Cat.*; 68^v–75^v *De Int.*;

75^v–82^v **Div.** *expl.* imperf. 'in partes eas que sibi sunt similes' (888A).

GLOSS

User's annotations to *Isag.* and *Cat.* No annotations to *De Int.* or *Div.*

DECORATION

C(um), bishop blessing, blue, red, green, ochre (fol. 49^r); *E(quivoca)*, doctor writing with scroll, yellow, green, red (56^r); *P(rimum)*, not historiated, green, yellow (68^v); *Quam*, not historiated, red, blue (75^v).

PROVENANCE

German. 'Montis S. Georgii II.lx67' (fol.1^r: s. xviii–xix); Asher, 8 October 1850.

BIBLIOGRAPHY BL, *Cat. Add.* (1868), p. 101; *AL*, 2044.

88. MS London, BL, Add. 18374
Logica vetus et nova

s. xiii 1/2

Parchment; ii + 319 + i fols.
A (s. xiii): page 342x235mm; text 2 cols, each 198x60mm; 34 lines.
B (s. xiii 1/2): page 340x230mm; text 2 cols, each 178x55mm; 31 lines.
Binding with clasps fastening on front, blind-stamped leather on wood, with ten metal studs (missing) and two studs on lower edge, back and front (present). Label from binding now mounted fol. 1^r: *'methaphisica, phisica, et / Quaedam alia Aristotelis opuscula.1534.'* with monogram.
A striking teaching volume.

CONTENTS

A: fols 2ra–90vb Aristotle, *Metaphysics*; 91ra–158ra idem, *Physics*.
B: fols 159ra–64va *Isag.*; 165ra–76vb *Cat.*; 177ra–83vb *De Int.*; 184ra–88vb *Liber sex principiorum*; 189ra–96rb *Div.*; 196va–214rb *Top. Diff.*; 214va–28vb *Soph. Elench.*; 228vb–68vb *Topica Aris.*; 269ra–300va *Prior Anal.*; 301ra–19vb *Post Anal.*, *expl.* imperf. 'circa intelligencias – quibus'.

GLOSS

A: users' annotation throughout section.
B: extensive two-column user's gloss to all treatises except *Div.* and *Top. Diff.*

DECORATION   A: good late abstract initial: blue, red, gold with grille-work
                  and half-border (fol. 2ra).
                  B: Dominican teaching (fol. 159ra); competent opening
                  initials with gold to all texts; further initials fols 288vb
                  (dragon) and 313ra.

PROVENANCE   Vienna Dominicans: 'Liber iste est conuentus fratrum ordinis
                  predicatorum in Wienna' (fol. 196^{v}: s. xiv); Ioanes Menginus
                  (fol. 2^{r}: s. xvi). *Ex libris* fols 2^{r}, 159^{r}, 196^{v}. Donation note:
                  'Hunc librum qui fuit domini Simonis Hawnspuchlis sacerdotis
                  pie memorie dedit conuentui wyen Servacius Cirurrgicus pro
                  salute anime eiusdem d. Simonis' (fol. 158^{v}: s.xiv).

BIBLIOGRAPHY   BL, *Cat. Add.* (1868), pp. 104–5; *AL*, 291.

89. MS London, BL, Add. 19585
DCPhil.   s. xiv

Parchment; ii + 96 + ii fols; page 374x269mm; text 237x78mm; text and
commentary 269x226mm; 64 lines (gloss text varies); same scribe for text and
commentary. Central text with half-spaced surrounding commentary.
The size and layout of this MS are similar to MS London, BL, Add. 27875,
also Trivet. The initials are in a different style, but they divide the text in the
same way.
A very swagger example of a standard type of manuscript.

CONTENTS   Fols 2ra–9ra Index to *DCPhil.*, *inc.* 'Abiectio est quo magis…
                  Zephyrus'; 10$^{ra–vb}$ Trivet's preface; 11^{r}–96^{v} *DCPhil.*, with
                  Trivet's commentary.

GLOSS   Trivet.

DECORATION   Fine border (fol. 10^{r}: initial missing) and opening initials to
                  DCPhil. with gold (bk V initial missing); portrait of Boethius
                  (fol. 11^{r}). Good minor initials and diagrams; cf. artist of MS
                  Add. 17298.

PROVENANCE   Italian (illumination). Purchased at Dr. Hawtrey's sale at
                  Sotheby's, 4 July 1853, lot 445.

BIBLIOGRAPHY BL, *Cat. Add.* (1868), p. 256; Kottler, N; Minnis, *Chaucer*, p. 136n. See pl. 2.

90. MS London, BL, Add. 19726
DCPhil.

s. xi

Parchment; 98 fols, of which 1 and 98 are s. xiv liturgical flyleaves.
A (s. xi): page 276x199mm; text 195x145mm; 31 lines; one scribe (text).
B (s. xi): page 276x197mm; text 195x150mm; 27 lines; one scribe.
Greek completely unsure. Binding (s. xv): tooled white leather on wood with five brass studs back and front and (lost) central clasp fastening on front cover. Label on front cover: 'Boecius de consolacione phylosophie. Ibidem uita / Columbe confessoris'. Colophon, fol. 57ʳ: 'Qui uitium superare cupit uirtutibus almis / Sepe legat uires quas continet iste libellus.' Dialogue in text marked B and)-(.

CONTENTS A: fol. 1ʳ⁻ᵛ service-book (s. xiv flyleaf); 2ʳ–57ʳ *DCPhil.*, glossed; 57ᵛ liturgical fragment (cf. Song 4:6–8), neumed (s. xv). B: fols 58ᵛ–97ʳ Adamnan, *Vita Columbae*, ed. Anderson and Anderson, 1961, without this MS, but see Esposito (1937); 98ʳ⁻ᵛ service-book, with historical note on AD 595 (s. xiv flyleaf).

GLOSS A: plentiful interlinear annotation; in parts, extensive marginalia related to text by Greek letters and Tironian notes (s. xi–xii). B: very little.

DECORATION A: initials with interlace, touched with green and yellow or with red; other initials with finely-drawn birds and animals; in brown penwork, 'insular' style. B: *B(eati)* fol. 59ʳ fine line-drawn red initial with primitive acanthus (cf. Harley 2904, fol. 4ʳ: Temple no. 41, pl. 141); otherwise simple red minor initials.

PROVENANCE Tegernsee, OSB (dioc. Freising). Edwin Tross, Paris; acquired 14 January 1854.

BIBLIOGRAPHY BL, *Cat. Add.* (1854–60), p. 2; M. Esposito, 'Notes on Latin Learning and Literature in Mediaeval Ireland: V', *Hermathena*,

1, 1937, p. 153, repr. in *Latin Learning in Mediaeval Ireland*,
ed. M. Lapidge, London, 198; Troncarelli, *Boethiana*, no. 84;
Krämer, ii. 754; Minnis, *Chaucer*, p. 195n.

91. MS London, BL, Add. 22766
DCPhil.   s. xiv

Parchment; iv + 47 + iv fols; page 234x166mm; text 147x83mm; 25 lines,
ruled for gloss; one scribe for text, except at fol. 1^r, which is rewritten in s.
xvi. Gloss added intensively in a minute cursive.
Extra lines at end of three metra introducing next prose: 'Quas ueris placidas
tempori lyras' (I.m.ii, fol. 2^r); 'Operis tanti pars non uilis / Homines quantum
fortune salo' (I.m.v, fol. 6^v); 'Discens equora uentus' (II.m.iv, fol. 12^v).
Glossator's colophon fol. 46^v: 'Explicit scriptum super libro (*sic*) de consolatione Boetii secundum magistrum Nicholaum Troveth ordinis fratrum
predicatorum. Amen.'

CONTENTS   Fols 1^r–47^r *DCPhil.*, with Trivet's commentary.

GLOSS   Trivet.

DECORATION   Beginning of each book, a blue initial with detailed red
                infilling; minor initials red, with yellow touches in offset ma-
                juscules. Diagrams fols 1^v, 6^r.

PROVENANCE   Italian inscription, 17 June 1460 (fol. 47^r). 'Iste liber est
                Thome de Inghraneniis de uulterris', probably Tommaso 'Fed-
                ra' Inghirami, 1470–1516 (fol. 47^v: s. xvi). Libri sale 1859, lot
                1751.

BIBLIOGRAPHY BL, *Cat. Add.* (1854–60), p. 729; Kottler, L.

92. MS London, BL, Add. 27625
DCPhil.   s. xiv

Parchment, with some paper in A; iii + 84 + iii fols.
A (s. xv 2/2): page 199x135mm; text 152x100mm; 22 lines; one scribe: 'EGO

F. FECI HOC OPUS' (fol. 25ᵛ).
B (s. xiv): page 199x135mm; text 150x80mm; 29–31 lines; several hands, deteriorating badly towards the end.

CONTENTS   A: fols 1ʳ–25ᵛ Galterus Anglicus, *Aesop*, versified (Hervieux, i. 570).
                B: fols 26ʳ–84ᵛ **DCPhil.**

GLOSS   Some annotation throughout in various hands; nothing system-atic.

DECORATION   Plain red or blue initials with simple penwork flourishing.

PROVENANCE   Purchased from J. Schönblum, 1867.

BIBLIOGRAPHY   BL, *Cat. Add.* (1854–75), p. 341.

93. MS London, BL, Add. 27875
DCPhil.
                                                                      s. xiv

Parchment; ii + 88 + ii fols; page 360x253mm; text 205x107mm; text and commentary 300x206mm; 64–69 lines commentary (text variable); one scribe (text and commentary). Colophon, 'Explicit expositio super librum boecii de consolatione secundum fratrem Nicholaum Treveth anglicum ordinis fratrum predicatorum sacre scientie professorem' (fol. 84ᵛᵃ).
A luxury volume with fine initials throughout.

CONTENTS   Fols 2ʳ–84ᵛ **DCPhil.**, with Trivet's commentary; 85ʳᵃ⁻ᵛᵇ frag-ment of *Moralium dogma philosophorum* (ed. Holmberg, pp. 5–12) added in a cursive hand; 88ʳ⁻ᵛ moral excerpts from classical authors (s. xv).

GLOSS   Trivet, *inc.* imperf. 'per Ysidorum Ethimologiarum libro iᵒ cap.ᵒ xxvᵒ tum quia incipit a planctu'.

DECORATION   The opening folio is lost. Text (fol. 2ʳ) frame illuminated with gold: tortoise chases bear, basset-hound chases rabbit, monkey plays bagpipes. Major initials with half frame to text at fols 18ʳ, 31ᵛ, 52ᵛ, 71ᵛ; high quality minor initials with gold throughout. Diagrams.

PROVENANCE   Purchased from Hazlitt, 25 April 1868.

BIBLIOGRAPHY BL, *Cat. Add.* (1854–75), pp. 368–69; Kottler, S.

94. MS London, BL, Add. 45026
DCPhil.   S. XV

Paper; i + 210 + i fols; page 211x154mm; text 129x65mm; 18 lines, ruled for gloss; fols 2–117 by several scribes writing a good humanistic cursive; fols 121–206 in other hands, of good quality but not humanistic. Contemporary German binding of tooled white leather (showing three roses vertically) on boards; two brass clasps; label on front cover, 'Boecius. De Consolatione Philosophica. MS.' Fol. 117ʳ two verse colophons in red (Walther 19805, 19815).
Contents-list (fol. 1ʳ), in same hand as *ex libris*.
An entirely homogeneous MS.

CONTENTS   Fol. 1ʳ contents-list, s. xv (as now); 2ʳ–117ʳ ***DCPhil.***; 121ʳ–47ʳ
              De modis cognoscendi deum, inc. 'Triplici pater reuerende
              existente gaudio noui seculi'; 147ʳ–56ʳ Petrarch, *Familiares*
              x.*3, imperf.; 156ᵛ–70ᵛ Thomas à Kempis, six letters; 170ᵛ–85ᵛ
              Bonaventure, *Regula Nouitiorum*; 186ʳ–90ʳ William of Au-
              vergne, *De septem astuciis diaboli*, part of his *De vitiis et
              virtutibus*; 190ᵛ–206ʳ Richard of St Victor, *De sex gradibus
              uiolente caritatis.*

GLOSS   None.

DECORATION   Plain red initials (e.g., *C(armina)*: fol. 2ʳ); occasional touches
              of yellow, consistent throughout the book. Many initials not
              supplied.

PROVENANCE   German. *Ex libris* of the Augustinian canons of St John the
              Baptist, Rebdorf, dioc. Eichstätt (fol. 1ʳ: s. xv).

BIBLIOGRAPHY BL, *Cat. Add.* (1936–45), pp. 70–71; Krämer, ii. 671.

ARUNDEL

The library of Thomas and Henry Howard, earls of Arundel (Sussex) was divided between the Royal Society and the College of Arms in 1666. The Royal Society bequest was purchased by the British Museum in 1831.

Catalogue of Manuscripts in the British Museum new series I (1840): i, *Arundel Manuscripts* (1834). Indexed jointly with the Burney manuscripts in I.iii (the same folio volume).

95. MS London, BL, Arundel 77
Mus.
                                                                    s. xi

Parchment; iii (modern) + 98 + iii (modern) fols.
A (s. xi): page 318x230mm; text 235x146mm; 38 lines; two main scribes (fols 6^v–38^v and 39^r–62^v).
B (s. xi): page 316x234mm; text 235x144mm; 38 lines; several scribes.
Diagram, fol. 19^r (paper), s. xvii addition. *Tituli* fols 6^v, 62^r. Latin interlinear translation to Greek, I.i.
A fine, stately manuscript.

CONTENTS	A: fols 1^r–3^r note on music; 3^v–6^r Gregory VII, letter to Hermann, bishop of Metz (*Reg.* vii. 21), *expl.* imperf.; 6^v–62^r *Mus.* (incl. inserted paper fol. 19: humanist diagram of music). B: fols 63^v–87^v *Scolica Enchiriadis de musica*; 87^v–91^v treatise on the monochord; 92^r–98^r list of antiphons and graduals etc., some neumed.
GLOSS	Extensive marginal glosses to *Mus.* fols 6^v–28^v (II.28 text 'quam dimidia') related to text by Greek letters, Tironian notes etc.
DECORATION	A: plain red capitals and rubrication, those at the beginning touched with silver (e.g., fol. 6^v); competent diagrams, some touched with yellow; s. xv capitulation throughout. B: plain red capitals.
PROVENANCE	Arundel bequest to the Royal Society of London (stamp, fol. 1^r).

BIBLIOGRAPHY *Musica et scolica enchiriadis*, ed. H. Schmid, Munich, 1981, MS Do; White, in Gibson, pp. 162–205, at 192n; Bower, no. 40; Bernhard and Bower, La.

96. MS London, BL, Arundel 179
DCPhil.   s. xiv

Parchment; i + 39 + ii fols; page 283x209mm; text 180x102mm; 33 lines, ruled for gloss; one scribe throughout. *Titulus* fol. 39ᵛ. Very economical on parchment: *metra* in double columns and any extra half-line used to begin *prosa*.
Standard quarto volume, well used (see annotation).

CONTENTS   Fols 1ʳ–39ᵛ *DCPhil.*

GLOSS   Several readers have added notes in the ample margins, but there is no systematic gloss.

DECORATION   Competent main initials blue or red with penwork flourishes at beginning of bks I–V (bk V with violet touches). Rubrication from fol. 28ʳ onwards, also with violet touches.

PROVENANCE   German. Mainz Carthusians: 'Iste liber est Carthusiensium Maguncie' (fol. 1ʳ). Arundel bequest to the Royal Society of London (stamp, fol. 1ʳ).

BIBLIOGRAPHY Kottler, A; Krämer, ii. 533.

97. MS London, BL, Arundel 339
Arith.   s. xii

Parchment; ii + 153 + ii fols; page 201x145mm; text 143x92mm; 45 lines. Transliterated Latin-Greek colophon (fol. 68ʳ).
A fine collection of quadrivial texts, including good coloured line-drawings in Hyginus.

CONTENTS   Fol. 1ʳ schema of *artes*; 1ᵛ–31ʳ *Arith.*; 31ᵛ–36ʳ mnemonic verses on arithmetic (fols 31ra–34va) and the computus (fols 34va–36ra), including Walther 1611 (fol. 31va) and 10233 (fol. 34va); 36^{v}–40^{v} *Liber iudiciorum Mesehalle*; 41^{r}–49^{r} Gerbert, *Geometry* (Bubnov, pp. 48–97); 49^{r}–59^{r} Ps.-Boethius, *Geometry* (Folkerts a); 59^{r}–68^{r} Hugh of St Victor, *Practica geometrie* (Goy 2.2.1.3); 68^{v}–69^{r} Arithmetical notes and diagrams; 69va–71rb Chalcidius' commentary on *Timaeus*, excerpts (Waszink, p. cviii); 71^{v}–89^{v} Hyginus, *Astronomicon*, glossed; 90^{r}–97^{v} *Liber de Wazalkora* (an astrolabe); 98^{r}–104^{r} Guy of Arezzo, *Micrologus* (Smits van Waesberghe MS Lo6); 104^{r}–9^{v} three *opuscula* of Guy of Arezzo (Smits van Waesberghe Lo6); 109^{v}–10^{r} *Mensura fistularum*, and *Organistrum* (includes Schaller 16894) neumed; 110^{v}–20^{r} *Timaeus*, glossed with excerpts from William of Conches, *Philosophia Mundi* (Waszink, p. cviii); 120^{v} diagrams of the soul and the elements; 121^{r}–51^{r} Macrobius, *In somnium Scipionis*, glossed; 151^{v} obit–list of Kastl; 152$^{va–vb}$ 'Pluuiarum diverse sunt cause'; *expl.* 'subditos montes causam esse'; 153^{r} diagram of zodiac.

GLOSS   Extensive gloss mainly to bk I, fols 1^{v}–14^{v}, thinner thereafter.

DECORATION   Many unfamiliar pastel green, blue, red abstract initials. Mediocre diagrams in red, many touched with green and blue. Fine zodiac drawings fols 73^{r}–85^{r}, red, pink, green, blue.

PROVENANCE   German. Kastl OSB, dioc. Eichstätt, near Regensburg (fol. 151^{v} obit-list in which last obit is 1222); Willibald Pirkheimer (d. 1530).

BIBLIOGRAPHY   Bubnov, p. xxxviii; Saxl and Meier, III.i.93–98; J. Smits van Waesberghe, *Guidonis Aretini Micrologus*, sine loco, 1955, pp. 30–31 (Lo6); *Conches*, p. 319; Folkerts, a, pp. 18–19; Krämer, i.389.

98. MS London, BL, Arundel 348
2 in Int.
                                                    s. xii 1/2

Parchment; i + 276 + i fols.
A (s. xii 1/2): page 208x107mm; text 132x60mm; 30 lines, ruled to permit annotation; same or similar minute hands throughout.

B (s. xii): page 202x115mm; text 140x64–72mm; 28 lines; various contemporary scribes.

C (s. xii 1/2): page 203x120mm; text 158x92mm; 31 lines, ruled with a stylus; one scribe.

Colophon, fol. 234ᵛ.

A tall, narrow *artes* manuscript.

CONTENTS A: fols 1ʳ–51ᵛ Cicero, *De inventione*; 51ᵛ–101ᵛ Ps.-Cicero, *Ad Herennium*.
B: fols 102ʳ–79ᵛ Thierry of Chartres, commentary on *De inventione*, *expl.* imperf. 'ad necessitatem de presenti' (2. 56. 170).
C: fols 180ʳ–276ᵛ *2 in Int.*

GLOSS None.

DECORATION A: initials in red, ochre, quite ambitious, with interlace; poor quality.
B: none.
C: plain and poor red initials marking the beginning of each book.

PROVENANCE Arundel bequest to the Royal Society of London (stamp, fol. 1ʳ).

BIBLIOGRAPHY *AL*, 293; K. M. Fredborg, *The Latin Rhetorical Commentaries by Thierry of Chartres*, Toronto, 1988, MS A.

99. MS London, BL, Arundel 383
Logica vetus et nova   s. xiii 2/2

Parchment; i + 296 + i fols; page 237x171mm; text 135x82mm; 24–27 lines, ruled for gloss; several similar hands.

CONTENTS Fols 2ʳ–12ᵛ *Isag.*; 13ʳ–32ᵛ *Cat.*; 33ʳ–44ᵛ *De Int.*; 45ʳ–53ᵛ *Liber sex principiorum*; 54ʳ–65ᵛ *Div.*; 66ʳ–103ᵛ *Top. Diff.*; 104ʳ–17ᵛ Thomas Aquinas, *De ente et essentia*; 118ʳ–71ᵛ *Prior Anal.*; 172ʳ–206ᵛ *Post. Anal.*; 207ʳᵃ⁻ᵛᵇ notes on logic; 208ʳ–78ᵛ *Topica Aris.*; 279ʳ–94ᵛ *Soph. Elench.* (lacuna at 290ᵛ–291ʳ = 173a30 / 181b10).

GLOSS   Extensive users' annotation in several hands to all but *Div.* and
                       Thomas Aquinas; rare annotations for *Top. Diff.*

DECORATION   Red and blue initials with penwork flourishing.

PROVENANCE   Pressmark Z 217 (fol. 1ʳ: s. xv); Arundel bequest to the Royal
                       Society of London (stamp, fol. 2ʳ).

BIBLIOGRAPHY *AL*, 294.

100. MS London, BL, Arundel 392
Logica nova et vetus
s. xiii

Parchment; i + 206 + ii fols.
A: page 220x155mm; text 126x54mm; 37 lines; similar scribes.
B: page 218x151mm; text 123x54mm; 36 lines; distinct but contemporary
scribes.
C: page 209x145mm; text 125x68mm; 35 lines; similar scribes.
D: page 210x156mm; text 153x105mm; 31 lines; one scribe.
A–C ruled to permit annotation.

CONTENTS   A: fols 1ʳ–45ʳ ***Topica Aris.***, *inc.* imperf. I.iv 'omnia accidit'
                       (lacks end of iv and beginning of v: fols 25–6); 45ʳ–59ʳ ***Soph.***
                       Elench.; 59ʳ–60ᵛ misc.
                       B: fols 61ʳ–94ʳ ***Prior Anal.***; 95ʳ–122ᵛ *Post. Anal.*, *expl.*
                       imperf. 'ostensum est autem' (96a1); 123ʳ–28ᵛ ***Isag.***;
                       128ᵛ–38ᵛ ***Cat.***; 139ʳ–44ʳ *Liber sex principiorum*;
                       144ᵛ–50ᵛ ***De Int.***; 151ʳ–58ᵛ ***Div.***
                       C: fols 159ʳ–79ᵛ Aristotle, *De anima*; 179ᵛ–82ʳ idem,
                       De memoria; 182ᵛᵃ⁻ᵛᵇ notes.
                       D: fols 183ʳ–206ᵛ Ps.-Albert the Great, *Physica* (ex-
                       cerpts).

GLOSS   A–D: extensive users' annotation throughout.

DECORATION   A: modest red and blue initials with penwork flourishings.
                       B: rather better red and blue initials with quite elabo-
                       rate penwork infill.
                       C: one plain blue initial with red flourishing

(unfinished: fol. 159^r).
D: green and red initials with penwork flourishing and infill.

PROVENANCE   'Iste liber est Guilelmi de quercu' (fol. 181^v: s. xiv).

BIBLIOGRAPHY   *AL*, 295; Burnett, *Glosses*, p. 133n.

101. MS London, BL, Arundel 514
DCPhil. (three copies)   s. ix–x; s. xiv

Parchment; ii + 173 + ii fols; 8 volumes bound together.
A (s. xiii 1/2): page 200x134mm; text 137x75mm; 29 lines; several scribes.
B (a. 1331): page 192x132mm; text 132x88mm; 30 lines; one scribe.
C (s. xiv 1/2): page 196x136mm; text 116x80mm; 2 cols; 41 lines; one scribe.
D (s. xiii 2/3): page 200x140mm; text 140x80mm; 26 lines; two scribes.
E: (s. xiv): page 202x137mm; text 135x92mm; 32 lines; one scribe.
F (s. ix/x): page 202x144mm; text 163x95mm; 27 lines; at least two similar scribes.
G (s. ix/x): page 203x145mm; text 165x96mm; 27 lines; one scribe.
H (s. xiv): page 203x127mm; text 152x72mm; 28 lines; one scribe.
Colophon bk II (fol. 115^r); colophon bk IV (fol. 147^v); neumes to III.m.ix.1–2 (fol. 160^v).

CONTENTS   A: fols 1^r–36^v Priscian, *Institutiones* xvii–xviii.157, glossed (Passalacqua 310).
B: fols 37^r–53^v Aristotle, *De anima*, glossed.
C: fols 54ra–64vb Pons of Provence, *Summa dictaminis de competenti dogmate*; 64vb–69ra idem, *Summa de constructione*; 69va–99rb idem, *Epistolarium*; 99rb canon law note dated 1342.
D: fols 100^v–7^v Ps.-Boethius, *De disciplina scolarium*, imperf. *ad in.* and *ad fin.* (Weijers, no.46), few glosses.
E: fols 108^r–44^v ***DCPhil***. I–IV.m.vi.7, very few glosses.
F: fols 145^r–52^v ***DCPhil***. IV.pr.vi.151 – V.pr.iv.92, glossed.
G: fols 153^r–60^v ***DCPhil***. III.pr.ii.16 – III.m.ix.24, glossed.

H: fols 161^r–73^r John of Garland, *Liber synonymorum* (Walther 374).

GLOSS

E: rare.

F: frequent users' annotation; syntax-marks in text.

G: frequent users' annotation, related to the text by musical notation-marks.

DECORATION

E: plain brown ink initials.

F: simple red initial and rubrication (fol. 147^v).

G: none.

PROVENANCE

Mainz Carthusians. 'Liber Carthus. prope Magunt.' (fol. 1^r); Arundel bequest to the Royal Society of London (stamp, fol. 1^r).

BIBLIOGRAPHY

H.-G. le Saulnier de Saint-Jean, 'Pons le Provençal maître en *Dictamen*', *Ecole des Chartes positions des thèses*, Paris, 1957, pp. 87–92; Bergmann, no. 408 (Frankish); Passalacqua, 310; Watson, *London*, 494 (C only); Troncarelli, *Boethiana*, no. 76; Krämer omits.

BURNEY

The library of Charles Burney, classicist, was purchased by the British Museum in 1818.

Catalogue of Manuscripts in the British Museum, new series I (1840): ii, *The Burney Manuscripts* (1840). Indexed jointly with the Arundel manuscripts in I.iii (the same folio volume).

102. MS London, BL, Burney 65
Topica Aris.

s. xiii

Parchment; iv + 76 + ii fols; page 211x153mm; text 109x60mm; 24 lines, ruled for gloss. Two very similiar scribes, changing at 36^v–37^r. Note older foliation: old fols 133–208 = new fols 1–76; the preceding texts in this collection have not been identified.

CONTENTS Fols 1ʳ–76ᵛ **Topica Aris.** Two MSS overlapping: 1ʳ–36ᵛ i–v.2, *expl.* 'Deinde destruenti' (p. 90, line 22); 37ʳ–76ᵛ v.2–viii, *inc.* 'destruʃenti quidem' (p. 90, line 8).

GLOSS Rare, e.g., fols 2ʳ (pencil), 66ʳ–70ᵛ.

DECORATION Good initial **P***(ropositum)* with gold (fol. 1ʳ). Red and blue penwork initials with elaborate flourishing at the beginning of bks ii–iv; v missing, vi–viii less grand. The initials change with the second scribe. Red and blue paraph signs within text.

PROVENANCE ? Italian (parchment).

BIBLIOGRAPHY *AL*, 297.

103. MS London, BL, Burney 129
DCPhil.
s. xiv 2/2

Parchment; iv + 56 + iv fols; page 269x170mm; text 191x103mm; 28 lines; same or similar scribes. *Titulus* (fol. 1ʳ).

CONTENTS Fols 1ʳ–56ᵛ **DCPhil.**

GLOSS Extensive gloss fols 1–2: *inc.* 'Volens igitur Boecius agere de consolatione philosophica primo inducit personam talem consolationem indigentem'; *expl.* imperf. I.pr.i.3 'uisa est mulier'. Interlinear Latin and Italian notes (translation and comments) fols 1–22, and occasionally thereafter. Cf. William of Conches.

DECORATION Red, blue, ochre with distinctive jagged pattern **C***(armina)*: fol. 1ʳ). Initials to bks II–V similar, without ochre but some use of brown ink. Modest grille-work in smaller initials.

PROVENANCE N. Italy. 'Franceschini de amicinis de legnano' (fol. 56ᵛ: s. xvⁱⁿ).

BIBLIOGRAPHY Kottler, Bu.

104. MS London, BL, Burney 130
DCPhil.

s. xiv^{ex} / xv^{in}

Parchment; iii + 49 + ii fols; page 265x176mm; text 180x110mm; 32 lines; several similar scribes. *Titulus*, fol. 3^r.

CONTENTS   Fols 3^r–47^v *DCPhil.*

GLOSS   None.

DECORATION   Half-border (fol. 3^r: s. xv) with portrait of Boethius holding book; shield (black and white quarters with pale green bar). Otherwise good quality red and blue initials with delicate penwork.

PROVENANCE   N. E. Italy; ? Padua. Silvester de Landis (fol. 47^v: s. xv). Bought in Padua from the library of Frederico Ceruti of Verona in 1629 (fol. 2^r).

BIBLIOGRAPHY   Kottler, Bur.

105. MS London, BL, Burney 134
Top. Diff. IV

s. xv

Paper; iv + 59 + iv fols; page 200x150mm; text 151x101mm; 23 lines; one scribe, writing a clear humanistic cursive. Fluent cursive Greek in marginal headings, fols 31^v–32^r.

CONTENTS   Fols 1^r–29^v Censorinus, *De die natali*; 30^r–37^r Priscian, *Prae-exercitamina*; 37^v–47^r *Top. Diff. IV*; 48^r–59^v Censorinus, *De origine primi hominis*.

GLOSS   None.

DECORATION   Red ink rubrication and some plain initials.

PROVENANCE   Unknown.

BIBLIOGRAPHY   None.

106. MS London, BL, Burney 275
Logica vetus et nova, Arith., Mus.   s. xiv 2/3

Parchment; iii (modern) + 561 + iv (modern) fols; page 410x290mm; text 2
cols, each c. 255x70mm; 59 lines; one scribe.
Designed as a set of texts; lavishly and consistently illustrated in an unwieldy
luxury volume.

CONTENTS   Fols 3ra–119vb Priscian, *Institutiones* i–xviii.208, lacking pref-
                 ace (Passalacqua, no. 318); 120ra–43ra Cicero, *De inuentione*;
                 143ra–65vb Ps.-Cicero, *Ad Herennium*; 166ra–69va *Isag.*;
                 169vb–76rb *Cat.*; 176va–80rb *De Int.*; 180va–83vb *Liber sex prin-
                 cipiorum*; 184ra–205ra *Prior Anal.*; 205rb–18va *Post. Anal.*;
                 218va–44ra *Topica Aris.*; 244va–52rb *Soph. Elench.*; 252va–56va
                 Div.; 256vb–65ra *Top. Diff I–III.*; 265rb–78ra *Syll. Hyp.*;
                 278ra–88rb *Syll. Cat.*; 288va–92vb Cicero, *Topics*, *expl.* imperf.
                 'loci maxime valeant' (98.3); 293ra–335rb Euclid (Burnett 59);
                 336ra–58rb *Arith.*; 358vb–59ra *Saltus Gerberti*; 359va–90rb *Mus.*;
                 390va–560vb Ptolemy, *Almagest*.

GLOSS   Virtually no annotation or sign of use.

DECORATION   Major initials at the beginning of each treatise, with gold,
                 several with full border and grotesques (scenes of hunting,
                 single combat and parodic animals), some showing a lady
                 holding a tree with the contents of the next treatise written on
                 the leaves; others show teacher and pupils. Minor abstract
                 initials in gold, purple, brown, blue, pink. Further initials in
                 red and blue with elaborate penwork. Heraldry (fols 94^r, 120^r,
                 166^r, 184^r, 336^r, 359^v). The opening page, no doubt splendid,
                 has been removed. Competent diagrams and tables.

PROVENANCE   Written and illuminated for Pope Gregory XI (fol. 2^v), whose
                 successor, Clement VII, gave it to Jean, duc de Berry, in 1387
                 (fol. 560^v); Albi, chapter library (Delisle).

BIBLIOGRAPHY   Bubnov, pp. 32–35 (*Saltus Gerberti*); L. Delisle, *Recherches
                 sur la librairie de Charles V*, 2 vols, Paris, 1907, ii.264–65,
                 314, no. 257; *AL*, 298; M. Meiss, *French Painting in the Time*

of Jean de Berry: The Late Fourteenth Century and the Patronage of the Duke, London, 1967, p. 310; Bergmann, 409; Bolton, p. 58; White, in Gibson, pp. 162–205, at 195, n. 56 (*Saltus Gerberti*); H. L. L. Busard, *The First Latin Translation of Euclid's Elements, Commonly Ascribed to Adelard of Bath*, Toronto, 1983, p. 25; Burnett, *Adelard*, p. 182, no. 59; Troncarelli, *Boethiana*, no. 77; Bower, no. 41.

EGERTON

Francis Henry Egerton, 8th earl of Bridgewater, donated manuscripts and a substantial trust fund in 1829. This 'Bridgewater Fund' is still used for the purchase of manuscripts, which are then accessioned as 'MS Egerton'.

107. MS London BL, Egerton 267
DCPhil.

S. X

A book of unrelated fragments; page not measurable; text 200x106mm; 20 lines (text). Inner margin and upper and lower margins missing, but text complete. Outer margin survives. Ruled for gloss.

CONTENTS   Fol. 37^{r-v} *DCPhil.* I.pr.iv.122 'Pro uerae' to line 162 'esse aduersae'.

GLOSS   Systematic gloss, related to text with Greek reference signs. Some interlinear annotation.

DECORATION   None visible.

PROVENANCE   Unknown.

BIBLIOGRAPHY   BL *Cat. Add.* (1834), p. 8; Bolton, p. 58; Troncarelli, *Boethiana*, no. 77.

108. MS London, BL, Egerton 628
Vitae I, VII, DCPhil.   s. xiii 2/2

Parchment; iii + 236 + ii fols; page 330x225mm. Text ruled variously for the job at hand: fols 5ʳ–161ᵛ text 2 cols, each 235x78mm, 34 lines (18 lines text, with half-spaced commentary); fols 162ʳ–94ᵛ text 2 cols, each 230x71mm, 34 lines; fols 195ᵛ–236ᵛ text 2 cols, each 239x71mm, 45 lines. Two main scribes, changing at fol. 195ᵛ. *Titulus* bk I (fol. 5ʳᵃ) only. The text and lay-out of fols 5–161 is close to MS Royal 15 B. III.
One, planned volume.

CONTENTS
Fol. 1ᵛ list of contents (added: s. xiii); 2ᵛ *schema* of learning, with special reference to music; 3ʳᵃ–4ʳᵇ Lupus, *De metris*, with brief addition; 4ʳᵇ⁻ᵛᵃ *Vitae I, VII*; 5ʳᵃ–161ᵛᵇ *DCPhil.*, with intercalated commentary, *inc.* 'Mos auctorum est operi suo prologos prescribere quibus lectores attentos beniuolos dociles-que reddant'; *expl.* 'spectator est et iudicator'; 162ʳᵃ–64ᵛᵃ commentary on III.m.ix, *inc.* 'Rationem dicit sapientiam dei' [Silk, *Commentaries*, pp. 332–39; also in MS Royal 15 B. III]; 165ʳᵃ–94ʳᵇ Ps.-William of Conches's commentary on *DCPhil. I–IV*; 194ʳᵇ–95ʳᵃ commentary on *DCPhil.* IV.m.vii, *inc.* 'Vere ut superius dictum est laborandum est pro eterna felicitate'; 195ᵛᵃ–227ᵛᵇ Augustine, *Contra Maximinum*; 227ᵛᵇ–30ᵛᵃ Ps.-Augustine, *Contra Pascentium* [= *CPL* 366]; 230ᵛᵃ–36ᵛᵇ Augustine, *Contra Felicianum*.

GLOSS
See contents.

DECORATION
The red and blue penwork initials at beginning of bks I–II, IV–V, and at III.m.ix of *DCPhil.* are from the workshop that produced the principal manuscripts of Vincent of Beauvais; cf. MS London, BL, Add. 15407. Diagram of the four elements (fol. 162ᵛ).

PROVENANCE
'Liber sancte Marie de Camberone' (fol. 3ʳ; cf. fols 165ʳ, 188ʳ, 224ʳ). St Mary, Cambron, a Cistercian house in the diocese of Cambrai.

BIBLIOGRAPHY
BL *Cat. Add.* (1838), p. 24; H. F. Stewart, 'A Commentary by Remigius Autissiodorensis on the *De consolatione philo-sophiae* of Boethius', *Journal of Theological Studies*, 17, 1917,

pp. 22–42 (22); P. Courcelle, 'Étude critique sur les commentaires de la Consolation de Boèce (IXᵉ–XVᵉ)', *Archives d'histoire doctrinale et littéraire du Moyen Âge*, 12, 1939, pp. 5–140 (130); H. Thoma, '*Codices Camberonenses* in the British Museum', *Revue Bénédictine*, 65, 1955, pp. 270–77 (273); Courcelle, p. 409; A. Stones, *The Minnesota Vincent of Beauvais Manuscript and Cistercian Thirteenth Century Book Decoration*, Minneapolis, 1977. See pl. 4.

109. MS London, BL, Egerton 832
DCPhil.

S. XV

Paper; v + 321 + v fols; page 140x75mm; text 105x52mm; 33 long lines; one clear cursive hand.
Pocket sized volume.

CONTENTS   Fols 1ʳ–4ᵛ 'Historia Susanne metrice composita' (Walther 8119); 5ʳ–141ʳ 'Incipit prephatio magistri Marcialis in librum de doctrina cordis'; 142ʳ–61ʳ *Floretus, inc.* 'Collige quos fidei floretus dat tibi flores'; 161ʳ–71ʳ Alan of Lille, *Parabolae*; 171ᵛ–87ʳ Galterus Anglicus, *Aesop*, versified; 187ᵛ–94ᵛ Horace, *Ars poetica*; 195ʳ–264ᵛ *DCPhil.*; 265ʳ–69ᵛ Gregory the Great, excerpts from *Cura pastoralis* and other works; 270ʳ–318ᵛ Alan of Lille, *Regulae caelestis iuris*; 319ʳ–20ᵛ contents-list of fols 5–141 in another hand.

GLOSS   None.

DECORATION   Simple but competent red ink initials throughout. A few major initials red and black.

PROVENANCE   Bib. Hall 299 (fol. 1ʳ). Purchased from T. Rodd, 11 August 1840 (fol. vʳ).

BIBLIOGRAPHY   BL, *Cat. Add.* (1840), p. 17; Hervieux, i.565 (Aesop).

HARLEY

The library of Robert and Edward Harley, 1st and 2nd earls of Oxford, was purchased for the newly founded British Museum in 1753. The catalogue by Humfrey Wanley (d. 1726) was completed and published in 1808–12. The provenances of the 7660 manuscripts were analysed by C. E. Wright in 1972.

A Catalogue of the Harleian Manuscripts in the British Museum, 4 vols, London, 1808–12; C. E. Wright and R. C. Wright *The Diary of Humfrey Wanley 1715–1726*, 2 vols, London, 1966; C. E. Wright, *Fontes Harleiani*, London, 1972.

110. MS London, BL, Harley 549
Arith.   s. xii 2/3

Parchment; iv + 60 + iii fols; page 204x133mm; text 140x79mm; 28 lines; one scribe.
A practical book of arithmetic, with lovely decorative touches.

CONTENTS   Fols 1^v–57^v **Arith.**; 58$^{ra–vb}$ fragment of religious epic, added s. xii^{ex}, *inc.* 'Da fontem mihi Christe nouum uero postulat usus'; *expl.* 'Ad uirtutis ortus uirtuti reddita merces'; 59$^{r–v}$ rough diagrams (s. xvi).

GLOSS   None.

DECORATION   Initials touched with gold (fols 1^v, 14^r, 21^r); diagrams throughout touched with red, green, yellow, blue; two eagles red, blue, ochre, gold (fol. 1^v); red, blue, green, ochre, gold diagram set as a circle with three dogs and a hare chasing round it, four fishes inside (fol. 14^r); dragon initial (same palette; fol. 21^r). Line drawing of man rowing boat, in which sits lady with gaming-board, added ? s. xiii (fol. 1^r). Good single colour minor initials throughout.

PROVENANCE   English notes (fol. 58^v: s. xiv+). Rogerus bedford (fol. 57^r: s. xv); John Dee (fol. 2^r); Simonds d'Ewes, A 894 (acquired 1626: Watson).

BIBLIOGRAPHY A. G. Watson, *The Library of Sir Simonds d'Ewes*, London, 1966, p. 205; Wright, *Fontes*, p. 382; R. J. Roberts and A. G. Watson, *John Dee's Library Catalogue*, London, 1990, M. 114, p. 122.

111. MS London, BL, Harley 1737
Arith.

s. xii 1/2

Parchment; ii + 33 + ii fols; page 215x133mm; text 136x72mm; 33 lines; quires marked in Roman numerals at the beginning; careful punctuation and correction; scribe changes at fol. 27^r.
Pages repeatedly missing; a well-used MS that has eventually fallen apart and had pages removed.

CONTENTS   Fols 1^r–33^v *Arith.* with many folios missing. Now contains: I.12–15 (fol. 1^{r-v}), 17–23 (fols 2^r–4^v), 25–28 (fols 5^r–7^v), I.32–II.1 (fols 8^r–9^v), II.3–23 (fols 10^r–15^v), 24–51 (fols 16^r–32^v), 54–end, with diagram (fol. 33^{r-v}).

GLOSS   Considerable users' annotation s. xii and later.

DECORATION   Simple red initials and diagrams throughout.

PROVENANCE   Henry Worsley. 93.A.8/1737 (fol. 1^r).

BIBLIOGRAPHY Wright, *Fontes*, p. 400.

112. MS London, BL, Harley 2364
DCPhil.

s. xv

Paper; iii + 108 + ii fols.
A: page 142x95mm; text 100x67mm; 26 lines; one cursive hand.
B: page 142x95mm; text 97x61mm; 29–32 lines; one small even cursive hand.
Moral or devotional headings to some proses, fols 10^r, 21^r, 23^r, 30^v, 31^v, 43^v.
Pocket sized.

CONTENTS   A: fols 1^r–48^r *DCPhil.*, *expl.* imperf. IV.pr.iii.9 'omnia geruntur'.

B: fols 49^r–108^v six synodical sermons by master
Michael de Daley.

GLOSS   A few subject-headings (fols 1–7) and very occasional notes
                   thereafter.

DECORATION   No major initials. Rubricated; some passages underlined in red.

PROVENANCE   'Liber Samuelis Kanuti Rectoris de Combe Rawley in
                   Devonia' (fol. iii^v: Samuel Knott, d. 1687; nr. Honiton, East
                   Devon). Robert Burscough (d. 1709). Acquired for Harley 17
                   May 1715 (fols iii^r and 1^r).

BIBLIOGRAPHY   Bernard, *CMA*, II.i.7660; Wright, *Fontes*, p. 407.

113. MS London, BL, Harley 2510
Arith.   s. xii 1/2

Parchment; vi + 167 + iv fols.
A (s. xi): page 245x170mm; text 186x105mm; 27 lines; palimpsest on s. ix
Italian service-book.
B (s. xii): page 207x148mm; text 140x80mm; 30 lines.
C (s. xii): page 242x169mm; text 210x145mm; 2 cols; 60 lines.
D (s. xii 1/2): page 221x140mm; text 165x98mm; 39 lines; several similar
hands.
Titles of chapters often included in text, sometimes in capitals.

CONTENTS   A: fols 1^r–64^r Cicero, *De inventione*; 65^r–122^v Ps.-Cicero, *Ad
                   Herennium*.
                   B: fols 124^r–31^v Martianus Capella, *De nuptiis*
                   VIII.814–87 (Leonardi 99).
                   C: fols 132ra–5vb commentary on *De nuptiis* VIII.1–862
                   (s. xii: *Conches*, pp. 35–36).
                   D: fols 136^r–67^v *Arith.*

GLOSS   A few users' notes.

DECORATION   D: line drawn eagle vertically in *I(n)* (preface: fol. 136^r) red
                   and green. Well executed minor initials throughout in red or

green with simple leaf terminals; diagrams red, with (fol. 140^v) green.

PROVENANCE   A–C: Dominicans of Chartres: s. xiii; *ex libris* fols 123^v, 124^r, 132^r.
D: unknown.

BIBLIOGRAPHY   Leonardi, no. 99; Wright, *Fontes*, p. 410.

114. MS London, BL, Harley 2516
DCPhil.   s. xiv 2/2

Parchment; i + 39 + ii fols; page 243x165mm; text 170x115mm; 35 lines; one scribe. Catchwords. Colophon, fol. 39^r.
A standard s. xiv MS.

CONTENTS   Fol. 1^r (flyleaf) legal commentary; 2^r–39^r *DCPhil.* (fols 34–35 lacuna IV.m.vii.23 – V.pr.ii.4).

GLOSS   Miscellaneous interlinear annotation throughout; marginal comments sporadic and slight.

DECORATION   Major initials to bks I–IV, blue and red with elaborate flourishing; minor initials throughout blue and red, flourished.

PROVENANCE   English or French. Flyleaf contains Venetian law on debtors (fol. 1^r). Acquired for Harley, 20 January 1721/22 (fol. 1^r).

BIBLIOGRAPHY   C. Foligno, 'Codici di materia veneta nelle biblioteche inglesi', pt. 2, no. cxcii, *Nuovo Archivio Veneto*, n.s. 14, 1907, pp. 352–70 (367); Kottler, Hr; Wright, *Fontes*, p. 410.

115. MS London, BL, Harley 2517
DCPhil.   s. xiv 2/2

Parchment; iv + 55 + iii fols; page 255x170mm: text 152x120mm; 27 lines. One scribe called Franciscus: colophon 'Qui scripsit scribat et semper / cum

domino uiuat. Vivat in celis Franciscus / nomine felix' (fol. 55^v).
Quite swagger, of its kind.

CONTENTS   Fols 1^r–55^v **DCPhil.**

GLOSS   A few interlinear users' notes, some translating the Greek,
                  mainly bk I (fols 1^r–9^v).

DECORATION   Ambitious painted half frame with cornflowers red, green,
                  blue, black, gold (s. xv) added to fol. 1^r: cf. MS London, BL,
                  Harley 3557. Major initials striking: geometric red and blue
                  with floral flourishing. Minor initials red and blue with routine
                  penwork flourishing. In the metres the first letter in each line
                  touched with yellow.

PROVENANCE   Gold and white bookplate inside back and front covers:
                  'VIRTUTE ET fiDE'. John Gibson. Acquired for Harley, 17 June
                  1721 (fol. 1^r).

BIBLIOGRAPHY Kottler, Ha; Wright, *Fontes*, p. 410.

116. MS London, BL, Harley 2518
DCPhil.   s. xiv

Parchment; ii + 31 + ii fols; page 257x168mm; text 187x130mm; 38 lines; one
scribe.
Cramped.

CONTENTS   Fols 1^r–31^r **DCPhil.** (fols 27–30 *rectius* 28, 27, 30, 29).

GLOSS   Some interlinear users' notes throughout. Some marginalia fols
                  1–2.

DECORATION   Major initials red and blue with penwork flourishing at the
                  beginning of each book of *DCPhil*. Minor initials, plain red
                  and blue with simple flourishing.

PROVENANCE   English or French. Italian epigram (s. xv) and 'Laurentius de
                  Lucca' (s. xiv^{ex}): both fol. 31^v. 'Arma Nobilis viri domini
                  batiste de bentivoliis' (fol. 31^r: s. xv). John Gibson. Acquired

for Harley, 13 February 1723/4 (fol. 1^r).

BIBLIOGRAPHY Kottler, H; Wright, *Fontes*, p. 410.

117. MS London, BL, Harley 2519
DCPhil.
                                                                        S. XV

Parchment; ii + 81 + ii fols; page 248x165mm; text 145x97mm; 23 lines; one
cursive scribe.
Colophon: 'Explicit liber Anicii Manlii Severini Boecii exconsularis ordinarii
patricii de consolacione philosophie manu W. fferoi' (fol. 80^v).
A luxury MS that has been left unfinished.

CONTENTS   Fols 1^r–2^r Trivet's prologue; 2^r–3^r Trivet's *accessus*; 3^v–13^v
                  Index, *inc*. 'Accusare non potuit in causa'; *expl*. 'Nec ymagine
                  nec sensibus…prosa quarta et cetera'; 14^r–80^v *DCPhil.*; 81^v
                  English poem.

GLOSS   Virtually none.

DECORATION   Planned, but not supplied. Bust of Christ (fol. 30^r); poor
                  drawing of man with triple crown (fol. 37^r).

PROVENANCE   English. 'Emptus a magistro Ward' c. 1500, and 'Thomas
                  Webster' s. xvi^{in} (both fol. 81^v). Ambrose Bonwicke,
                  headmaster of Merchant Taylors, 1686–91. Acquired for
                  Harley, 11 September 1725 (fol. 1^r).

BIBLIOGRAPHY Bernard, *CMA*, II.i.8722 (Bonwicke); Wright, *Fontes*, p. 410;
                  A. G. Watson, 'Harley Manuscripts', *Journal of the Society of
                  Archivists*, 4, 1973, p. 606.

118. MS London, BL, Harley 2559
DCPhil., Vita VII
                                                                        s. xiii

Parchment; iv + 34 + iii fols; page 220x150mm; text 151x97mm; 32 lines
ruled for gloss in outer margin of each page; one scribe. *Tituli* and colophons
to bks I–V of *DCPhil.*

CONTENTS   Fols 1^r–34^r **DCPhil.**; 34^r *Accessus* fragment and **Vita VII** by the gloss hand.

GLOSS   *Inc.* 'Boetius tractaturus de philosophica consolatione primitus ostendit se talem qui indigeat consolatore, ostendens se miserum'. Marginal commentary sporadic after fol. 2^r, except at fol. 18 (III.m.ix) and fols 27–28, 30 (IV and V); plentiful interlinear notes throughout. The commentary is William of Conches, as is *Vita VII*, the *accessus* and the commentary on the *titulus* (fol. 34^r).

DECORATION   Major initials plain red with internal white decoration; otherwise competent plain red initials and rubrication throughout. Red paraph signs in the marginal commentary.

PROVENANCE   J. G. Graevius (d. 1703). Acquired for Harley 6 August 1724 (fol. 1^r).

BIBLIOGRAPHY   A. C. Clark, 'The Library of J. G. Graevius', *Classical Review*, 5, 1891, pp. 365–72, at 369; Wright, *Fontes*, p. 411; Minnis, *Chaucer*, p. 189n.

119. MS London, BL, Harley 2685
DCPhil.
s. ix/x

Parchment; ii (modern) + ii + 102 + iii (modern) fols; page 344x256mm; text 2 cols, each 273x90mm; 46 lines; several similar hands. *Tituli* in red capitals for bks II, III, V. Colophons. Neumes, I.m.v (fol. 3ra).
A handsome folio volume.

CONTENTS   Fols 1ra–23va **DCPhil.**; 24ra–35vb Fulgentius, *Mythologiae*; 35vb–39rb idem, *Expositio Virgiliane continentiae secundum philosophos moralis* (antique colophon fol. 39rb); 39rb–102rb Martianus Capella, *De nuptiis* (Leonardi 101).

GLOSS   *DCPhil.* untouched except for glosses on fols 1^r–3^r; the Old High German glosses are later in the MS. Greek given red interlinear Latin translation.

DECORATION   Plain offset red capitals opening each prose and metre. Good rustic capitals for *tituli*.

PROVENANCE   ? Cologne cathedral: 'LIBER MAIORIS EC' (fol. ii^r: s. xv). J. G. Graevius (d. 1703); Acquired for Harley, 20 October 1725 (fol. ii^r).

BIBLIOGRAPHY A. C. Clark, 'The Library of J. G. Graevius', *Classical Review*, 5, 1891, pp. 365–72, at 370 and 372; K. Löffler, *Kölnische Bibliotheksgeschichte im Umriss*, Cologne, 1923, pp. 26, 74; Leonardi, no. 101; Wright, *Fontes*, p. 414; Bergmann, 413; Troncarelli, *Boethiana*, no. 78; Krämer, ii.417.

120. MS London, BL, Harley 2688
Mus.

s. xii 1/2

Parchment; iii + 66 + ii fols.
A (s. xii): page 277x193mm; text 2 cols, each 239x80mm; 50 lines.
B (s. x): page 270x222mm; text variable; lines variable.
C (s. ix): page 320x245mm; text 240x115mm; text and gloss 286x180mm; 28 lines (text).
D (s. ix): page 357x275mm; text 258x196mm; 33 lines.
E (s. xii 1/2): page 345x230mm; text 268x150mm; 48 long lines; one scribe.
Chapter headings in small red capitals (no capitula to I).
A composite MS in which the sections are entirely unrelated, acquired by Harley at different times. Colophon and *titulus*: bk II, fol. 61^r.
E was once a fine MS; cf. MS Oxford, Bodleian Library, Laud. Lat. 49.

CONTENTS   A: fols 1^r–16^r Liutprand, *Antapodosis*, *expl.* imperf.
B: fols 17^r–22^r *tabula uentorum*; hymns to Michael; 18^v John Scot Eriugena, epitaph for Hincmar; *Idiomata generum* (Dionisotti).
C: fols 23^r–29^r Horace, *Epodes* 8.12–17.81; 29^r–30^v idem, *Carmen saeculare*; 30^v–43^v idem, *Epistles*; 43^v–46^v idem, *Satires* I. i.1 – ii.64 (all quite extensively glossed).
D: fols 47^r–54^v Priscian, *Institutiones* iv–v.
E: fols 55^r–66^v *Mus.* I–II.31.

GLOSS   E: a few substantial glosses. Related to text by Greek letters in
                 narrow column between text and gloss.

DECORATION   B: drawing of Philosophy (fol. 22ᵛ: see Ganz), originally in
                 MS Harley 3095.
                 E: poor quality ink initials. Simple main capitals
                 touched with red and some buff, blue, yellow.
                 Diagrams in red and blue.

PROVENANCE   A: acquired by Harley, 20 October 1725.
                 B: Cologne, judging by 'HA ARCHIEPISCOPUS' (i.e.,
                 Hadebold: 819–42, fol. 19ʳ). J. G. Graevius (d. 1703).
                 Acquired by Harley, 6 August 1724.
                 C, D: acquired by Harley, 6 August 1724.
                 E: French. Acquired by Harley, 13 August 1724.

BIBLIOGRAPHY   A. C. Clark, 'The Library of J. G. Graevius', *Classical Review*
                 5, 1891, pp. 365–72 (367, 369–70); Wright, *Fontes*, p. 414;
                 Passalacqua, no. 323; Ganz, in Gibson, pp. 275–77; A. C.
                 Dionisotti, 'Greek Grammars and Dictionaries in Carolingian
                 Europe', in *The Sacred Nectar of the Greeks*, ed. M. W. Her-
                 ren, London, 1988, pp.1–56 (16–17); Bower, no. 42; Krämer,
                 ii.417; Bernhard and Bower, Lha.

121. MS London, BL, Harley 2713
1 in Isag.
                                                                    s. xii

Parchment; iv + 64 + iii fols.
A (s. ix): page 180x120mm; text 150x85mm; 22 lines.
B (s. xii): page 180x106mm; text 157x88mm; 46 lines; 'écriture micro-
scopique'.
C (s. xii): page 162x110mm; text 127x83mm; 29 lines.

CONTENTS   A: fols 1ʳ–34ᵛ Isidore, *Etymologies* I, with lacunae.
                 B: fols 35ʳᵃ–41ʳᵇ continuous commentary on Priscian,
                 Institutiones xvii–xviii: *inc.* and *expl.* imperf.; 41ᵛ–42ᵛ
                 Notes, *inc.*'Inuisibilia dei'.
                 C: fols 43ʳ–64ᵛ *1 in Isag.* i.1–21, *expl.* imperf. 'diffinire'
                 65/10.

GLOSS   Occasional subject-headings in margin, e.g., 'questio. utrum essent corporalia an incorporalia' (fol. 50ᵛ: i.10, 26/13–14). Textual corrections added in margin.

DECORATION   A: fine opening **D** (fol. 1ʳ) now cut out. Good minor initials green, yellow, and silver, with Celtic interlace.
                 C: small but highly competent red abstract initial fol. 43ʳ.

PROVENANCE   A, B, C owned by J. G. Graevius (d. 1703). Acquired by Harley, 20 October 1725.

BIBLIOGRAPHY   A. C. Clark, 'The Library of J. G. Graevius', *Classical Review* 5, 1891, pp. 365–72 (370); Wright, *Fontes*, p. 415.

122. MS London, BL, Harley 3068
DCPhil. I–II   s. xii 1/2

Parchment; ii + 67 + ii fols; page 260x108mm; text 205x80mm; 58 lines, ruled with a stylus; one scribe for the *DCPhil.*; 6ᵛ–67ʳ written by the scribe Arnulf and several others. *Titulus* (fol. 1ʳ); scribal colophon to Augustine sermons fol. 67ʳ.
A tall, narrow MS.

CONTENTS   Fols 1ʳ–6ʳ **DCPhil**. I–II.pr.v.9; 6ᵛ–45ʳ *Ephraem Latinus* (*CPL* 1143); 45ʳ–62ᵛ *De exemplis patrum, inc.* 'Scio uere multum esse beatum'; *expl.* 'de quibus nos redemit ipse'; 62ᵛ–67ʳ Augustine, two sermons; 67ʳ six-line verse colophon; *inc.* 'Libri perscriptor qui sic et constitit actor / Dicitur Arnulfus'; 67ᵛ two prayers (s. xii).

GLOSS   None.

DECORATION   Simple but well designed red initials to each prose and metre. Offset capitals touched with red to each line of metres and to sections of proses. **C**(*armina*) and **H**(*ec*) slightly more ornate (fol. 1ʳ).

PROVENANCE   German? 'Ex libris Aegidii Haguniis' (fol. 1ᵛ: s. xvi); de Rochefleur (fol. 2ʳ).

BIBLIOGRAPHY *Colophons*, 1430; Troncarelli, *Boethiana*, no. 79.

123. MS London, BL, Harley 3082
Op. Sac. I–III, V   s. xii 2/2

Parchment; ii + 138 + ii fols; page 290x207mm; text 220x45mm; text and
commnentary 220x151mm; 15 lines of text; 29 lines of commentary, ruled at
half spacing; fol. 138 is a replacement (s. xvi); one scribe.
A good solid library volume.

CONTENTS   Fols 1ra–138rb *Op. Sac. I–III, V,* with commentary of Gilbert
                of Poitiers.

GLOSS   See contents.

DECORATION   Initials fol. 1ra, 2rb, 4ra only; line-drawn red and pale green,
                with acanthus leaves.

PROVENANCE   ? French. J. G. Graevius (d. 1703).

BIBLIOGRAPHY A. C. Clark, 'The Library of J. G. Graevius', *Classical Review*
                5, 1891, pp. 365–72 (370); Häring, *Gilbert*, p. 21; Wright,
                Fontes, p. 422; Häring, no. 68. See pl. 5.

124. MS London, BL, Harley 3095
DCPhil., Op. Sac., Vitae I–II   s. ix

Parchment; ii (modern) + i + 149 + ii (modern) fols; page 276x218mm; text
175x117mm; 20 lines.
Metres identified with scansion marks. *Tituli* and *colophons* to *DCPhil.* I–V.
Tituli to *Op. Sac.* Rhetorical labels, e.g., YRONIA (I.pr.iv.10: fol. 7^{r}). 'Boethius'
(**B**) and 'Philosophia' (**Ph**) named in dialogue.

CONTENTS   Fol. 1^{v} *Vitae I–II*; 1^{v}–2^{r} commentary on *titulus, inc.* 'Boetius
                dignitatibus summis excelluit utraque lingua peritissimus
                orator. Qui regem Theodricum cum in senatu pro consulatu
                filiorum luculenta oratione laudauit'; *expl.* 'quemadmodum
                socerum abreauit'; 2^{v}–110^{v} *DCPhil.*; 47^{r}–61^{v} two commentaries

on III.m.ix (Huygens): 47^r–59^r *inc.* 'Quamuis hic sator pro conditore non proprie sed metaphorice positum uideatur'; *expl.* 'atque de his censui reticere'; 59^v–61^v *inc.* 'Inuocatio haec philosophiae ad integrum'; *expl.* 'ubi intelligitur presentia dei'; 111^r list of Byzantine offices; 111^r Eugenius of Toledo, *Hex-aëmeron ii* (Schaller 12551); 111^v liturgical material, neumed, in another, slightly later hand; 112^v diagram of the heavens; 113^v–49^v *Op. Sac. I–V*.viii.95.

GLOSS   Extensive marginal and interlinear Carolingian gloss to *DCPhil.* (cf. Silk) and to *Op. Sac.* Latin and Greek alphabetical reference-signs. Nota signs.

DECORATION   Plain red initials at the beginning of each prose and metre; good capitals for *tituli*, colophons and rhetorical labels. Simple diagram fol. 112^v; drawing of Philosophia now MS London BL, Harley 2688, fol. 22^v. Red leaf motifs divide 2–col. metres. Drypoint knot-patterns in margins, esp. fols 119^v–32^r.

PROVENANCE   French. 'RVOTBERTI LIBER. NON EST ALIVS HVIC SIMILIS' (fol. 89^r). Acquired by Harley, 20 October 1725 (fol. 1*).

BIBLIOGRAPHY   Silk, *Commentarius*, h; R. B. C. Huygens, 'Mittelalterliche Kommentare zum *O qui perpetua*', *Sacris Erudiri*, 6, 1954, pp. 373–427 (383–404); Courcelle, pp. 406–8; Wright, *Fontes*, p. 422; Bergmann, no. 418; Troncarelli, *Boethiana*, no. 80; Krämer, ii.417 (Cologne); Troncarelli, 'Opuscula', p. 16. See pl. 6.

125. MS London, BL, Harley 3272
Logica vetus et nova   s. xiv 1/2

Parchment; vi + 227 + iv fols.
A (s. xiv 1/2): page 240x183mm; text 118x60mm; 24 lines.
B (s. xiv 1/2): page 260x188mm; text 145x82mm; 29 lines.
C (s. xiv 1/2): page 255x178mm; text 132x66mm; 26 lines.
D (s. xiv 1/2): page 255x177mm; text 125x70mm; 29 lines.
E (s. xiv^{in}): page 255x190mm; text 2 cols, each 180x50mm; 32 lines. Scribal colophon 'per manus Volperti de Wolmarkusen Anno domini M ccc iii' (fol. 227rb).

CONTENTS   A: fols 1^r–10^v *Isag.*, glossed; 11^r–30^v *Cat.*, glossed; 31^r–42^v *De Int.*, glossed; 43^r–52^r *Liber sex principiorum*, glossed; 52^v–64^r *Div.*, glossed; 64^r–70^r *Top. Diff.* with *lacunae*, glossed; 70^v–72^v notes.
B: fols 73^r–99^v *Prior Anal.*, glossed; 100^r–20^v *Post. Anal.*, glossed.
C: fols 121^r–42^v *Soph. Elench.*, glossed; 143^{r-v} notes.
D: fols 144^r–207^r *Topica Aris.*, glossed.
E: fols 208ra–27rb Aristotle, *De anima* I–III, glossed; 227^{rb-vb} unidentified text.

GLOSS   See contents.

DECORATION   A–D: flourished red initials, *tituli* and explicits by the same hand.
E: red and blue flourished initials (fols 208ra, 213va).

PROVENANCE   Unknown.

BIBLIOGRAPHY   Watson, *London*, 744 (E only); Burnett, *Glosses*, p. 132n.

126. MS London, BL, Harley 3302
DCPhil.   s. xiv

Parchment; ii + 66 + ii fols; page 285x189mm; text 166x85mm; 28 lines; ample margin left for gloss; same or very similar Italian hand throughout.

CONTENTS   Fols 1^r–66^v *DCPhil.*

GLOSS   None.

DECORATION   Border (fol. 1^r) and half-border (fol. 10^v); minor initials at the beginning of each prose and metre in red and blue with contrasting penwork flourishing; competently done. Initials with figures at the beginning of each book (all with gold): Boethius (fol. 1^r: damaged); man with book (fol. 10^v); standing figure with book (fol. 22^v); green-clad tonsured man with book (fol. 40^v); Philosophy with rod (fol. 56^v).

PROVENANCE   Bologna (illumination). 'Questo libro é...' (fol. ii^r: s.
xvii–xviii). Acquired by Harley 13 February 1723/4 (fol. ii^r).

BIBLIOGRAPHY   Wright, *Fontes*, p. 425.

127. MS London, BL, Harley 3509
Top. Diff. IV

s. xii 2/3

Parchment; iii + 86 + iv fols; page 200x130mm; text 155x92mm; 33 lines;
several similar scribes. Ruled with a stylus.

CONTENTS   Fols 1^r–2^v flyleaves: canonistic notes; 3^r–43^v Cicero, *De inventione*; 44^r–48^v *Top. Diff. IV*; 48^v–84^v Ps.-Cicero, *Ad Herennium*; 85^r–86^v flyleaves: canonistic notes.

GLOSS   A few notes to *Top. Diff.*, more to *De inventione* and *Ad
Herennium*.

DECORATION   Major initials green and red or red and yellow with foliate
embellishment: fols 3, 21^v, 44^r (plain green), 48^v, 61^r (red with
penwork flourishing).

PROVENANCE   Acquired by Harley, 21 December 1723 (fol. 1^r).

BIBLIOGRAPHY   Wright, *Fontes*, p. 429.

128. MS London, BL, Harley 3557
DCPhil.

s. xiv/xv

Parchment; iv + 48 + ii fols; page 260x190mm; text 162x111mm; 31 lines;
ample margins left for annotation; ruled for gloss; one Italian scribe. *Titulus*
added by glossator (fol. 1^r). Hebrew pledge-note (fol. 48^v).
A standard s. xiv–xv vol. with illumination, very like Harley 3302.

CONTENTS   Fols 1^r–47^v *DCPhil.*

GLOSS   Gloss added fairly extensively in the margin and interlinearly.

Some glosses are in a clear humanistic cursive, the hand of Pietro da Montagnana of Padua, who has also corrected the Greek (e.g., I.pr.iv.2–3 and I.pr.v.12: fols 3ᵛ, 6ᵛ).

DECORATION   Half border (fol. 1ʳ) and major initials with gold at the beginning of each book. Gold balls with flying sparks. Minor initials red and blue with red, blue and mauve penwork flourishes; cf. MS Harley 2517.

PROVENANCE   North Italian. *Ex libris* Antonio de ? miel (fol. 48ᵛ: s. xvi). Acquired for Harley, 20 January 1721/22.

BIBLIOGRAPHY Wright, *Fontes*, p. 430; R. W. Hunt, 'Pietro da Montagnana: A Donor of Books to San Giovanni di Verdara in Padua', *Bodleian Library Record*, 9, 1973–78, pp. 17–22 and pl. vi.

129. MS London, BL, Harley 3595
Arith., Mus.   s. xi

Parchment; iv (modern) + 73 + iv (modern) fols.
A: *Arith.* page 288x203mm; text 212x143mm; 30 lines. *Mus.* page 282x197mm; text 202x145mm; 29 lines; very neat scribe.
B: page 280x183mm; text 220x132mm; 43 lines.

CONTENTS   A: fols 1ʳ–48ᵛ **Arith.** with extensive *lacunae* in bk I (geometrical fragment, fols 5ᵛ–6ʳ); 49ʳ⁻ᵛ astronomical fragment with drawings; 50ʳ–56ᵛ **Mus.** (disordered fragments). B: fols 57ʳ–73ᵛ Ps.-Boethius, *Geometria*.

GLOSS   Fol. 1ʳ⁻ᵛ heavy; 3ᵛ–4ᵛ, 9ᵛ–14ʳ, 17ʳ–18ʳ some; scattered glosses throughout *Arith.*; *Mus.* 51ᵛ–52ᵛ, 55ʳ–56ʳ.

DECORATION   Perseus with Gorgon's head (fol. 49ʳ); seven stars as female busts in circles (fol. 49ᵛ). Simple capitals in scribe's ink and his hand; otherwise no decoration. Plentiful, coarse diagrams and tables in orange-red.

PROVENANCE   'E. Benzelius' (fol. 1ʳ: s. xvii); J. G. Graevius (d. 1703). Acquired for Harley, 20 October 1725 (fol. 1ʳ).

BIBLIOGRAPHY   A. C. Clark, 'The Library of J. G. Graevius', *Classical Review*
5, 1891, pp. 365–72 (371); Folkerts, h, pp. 4–5; Wright,
Fontes, p. 431; Bower, no. 43; Bernhard and Bower, Lh.

130. MS London, BL, Harley 4092
DCPhil.
                                                                s. xii 1/2

Parchment; v + 158 + iv fols.
A (s. xii): page 202x130mm; text 150x80mm; 32 lines.
B (s. xii 2/2): page 197x130mm; text 150x70mm; 34 lines.
C (s. xii 1/2): page 200x130mm; text 132x63mm; 25 lines; several scribes (at
least one s. xii 1/4).
Metres occasionally written as prose, e.g., IV.m.i (fol. 135^{r-v}).

CONTENTS   A: fols 1^r–2^v Prudentius, *Psychomachia, inc.* line 801; 3^r–38^v
Sedulius, *Carmen paschale*, hymns and poems.
B: fols 39^r–83^v Bernard of Morlás, *De contemptu
mundi* (Wright's MS **B**); 84^r–86^v Walther 15676.
C: fols 87^r–157^v *DCPhil.* Folio missing between fols
94^v–95^r (I.pr.iv.173: 'securitate' to I.pr.v.1 'illa uultu
placido'). Fol. 135^v: error in copying III.m.xii which
has gone wrong for eight lines, all crossed out, arises
from a three-column original. 158^r s. xiv contents-list:
'Epigramatum Prosperi de uirtutibus / Prudens
Clemens de uirtutibus et uiciis / De poetria efflactus
Tarte (sic) / Boicius de consolacione philosophie /
Plato de [blank]'.

GLOSS   Sporadic users' notes s. xiii and later.

DECORATION   C: good unambitious 'monastic' s. xii 1/2 initials at the
beginning of proses and metres: green, red with simple leaf
terminals. No special initials to begin a new book. Offset
initials common until fol. 151^r.

PROVENANCE   Acquired by Harley, 17 May 1715 (fol. 1^r).

BIBLIOGRAPHY   T. Wright, *The Anglo-Latin Satirical Poets and Epigram-
matists of the Twelfth Century*, 2 vols, London, 1872,

pp. 3–102; Wright, *Fontes*, p. 439; Troncarelli, *Boethiana*, no. 81.

131. MS London, BL, Harley 4725
Op. Sac. I–II   s. xiii 2/2

Parchment; iii (modern) + ii + 223 + i + iii (modern) fols. Page 200x148mm, except for B = 195x148mm.
A (s. xiii 2/2): text 2 cols, each 163x50mm; 41 lines; one scribe for *Op. Sac.*; fols 20^r–47^v were once part of another MS, *paginated* (arabic nos) 128–183.
B (s. xiii mid): text 135x80mm; 46 lines; double frame ruled; one minute hand.
C (s. xiii 2/2): text 2 cols, each 130x50mm; 35 lines; one or two scribes.
D (s. xiii 1/2): text 168x104mm; 29 lines; three or four scribes.
E (s. xiii 1/2): text 146x90mm; 24 lines; double panel ruled; one scribe.
F (s. xii^{ex}/xiii^{in}): text 170x115mm; 34–40 lines; two or three scribes.
G (s. xiv): text 2 cols, each 175x66mm; 39–43 lines; one scribe.
A–E were already assembled in s. xv (contents-list fol. v^v [=2*^{v}]). *Titulus* in red, fol. 45rb. Hebrew (fol. 205^v). Re-sewn onto separate supports for each quire and rebound, 1968.

CONTENTS   A: fols 1ra–10ra Bonaventure, *Meditationes*; 10ra–19vb
Testamenta XII patriarcharum (abridged); 20ra–45rb Augustine,
three treatises and three sermons; 45rb–47vb *Op. Sac.* **I–II**.39.
B: fols 48^r–55^r Cicero, *De amicitia*, abridged.
C: fols 56ra–81vb Gregory the Great, *Quomodo uen-
erandi sancti sunt*.
D: fols 82$^{r–v}$ list of definitions; 83^r–117^v Richard of St
Victor, *Benjamin Minor*; 117^v–18^r *Ratio nominum
filiorum Jacob*; 118$^{r–v}$ *Benedictiones filiorum Jacob*;
119^r *Oralis expositio Jacob et uxorum et filiorum eius*;
119^v–55^v John Beleth, *De ecclesiasticis officiis*.
E: fols 156^r–204^r Jacques de Vitry, *Life of S. Mary of
Oignes* (*BHL* 5516).
F: fols 206^r–10^v *De ligno crucis*; 210^v–11^v Augustine,
sermon; 211^v 'Dum medium silentium tenerent omnia'
(Wis. 18.14); 211^v–13^v 'Ibo mihi ad montem mirri'
(Song 4.6).
G: fols 214ra–23vb Thomas Ysmaelita, *Life of the
Virgin Mary*.

GLOSS   A: a few notes and corrections.

DECORATION   A: plain red capitals and some internal touches of red.

PROVENANCE   Durham. Thomas Swalwell, monk of Durham, 12 June 1513
                 (fol. 1^r); Sir Thomas Tempest (d. 1698), 4th baronet of Stella,
                 Co. Durham (fol. v^r [=2*^{r}]).

BIBLIOGRAPHY   Ker, *MLGB*, p. 73; Wright, *Fontes*, p. 447.

132. MS London, BL, Harley 5237
Mus.
                                                                  s. xii 2/2

Parchment; iv + 42 + iv fols; page 220x155mm; text 146x84mm; 34 lines.
Chapter titles in red.

CONTENTS   Fols 1^r–42^r *Mus.* I.22–II.30, III.1–IV.5, IV.6–V.2, V.4–9.

GLOSS   Some later (s. xiii) user's gloss fols 1–15 only.

DECORATION   Red or blue major initials with slight flourishing in the other
                 colour; high quality diagrams, e.g., 35^v–36^r, with occasional
                 use of red, green or blue.

PROVENANCE   Jo(hannes) Rippon' (fol. 42^r).

BIBLIOGRAPHY   Wright, *Fontes*, p. 454; Bower, no. 44.

LANSDOWNE

The library of William Petty, first marquess of Lansdowne, was purchased in
1807.

A Catalogue of the Lansdowne Manuscripts in the British Museum, London,
1819.

133. MS London, BL, Lansdowne 842A
Op. Sac., in Topica Cic., Mus.   s. xv 4/4

Parchment; ii (modern) + 163 + i + iii (modern) fols; page 325x220mm; text
220x125mm; 37 lines; drypoint ruled; written by Tommaso Baldinotti of
Pistoia *c*. 1473–85 (de la Mare). Headings to treatises in red capitals. *Tituli*
and colophons to *Op. Sac.* in red. Latin interlinear translation of Greek in *Mus.*
Mus. has red chapter headings.
Matching vol. with 842B; a very fine pair of humanistic books.

CONTENTS   Fol. 1ᵛ schematic table of contents (Gibson, frontispiece);
                  2ʳ–18ᵛ *Op. Sac. I–V* (III & IV run together); 19ʳ–27ᵛ Cicero,
                  Topica; 28ʳ–94ʳ *in Topica Cic.*; 94ᵛ–104ᵛ Marius Victorinus,
                  De definitionibus; 104ᵛ–6ᵛ additional material, *inc*. 'Topicorum
                  id est localium argumentatio triplex est'; *expl*. 'iudex iniquus
                  et conferendus est'; 107ʳ–63ᵛ *Mus.* (added to *expl*. 'longo-
                  bardorum invidia').

GLOSS   None.

DECORATION   The illumination, but not the diagrams, attributable to Vante
                  Attavanti (de la Mare). Floral half-border, gold, blue, rose,
                  green, grey, with roundels of plants, bees, fire; heraldic bottom
                  border; gold initial with parakeet (fol. 2ʳ). Elsewhere very
                  lovely gold initials with floral infilling and decoration. No
                  minor decoration, except for a few plain blue capitals in *Mus.*
                  Mus. also has diagrams in purple and brown.

PROVENANCE   Florence; made for Lorenzo de' Medici, c. 1473–85.

BIBLIOGRAPHY De la Mare, in Gibson, pp. xvii–xix; Bower, no. 45.

134. MS London, BL, Lansdowne 842B
Arith., DCPhil.   s. xv 4/4

Parchment; iii (modern) + i + 105 + iii (modern) fols (fols 50 & 66 doubled);
page 325x220mm; text 220x125mm; 37 lines; drypoint ruled; written by
Tommaso Baldinotti of Pistoia *c*. 1473–85 (de la Mare). Red headings to
treatises and chapters. *Tituli* to *DCPhil.* in red.

Matching vol. with 842A; a very fine pair of humanistic books.

CONTENTS   Fols 1^r–47^r **Arith.**; 47^v *uersus de Arithmetica*; 47^v verses
                  concerning Gerbert of Rheims; 47^v–49^r *Testamentum porcelli*;
                  48 an inserted paper part-sheet with note on contents by 'G.
                  N.'; 49^r–50^r *Breuis descriptio arithmetice*; 50^v quadrivial
                  schema; 51^r–65^v Ps.-Boethius, *Geometria*; 66^r–105^r **DCPhil**.

GLOSS   None.

DECORATION   The illumination, but not the diagrams, attributable to Vante
                  Attavanti (de la Mare). Very lovely gold initials with floral
                  infilling and decoration. Frequent plain blue capitals. Diagrams
                  in purple and brown.

PROVENANCE   Florence; made for Lorenzo de' Medici, c. 1473–85.

BIBLIOGRAPHY   Folkerts, pp. 19–20; de la Mare, in Gibson, pp. xvii–xix.

ROYAL MANUSCRIPTS

In 1757 George II transferred the manuscripts in the Royal Library to the
British Museum. They are well characterized by Warner and Gilson, *BL, Royal*
I, pp. xi–xxxii. Note that they include the libraries of John, Lord Lumley (d.
1609) and John Theyer (d. 1673).

Bernard, *CMA*, II.i.6371–6682 (Theyer library); G. F. Warner and J. P. Gilson,
Catalogue of Western Manuscripts in the Old Royal and King's Collections, 4
vols, London, 1921; S. Jayne and F. R. Johnson, *The Lumley Library: The
Catalogue of 1609*, London, 1956.

135. MS London, BL, Royal 7 D. VII
Topica Aris. V
                                                                    s. xiii

Parchment; flyleaf s. xiii. The top half of the page survives; page 140mm
wide; text 63mm wide. The fragment is the front flyleaf to a sermon collection
(paper, c. 1500).

CONTENTS   Fol. 1^{r-v} (flyleaf) *Topica Aris.* **V.**3–5; 2va–5vb index to
                  remainder of text; 6^r–244^v Peter of Rheims, O.P. (d. 1247),
                  Sermons; 245^r–58^r three further sermons; 258^v–59^r Peter
                  Damian, verse sermon (Lokrantz D. 5); 259^v Walther 5063.

GLOSS   A few user's glosses.

DECORATION   None.

PROVENANCE   Johannes Ryckes (s. xvi); John Denham, B.Th., canon of
                  Lincoln (d. 1533); Thomas Cantuariensis [i.e., archbp. Cran-
                  mer]; Lumley (all fol. 2^r).

BIBLIOGRAPHY   Bernard, *CMA*, II.ii 8175; BL, *Cat. Royal*, I.187; *AL*, 306;
                  Emden *BRUO*, pp. 569–70 (Denham); M. Lokrantz, *L'Opera
                  poetica di S. Pier Damiani*, Uppsala, 1964, pp. 144–50; Sch-
                  neyer, iv.756.

136. MS London, BL, Royal 8 B. IV
DCPhil. I–II   s. xii 1/2

Parchment; iv + 112 + v fols; page 195x120mm.
A (s. xii): text 153x57mm; 40 lines.
B (s. xiii): text 150x47mm; 38 lines.
C (s. xiii/xiv): text variable; lines variable.
D (s. xii 1/2): text 152x90mm; 35 lines, ruled with a stylus; several scribes.

CONTENTS   Fol. 1^r Suidas: list of 71 chapters; 1^v contents-list (s. xv)
                  covering A–C, to which the Boethius has been added later.
                  A: fols 2^v–5^r Walther 4477 (from this sole MS), notes
                  on Ps. 1 and ages of the world; 5^r–10^r Walther 20296;
                  10^r–18^r Hildebert, *Expositio misse* (Walther 17385).
                  B: fols 19^r–71^v Walter of Châtillon, *Alexandreis*, glos-
                  sed, *expl. imperf.* VIII.129 (noted by Colker, p. xxxiv).
                  C: fols 72^r–101^v Grosseteste material, including Suidas
                  (fol. 72^v s. xiv contents-list relating to A and C only).
                  D: fols 102^r–12^v *DCPhil.* I–II.pr.vi; lines 56–69
                  completed in s. xvi hand.

GLOSS   None.

DECORATION None. Some internal initials in scribe's ink but otherwise no initials, no rubrication. Diagram of elements, with notes: I.pr.vi *ad fin.* (fol. 107^r).

PROVENANCE C: Bury St Edmunds, S 184 (s. xv: fols 1^v, 72^v, 73^r). Given by Henry of Kirkestede (fol. 72^r). Lumley (fol. 2^r).

BIBLIOGRAPHY BL, *Cat. Royal*, I.219–20; S. Harrison Thompson, *The Writings of Robert Grosseteste*, Cambridge, 1940, pp. 63–64; Jayne and Johnson, *The Lumley Library*, no. 932; Ker, *MLGB*, p. 20; R. H. Rouse, 'Bostonus Buriensis and the Author of the *Catalogus Scriptorum Ecclesiae*', *Speculum*, 41, 1966, pp. 471–99 (p. 492); Troncarelli, *Boethiana*, no. 82; A. C. Dionisotti, 'Robert Grosseteste and the Greek Encyclopaedia', in *Rencontres de culture dans la philosophie médiévale: traductions et traducteurs de l'antiquité tardive au XIVe siècle*, ed. J. Hamesse and M. Fattori, Louvain-la-Neuve etc., 1990, pp. 337–53 (341–42 and 351–53); *Registrum Anglie*, p. 211.

137. MS London, Royal 12 D. II
Logica nova   s. xiv$^{in.}$

Parchment; iii + 212 + iv fols; page 244x179mm; text 128x67mm; 26 lines. Mnemonic marginal drawings frequent throughout *Topica Aris.* (fols 25–85), a few in *Soph. Elench.*

CONTENTS Fols 1–2, 211–12 (flyleaves) commentary on Peter Lombard, *Sententiae* (s. xiii); 3^r–24^r **Soph. Elench.,** *inc.* imperf. 'de agonisticis' 17/7; 25^r–112^r **Topica Aris.** (fols 87–112 supplied s. xv); 113^r–71^r **Prior Anal.**; 171^r–208^v *Post. Anal.*; 209^r Aristotle, *Ethica nova* (fragm.); 209^v–10^r commentary on *Post. Anal.*

GLOSS Extensive annotation throughout.

DECORATION One initial, red and blue (fol. 13^r). Many line-drawn heads, animals and grotesques in margins, e.g., fols 37^r, 39^r, 75^r. Man drinking: 'Ecce non desideratur uinum quia uinum sed quia dulce' (fol. 39^r = *Topica Aris.* II.3, 2–4/36).

PROVENANCE   English. 'Textus noue logice magistri Willelmi', 'Magister
              Willelmus Eure Eure' (s. xiv: fols 210^v–11^r), delegate of
              Oxford University, 1304 (d. by 1307).

BIBLIOGRAPHY BL, *Cat. Royal*, II.36–37; *AL*, 311; Emden, *BRUO*, pp. 652–53.

138. MS London, BL, Royal 13 E. X
Op. Sac. IV   1442 +

Parchment; 276 fols; page 444x290mm; text 2 cols, each 345x93mm; 55 lines.
Essentially this is using spare space in a MS with blank space left deliberately
in case more historical information should come to hand. Red *tituli*, but not in
Op. Sac.
The Black Book of Paisley.

CONTENTS   Fols 1ra–14ra Index to *Scottichronicon*; 14rb–27^r historical and
              genealogical prolegomena; 28^r–265rb *Scottichronicon*, I–XVI;
              265va–67va further historical material; 268ra Seneca, *Ad Lucil-*
              ium; 268ra–69rb *Op. Sac. IV*; 269rb–70ra Ps.-Bernard of Clair-
              vaux, *De formula honeste uite* (*PL*, 184: 1167–72); 270ra–71rb
              Letter of Prester John to Emperor Manuel Comnenus; 271va list
              of councils; 271$^{va–vb}$ Bridget of Sweden, *Revelations*.

GLOSS   None.

DECORATION   None. The MS as a whole has simple red and blue initials, but
              Op. Sac. has nothing.

PROVENANCE   Paisley Abbey, Cluniac (dioc. Glasgow): 'Iste liber est sancti
              Iacobi et sancti Mirini de Pasleto' (fol. 271vb). Thomas, Lord
              Fairfax (1650: fol. 15^r), from whom the MS passed to Charles
              II, whose cipher is on the binding.

BIBLIOGRAPHY BL, *Cat. Royal*, II.116–18; Ker, *MLGB*, p. 150.

139. MS London, BL, Royal 15 A. VIII
Top. Diff. IV   s. xii

Parchment; v + 238 + iv fols; page 195x122mm; text 147x90mm; 30 lines.

CONTENTS   Fols 1ʳ–20ʳ Cicero, *De amicitia*; 20ʳ–36ʳ idem, *De senectute*; 36ʳ–43ᵛ idem, *Paradoxa*; 45ʳ–87ʳ idem, *De officiis*; 87ᵛ–92ᵛ ***Top. Diff. IV*** (fills up the end of the quire); 93ʳ–143ᵛ Cicero, *Philippics*; 144ʳ–238ᵛ Terence.

GLOSS   None.

DECORATION   None.

PROVENANCE   Ownership note 1303 (fol. 91ᵛ); note in hand of Peter Young, tutor to James VI and father to Patrick Young, later royal librarian (fol. 87ᵛ); royal pressmark, a seal (red wax): ship (fol. 1ʳ).

BIBLIOGRAPHY   Bernard, *CMA*, II.i. 8627; BL *Cat. Royal*, II.144.

140. MS London BL, Royal 15 A. XXX
DCPhil.   s. xiv

Parchment; v + 184 + iv fols; page 227x165mm; text 166x110mm; 36 lines; one cursive hand throughout. Catchwords. Running heads in scribe's hand noting proses and metres.

CONTENTS   Fols 1ʳ–2ʳ Trivet's prologue; 2ʳ–3ʳ Trivet's *accessus*; 3ʳ–182ʳ ***DCPhil.***, with Trivet's commentary (omits V.pr.vi); 182ʳ Note of Boethius's family and works in another s. xiv cursive hand (cf. *Vita III*).

GLOSS   Trivet is complete.

DECORATION   Simple red ink initials at the beginning of each prose and metre. Rubrication of metres, and frequently within commentary.

PROVENANCE   Oxford. 'Iste liber pertinet mag. R. Wood ex dono Ricardi
                      Nercotes' (fol. 1^r: s. xvi. Richard Wode was Fellow of Lincoln
                      1505; Nercotes was Fellow of Exeter 1502); John Theyer's
                      book mark, no. 2 (fol. 1^r).

BIBLIOGRAPHY   Bernard, *CMA*, I.ii.6411; BL, *Cat. Royal*, II.150; Kottler, Y;
                      Emden, *BRUO*, p. 2070 (Wood).

141. MS London, BL, Royal 15 B. III
DCPhil., Vita VII   s. xiv

Parchment; v + 143 + vi fols; page 233x158mm; text 2 cols, each 171x48mm;
22 text lines and 42 gloss lines; one scribe for text and commentary.

CONTENTS   Fols 2ra–3ra *Vita VII* and *accessus*; 3ra–142va *DCPhil.*, lacking
                      III.pr.vi.14 – III.m.ix.2 (73^v/74^r), III.pr.x.9 – III.xi.114
                      (81^v/82^r), V.pr.v.44 – V.m.v.15 (138^v/39^r); *expl.* imperf.,
                      V.pr.vi.124 'euenire potuissent' (142^v).

GLOSS   Intercalated commentary throughout: Ps.-William of Conches
                      (Minnis).

DECORATION   *Schema* of the elements: fol. 79^r. Illuminated full border with
                      initial fol. 2^r (French) and half border with initial fol. 3^r.
                      Simple red or blue major and minor initials (fols 34^r, 61^v, 91^r,
                      122^v); red and blue paraph signs, lemmata underlined in red.

PROVENANCE   French (illumination). ? King's College, Cambridge (erased
                      inscription fol. 1^v); John Theyer, 17 July 1663 (fol. 75^r).

BIBLIOGRAPHY   Bernard, *CMA*, I.ii.6612; BL, *Cat. Royal*, II.153; Ker, *MLGB*,
                      p. 26; P. Dronke, 'L'amor che move il sole e l'altre stelle',
                      Studi Medievali, 6, 1965, pp. 389–442 (410–13); Courcelle, p.
                      409; Minnis, *Chaucer*, chap. 1 and App. I.

142. MS London, BL, Royal 15 B. IV
Prior Anal.

s. xiii/xiv

Fragment in a miscellany from Worcester, not certainly relating to rest of volume. Page 216x153mm; text 127x70mm; 29 lines.

CONTENTS   Fols 93^r–96^r *Prior Anal.* I. 32–45 (72/9–84/5), *inc.* 'Quomodo autem reducemus sillogismos'; *expl.* imperf. 'Eorum uero sillogismorum qui sunt in secunda.'

GLOSS   A few glosses, fol. 93^r, only.

DECORATION   None.

PROVENANCE   Unknown.

BIBLIOGRAPHY   BL, *Cat. Royal*, II.153–55; *AL*, 2046; Ker, *MLGB*, p. 208; Burnett, *Adelard*, no. 63.

143. MS London BL, Royal 15 B. IX
Mus.

s. xii 2/2

Parchment; iv + 79 + iv fols; page 245x169mm; text 177x105mm; 41 lines. Same or similar scribes throughout. Hebrew, fol. 78^v.
A coherent and elegant volume.

CONTENTS   Fols 1^v–2^v (flyleaves) aphorisms (s. xiii) and (2^v) note of contents in John Dee's hand; 3^r–49^v *Mus.*; 50^r two-line fragment on abacus; 51^r–60^v Hermann of Reichenau, *De mensura astrolabii*; *De utilitatibus astrolabii* (*PL*, 143:381–410); 61^r–69^v Gerbert, *Ad mensurandum cum quadrato astrolabii* (*PL*, 143:410D–11B) and *Geometria*, caps. 16–94; 69^v–70^r letter of Adelbold to Gerbert (*PL*, 140:1103); 70^r–v letter of Gerbert to Adelbold (*PL*, 139:151); 70^v–73^v arithmetical material; 73^v–77^r on the astrolabe; 77va–vb on algorism; 78^r–79^v (flyleaves) miscellaneous material, including notes by Theyer on the occult and fragment of commentary on Job (s. xiii 2/2).

GLOSS   Extensive, in scribe's hand.

DECORATION   Plain initials in red, green or blue at the beginning of each
                 section. Decorated diagram with dragon's head (fol. 10^r).
                 Abstract initial *O(mnium)*, red, blue, green, buff (fol. 3^r).

PROVENANCE   John Dee, M 74; Henry Fowler (1618: fol. 37^v); John Theyer
                 (fol. 2^r).

BIBLIOGRAPHY   Bernard, *CMA*, I.ii. 6625; Bubnov, pp. xxxvi–xxxviii; BL, *Cat.
                 Royal*, II.156–57; Bower, no. 46; R. J. Roberts and A. G.
                 Watson, *John Dee's Library Catalogue*, London, 1990, pp. 119
                 and 71, n. 38; Bernhard and Bower, Lry.

SLOANE

The library of Sir Hans Sloane was purchased for the newly founded British
Museum in 1753.

S. Ayscough, *A Catalogue of the Manuscripts Preserved in the British
Museum Hitherto Undescribed*, 2 vols, London, 1782; E. J. L. Scott, *Index to
the Sloane Manuscripts in the British Museum*, London, 1904; reprinted
Oxford, 1971.

144. MS London, BL, Sloane 1777
Op. Sac. V   s. xii 3/4

Parchment; 100 fols (folio missing between 90–91); page 173x117mm; text
144x91mm; 43 lines.

CONTENTS   A (s. xii 2/2): fols 1^r–47^r Becket correspondence (Duggan
                 omits).
                 B (s. xii 1/2): fols 48^r–71^v prayers, sentence-literature,
                 including (60ra–65va) continuous commentary on
                 DCPhil. III m. ix.

C (s. xii 2/3): fols 72^r–86^v *Querolus*, glossed; 86^v–90^v letters, including St Bernard, Alcuin to Fredegisus; 90^v–95^r **Op. Sac. V**, with lacuna from 'nutumque aspicere' to 'unde hec mensa' (p. 74, line 25 – p. 84, line 46); 95^r–99^r Hugh of St Victor, *De anima Christi*; 99^r–100^v idem, *De virginitate Marie*, *expl.* imperf.

GLOSS   None.

DECORATION   None.

PROVENANCE   English. B possibly Canterbury.

BIBLIOGRAPHY   Goy, 2.2.3.7–8; Rouse (*Querolus*), in *Reynolds*, pp. 330–32.

LAMBETH PALACE

Although Lambeth Palace was an archiepiscopal residence from the twelfth century and doubtless had books, Lambeth Palace Library as a place of study was founded by Archbishop Richard Bancroft (1604–10). The collection includes some Christ Church books, but more notably a major part of the monastic library of Lanthony (Gloucestershire). For a brief, clear overview see James and Jenkins, I, pp. v–vii. Archbishop Sancroft's re-establishment of the library in 1664 is discussed by N. R. Ker in Bill, I, pp. 1–51.

M. R. James and C. Jenkins *A Descriptive Catalogue of the Manuscripts in the Library of Lambeth Palace*, 2 vols, Cambridge, 1930–32; E. G. W. Bill, *A Catalogue of Manuscripts in Lambeth Palace Library*, 3 vols, Oxford, 1972–83.

145. MS London, Lambeth Palace Library, 67
Arith., Mus.
                                                          s. xii 1/2

Parchment; i (modern) + iv + 172 + i + i (modern) fols; page 350x250mm; text 230x150mm; 30 lines; one principal scribe with a fine hand; fols. 63^r line 7 to fol. 95^r very similar (same?) hand, but smaller; running headers in black. Sancroft binding.

CONTENTS   Fol. iii^v capitula of *Arith*.; iv^r list of Boethius' works by
                  'Boston of Bury' (s. xiv), i.e., Henry of Kirkstede, with
                  incipits; 1^r–62^v **Arith**. (fol. 33^r text missing, but figures
                  present); 63^r–v *Saltus Gerberti*; 64^r–91^v Adelard's astronomical
                  tables (as MS Oxford, Corpus Christi 283); 92^r–95^r Petrus
                  Alfonsi / Alkwariz mi, *inc.* 'Nunc demonstrandum est qua
                  ratione cuiuslibet planete medialitas reperiri querat'; *expl.* 'de
                  predictis signis et numero auferetur'; 96^r–172^r **Mus**.

GLOSS   Interlinear throughout *Arith*., in the same hand. Fewer glosses
                  for *Mus*., but when present they are quite substantial (e.g., fols
                  98^r–v, 107^r, 110^v ,132^r).

DECORATION   **I***(n dandis)* line-drawing of Boethius with book in left hand,
                  right hand raised to expound (fol. 1^r). Competent single-colour
                  (green, red, blue) paragraph initials throughout; red and blue
                  initial **O** (fol. 96^r). Diagram of planets/tones *secundum Tullium*
                  (fol. 111^v). *Mus*. lacks all but the simplest diagrams (fols.
                  156^r–72^v). Astronomical tables and diagrams in black, red,
                  blue, and green, beautifully produced.

PROVENANCE   Bury St Edmunds, B. 318 (fol. 1^r); John Dee (fol. iii^v).

BIBLIOGRAPHY   James and Jenkins, pp. 106–8; Ker, *MLGB*, p. 21; R. H.
                  Rouse, 'Bostonus Buriensis and the Author of the *Catalogus
                  scriptorum ecclesiae*', *Speculum*, 41, 1966, pp. 471–99, pl. IX;
                  Bolton, in Gibson, p. 432 (fol. 1^r, drawing); Burnett, *Adelard*,
                  no. 68; Bower, no. 48; R. J. Roberts and A. G. Watson, *John
                  Dee's Library Catalogue*, London, 1990, DM 87, p. 171;
                  Bernhard and Bower, Lpl; and see MS Royal 8 B. IV, above.

146. MS London, Lambeth Palace Library, 339
Logica vetus   s. xii 1/2

Parchment; i (modern) + ii + 174 + i (modern) fols; page 260x170mm; text
185x105mm; 29 lines; one scribe. Sancroft binding.
A fine monastic volume of *logica vetus*.

CONTENTS   Fols 1ʳ–10ᵛ *Isag.*; 10ᵛ–28ʳ *Cat.*; 28ᵛ–38ᵛ *De Int.*; 39ʳ–55ʳ M. Victorinus, *De definitionibus*, *expl.* imperf. (*PL*, 64:909C); 55ᵛ–68ᵛ *Div.* (with fragment of *Topica Aris.* IV embedded in it); 68ᵛ–101ʳ *Top. Diff.*; 101ᵛ–13ʳ Cicero, *Topica*; 113ᵛ–39ʳ *Syll. Cat.*; 140ʳ–72ᵛ *Syll. Hyp.*

GLOSS   Gloss, fols 20ʳ, 34ʳ, 52ᵛ, 68ᵛ, 113ᵛ, notably 118ʳ, 125ʳ. A much later glossing hand, fol. 1ʳ only.

DECORATION   High quality abstract initials consistent throughout in blue, red (some oxidized silver?), green and purple.

PROVENANCE   Lanthony, Can. Reg.: 'Liber Lanthonie iuxta Gloucestriam' (fol. 174ᵛ); *ex libris* on fol. 1ᵛ erased. No. 312 in Lanthony catalogue.

BIBLIOGRAPHY James and Jenkins, pp. 445–46; *AL*, 287; Ker, *MLGB*, p. 110; *AL*, V.1–3, pp. xxxviii–xxxix (La).

147. MS London, Lambeth Palace Library, 423
Logica nova

s. xiii

Parchment; ii (modern) + 208 + ii (modern) fols; three vols bound together; page 220x165mm.
A: text 115x70mm; 30 lines; wide margins for gloss.
B: text 110x65mm; 24 lines.
C: text 160x125mm; 2 cols; 62 lines.
Several good school hands.
A very personal, used schoolbook, with very scrappy parchment.

CONTENTS   A: fols 1ʳ–30ʳ *Prior Anal.*, with marginal and interlinear gloss, tree diagrams and diagrams in margins; 30ʳ–53ᵛ *Post. Anal.*, with almost no gloss; 55ʳ–97ᵛ *Topica Aris.* with considerable marginal and interlinear gloss; 98ʳ–114ᵛ *Soph. Elench.* with marginal and interlinear gloss; 115ʳ⁻ᵛ is an old cover sheet, with a circular maze and a small diagram of the planets on 115ʳ.
              B: 116ʳ–86ᵛ Priscian, *Institutiones* xvii–xviii.157, with marginal and interlinear glosses; 187ʳ–92ᵛ Donatus, *De*

barbarismo; 193^r–200^r Priscian, *De accentibus*;
200^v notes and *probationes pennae*.
C: 201ra–6ra grammatical text, *inc.* 'Sicut in montibus
sunt tria'; *expl.* 'In principio medio et fine'; 206rb
beginning of note in s. xiv hand to explain the calen-
dar tables which follow; 206^v–7^r unfinished calendar
tables and *probationes pennae* including 'Richard de
irlande'; 207^v–8^v alphabets, scrawls, bits of prayers,
drawing (?) cut out of 208^r.

GLOSS   See contents.

DECORATION   A: characteristic s. xiii blue and red pen-flourished initials;
                   some red paraph signs.
                   B: simple red and blue initials and paraph signs; some
                   scrappy pencil drawings of men and beasts on fols
                   157^r–63^v; fol. 186^v drawing of rampant horse.

PROVENANCE   Unknown.

BIBLIOGRAPHY James and Jenkins, pp. 584–85; Passalacqua, no. 335.

148. MS London, Lambeth Palace Library, 456
Logica vetus   s. xiii^{ex}

Parchment and paper; i (modern) + i + 220 + ii (modern) fols; pages of very
varied measurements; four vols bound together; vols A–C (s. xiii^{ex}) =
parchment (fols 1^r–126^v), D (s. xv) = paper, except outer and middle sheets of
first quire (fols 127, 136–137, 146 = parchment; 128–135, 138–145, 147–220 =
paper; James and Jenkins have excellent description and full quiring).
B: page 190x150mm; text 110x70mm; 22–31 lines; several small hands.

CONTENTS   A: fols 1^r–34^v Priscian, *Institutiones*, xvii–xviii.85.
                   B: fols 35^r–45^r *Isag.*, with marginal and interlinear
                   gloss; 45^v–60^v *Cat.* with sporadic glossing; 61^r–70^v *De
                   Int.*, with a few marginal glosses; 71^r–80^r *Liber sex
                   principiorum*, with very little gloss; 80^v–92^r *Div.*, with
                   wide margins for gloss which is hardly present;
                   92^r–106^v *Top. Diff.* I–III, 'eligitur similis enim est

navis civitati' (*PL*, 64:1197D), with short glosses.

C: fols 107ʳ–26ᵛ notes, mainly theological, very tightly abbreviated.

D: fols 127ʳ–220ᵛ various religious tracts, mainly in French.

GLOSS   See contents.

DECORATION   B: red and light blue initials, usually plain, and paraph signs. Ink diagram of a stylised tree explaining text (fol. 45ʳ); no decoration after fol. 96ʳ.

PROVENANCE   Buildwas, O. Cist. (Shrop.). D given by Archbp. Abbot (1611–33).

BIBLIOGRAPHY James and Jenkins, pp. 631–35; Ker, *MLGB*, p. 15; Ker, in Bill, *Catalogue*, i.16; Passalacqua, no. 336.

SION COLLEGE, f. 1630.

Founded as 'a college for the corporation of all the ministers, parsons, vicars, lecturers, and curates within London and suburbs thereof' (*DNB*, xxi.79), Sion College was a copyright library from 1710–1836.

Bernard, *CMA*, II.i.4065–4132; Ker, *MMBL*, i.263–91, with a history of the collection, pp. 263–64.

149. MS London, Sion College, Arc. L 40.2 / L 23
Op. Sac.
                                                             s. xiiiᵉˣ/xivⁱⁿ

Parchment; xvi (modern) + 155 + xvii (modern) fols; page: 330x235mm; text: 245x160mm; 2 cols; 60–64 lines; one neat scribe for Boethius. Parchment damaged by water and heavily restored. Rebound 1963.

CONTENTS   Fols 1ʳ–27ʳ John Damascene, *De fide orthodoxa*, with table of chapters (fol. 1^r); 29^r–94va short theological texts, mostly Augustine and Ps.-Augustine; 94ra–100vb *Op. Sac. I–V*; 100vb–1vb Gundissalinus, *De unitate et uno*; 102^r–36^v short theological texts; 137^r–55^v Richard of St Victor, *De trinitate I–VI*, *expl.* imperf. 'sine generacione pro', bk IV, chap. 17.

GLOSS   Very little annotation; marginal headings and notes of subject matter, all in the same later hand. A few pointing hands, but little evidence of use. The Augustine (fols 29^r–52^v) has 'Grossetestian' indexing symbols (Ker, p. 280).

DECORATION   Blue or red initials with blue and red scrolling; red and blue paraph signs. In the Boethius, space has been left between the *opuscula* for rubricated headings (as in the Richard of St Victor) which are not supplied.

PROVENANCE   English. Fol. 1^r 'Liber M' Johannis Gunthorp' ... a° x^i 1484', dean of Wells (1472–98).

BIBLIOGRAPHY   Bernard, *CMA*, II.i.4077; *DNB*, viii.794–95; S. H. Thomson *The Writings of Robert Grosseteste*, Cambridge, 1940, pp. 48–49; idem, in *Robert Grosseteste*, ed. D. A. Callus, Oxford, 1955, pp. 46–54; R. W. Hunt, ibid., pp. 123–26; Ker, *MMBL*, i.280–81.

WELLCOME HISTORICAL MEDICAL LIBRARY

Incorporates the Wellcome Historical Medical Library (opened to the public in 1949) and the Wellcome Historical Medical Museum.

S. A. J. Moorat, *Catalogue of Western Manuscripts on Medicine and Science in the Wellcome Historical Medical Library*, 3 vols, London, 1962–73. The second and third volumes (II.i–ii) contain manuscripts post-1650, with (II.ii) a *Catalogue of Additional Manuscripts Written Before 1651 A.D.* (pp. 1463–80); J. Symons, *A History of the Wellcome Institute for the History of Medicine*, London, 1993.

150. MS London, Wellcome Historical Medical Library, 55
Prior Anal., Isag., Cat., De Int.

                                                                                    1472–74

Paper; i + 203 fols; page 310x210mm; text 255x205mm; 28 lines; ruled for gloss; scribe, Johann Lindner of Münchberg, O.P. (later chaplain to Prince George of Saxony). Binding: s. xvi stamped half–leather on boards; two clasps, partly surviving. Paper label on front cover: 'Scolasticalia'. Colophons (fols 48ᵛ, 83ᵛ, 91ᵛ, 100ʳ, 148ᵛ, 175ᵛ, 203ᵛ), which show that, originally, the *Logica vetus* preceded the *Logica nova*.
A university text.

CONTENTS
Fols 1ʳ–17ᵛ ***Prior Anal.*** I. 1–26, *expl.* imperf. 'in omnibus figuris' 57/24; 18ʳ–48ᵛ *Post Anal.*; 49ʳ–59ʳ ***Isag.***; 59ᵛ–74ʳ ***Cat.***; 74ᵛ–83ᵛ ***De Int.***; 84ʳ–91ᵛ *Liber sex principiorum*; 93ʳ⁻ᵛ human bust with annotation; 94ʳ–99ᵛ Ps.-Albert the Great, *Parva philosophia naturalis* (abridged, incomplete and heavily glossed; *inc.* 'Natura est principium et causa mouendi'); 100ʳ summary of Aristotle, *Ethics*, I–VI; 101ʳ–48ᵛ Aristotle, *De caelo et mundo*; 149ʳ–75ᵛ idem, *De anima* (*nova translatio*); 176ʳ–83ᵛ Anon., *inc.* 'Principium autem questionis est apponere' (at end, in red, 'Sequitur 2ᵘˢ de anima'); 184ʳ–98ᵛ Aristotle, *De sensu et sensato*; 199ʳ–203ᵛ Peter of Spain, *Dialectica* (Hauréau II.39), *expl.* 'denominative dicitur predicari'; at end, in red, '1474'.

GLOSS
Logica vetus not glossed, except for the *Liber sex principiorum*. Extensive marginalia and sometimes interlinear annotation by the scribe of the *Analytics*. Glosses laid out neatly in both margins connected to the text by lemmata. Gloss often rubricated; reference signs and pointing hands.

DECORATION
Simple capitals in red or blue, sometimes with infilling and flourishing in the same colour or the alternate. Many initials not supplied. Most texts are at least partly rubricated and have red and blue paraph signs. Item 6 seems to have been decorated with items 1–2.

PROVENANCE
Written in Leipzig (colophons); signature of <Johann Conrad> Varrentrapp (1779–1860) inside upper cover; Phillipps 1145 (stamp, fol. iʳ). Unrelated to MS 56, *pace* Moorat (Ker, p. 395).

BIBLIOGRAPHY Moorat, *Catalogue*, I.39–41; Thorndike and Kibre, 901; Ker, *MMBL*, i.395.

151. MS London, Wellcome Historical Medical Library, 127
Top. Diff. IV   s. xv 2/3

Parchment; 49 fols; page 270x190mm; text 180x110mm; 29 lines; one cursive italic hand. Original stamped calf binding over wooden boards, worn; four clasps (top, bottom, and side), all missing. Pink titles and chapter headings to the treatises.
A fine humanist text.

CONTENTS   Fols 2^r–4^r Bede, *De natura rerum* and *De temporibus* (extracts); 4^r–32^r Censorinus, *De die natali*; 32^r–38^v Priscian, *Praeexercitamina*; 39^r–48^v *Top. Diff. IV*.

GLOSS   None; a few annotations to Bede.

DECORATION   Simple red or blue capitals.

PROVENANCE   Italy; from the library of I. T. Adams of Snaithfield, Sheffield.

BIBLIOGRAPHY Moorat, *Catalogue*, I.87–88.

152. MS London, Wellcome Historical Medical Library, 801A
Topica Aris. II–III   s. xiii^{ex}

Eight flyleaves, of which six are sequential fols of *Topica Aris.*, fols i^r–iv^v (beginning) and i^{r–v} and iv^{r–v} (end).
Parchment; page 203x144mm; text 135x85mm; 25 lines; one large, abbreviated, textualis hand.
Host book is two s. xii vols of the *Ars medicinae* and other texts, bound together in s. xiv (fol. v^{r–v}). Binding: white leather on wood with single clasp; chain marks.

CONTENTS   Fols i^r–iv^v and (at end) i^{r–v}, iv^{r–v} *Topica Aris.* ii.9–iii.6 (45/20–62/2).

GLOSS   Extensive user's annotation.

DECORATION   Red paraph signs within text; otherwise none.

PROVENANCE   Both host vols from Bury St Edmunds: M 27, a South Italian MS of the *Ars medicinae* (in Beneventan script), and B 357, modern theologians. St James' parish church, Bury. Acquired from Christie's, 1971.

BIBLIOGRAPHY   Moorat, *Catalogue*, II.ii.1464–67; A. G. Watson, *Supplement to N. R. Ker, Medieval Libraries of Great Britain*, London, 1987, p. 6.

PRIVATE OWNER

153. MS London, private owner, 1
De Int.
s. xiii

Parchment; 1 fol.; page 245x175mm; text 122x71mm; 27 lines; wide margins.

CONTENTS   *De Int.*, chapters 13–14, *inc.* 'Non necesse'; *expl.* 'quiddam non' (32/1–36/19).

GLOSS   Some later s. xiv notes.

DECORATION   One sound, unambitious red initial. Red minor initials and paraph signs.

PROVENANCE   English. Several s. xvi *ex libris*, including John Andrew, Queens' College, Cambridge. Dr Brian Lawn (Guardbook fragment, 46).

BIBLIOGRAPHY   None.

154. MS London, private owner, 2
Prior Anal.   c. 1300

Parchment; one fol.; page 250x185mm; text 134x79mm; 22 lines; wide margins.

CONTENTS   ***Prior Anal.*** II.16–17, 'in eo quod' to 'Manifestum'
                (124/1–126/26).

GLOSS   Many later s. xiv glosses.

DECORATION   Minor initial in blue with red penwork; blue and red paraph
                signs.

PROVENANCE   ? Italian. Dr Brian Lawn (Guardbook fragment, 47).

BIBLIOGRAPHY   None.

155. MS London, private owner, 3
Top. Diff. III–IV   s. xii/xiii

Four flyleaves in the binding of Ps.-Aristotle, *Problemata* (Lyons, c. 1505). The Boethius is fols ii–iii, xii–xiii of host book's vii + 212 + vii fols. Parchment; page 161x96mm (outer margin trimmed by c. 15mm); text 103x70mm; 21 lines; several similar scribes writing an ? Italian hand that faintly echoes Beneventan. Chapter headings and internal headings in red. An unambitious, plain book.

CONTENTS   ***Top. Diff.*** III–IV, fragments: fol. ii^r illegible; ii^v–iii^v IV (*PL*,
                64: 1207C–8D); xii^r–v III (*PL*, 64: 1203D–6B); xiii^r IV (*PL*,
                64: 1210D–11A); xiii^v illegible.

GLOSS   None.

DECORATION   Poor internal initials in red.

PROVENANCE   *Ex libris* for the host book, Richard Townley, 1702. Dr Brian
                Lawn.

BIBLIOGRAPHY None.

156. MS London, private owner, 4
DCPhil.
s. xiv mid

Parchment; single leaf; page 215x150mm; text 167x118mm; outer margin cropped by 3–4mm; 35 lines. Metre in left–hand col.; pr.x fills up right–hand col. then continues as long lines.

CONTENTS   *DCPhil.* III.pr.ix.51 'laborat' to III.pr.x.61 'summum'.

GLOSS   None, except for several pointing hands..

DECORATION   None.

PROVENANCE   German (script); Christopher de Hamel.

BIBLIOGRAPHY   Erik von Scherling, *Rotulus IV* (1937), no. 1999 (dealer's catalogue).

* 157. MS London, private owner, 5
Arith., Mus.
s. xv 1/4

Parchment; 118 fols; 2 cols; 40–42 lines; ruled in pencil; one clear cursive hand. Photographs of three pages (the incipits of Alchandreus, *De astrologia*, and *Arith.* and *Mus.*) in the Courtauld Institute, University of London. A single coherent MS.

CONTENTS   Alchandreus, *De astrologia*; *Arith.*; 70ʳ–118ʳ *Mus.*

GLOSS   None.

DECORATION   Miniatures by the 'Virgil master', active 1410–15 (Meiss). Alchandreus has half–page miniature and full border; *Arith.* and *Mus.* each have half–border and miniature at the top of first column: *Arith.* Boethius teaching a boy who presents writing tablets; *Mus.* Boethius teaching four adults with circular chart.

PROVENANCE   Paris (illumination). Phillipps 1351. Collection of the late
               Count Antoine von Seilern (currently inaccessible).

BIBLIOGRAPHY   M. Meiss, *French Painting in the Time of Jean de Berry: The
               Late Fourteenth Century and the Patronage of the Duke*, 2nd
               edn, London etc., 1967, p. 360; idem, *French Painting in the
               Time of Jean de Berry: The Limbourgs and their
               Contemporaries*, New York, 1974, p. 410; Bower, no. 47.

MAIDSTONE

KENT COUNTY RECORD OFFICE

158. MS Maidstone, Kent County Record Offices U 1121 M2B, pages 103–6
DCPhil.   s. xii 1/3

Parchment; the innermost bifolium of a quire; page 270x176mm; text
230x110mm; 28 lines. Used as wrapping for estate records of Cuckstane,
1584.

CONTENTS   *DCPhil.* IV.pr.vii.34 – V.pr.ii.2.

GLOSS   None.

DECORATION   Fine line–drawn dragon initial inhabited by rebeck player (p.
               104; opening of bk V).

PROVENANCE   Southern English, perhaps Christ Church, Canterbury.

BIBLIOGRAPHY   None.

MANCHESTER

CHETHAM'S LIBRARY, f. 1656.

Founded by a local businessman, Chetham's Hospital developed as a school and library, pari passu.

Bernard, *CMA*, II.i.7146–51; Ker, *MMBL*, iii.335–84, with a history of the collection pp. 335–36.

159. MS Manchester, Chetham's Library, 6682 (Mun. A. 7. 67)
Op. Sac.

s. xiii 2/2

Parchment; ii + 204 + ii fols; page 375x260 mm; text 2 cols, each 258x62mm; 68 lines. Small hands changing at fols. 109^r and 183^r. *Tituli* to *Op. Sac. II, V*. Binding s. xix.

CONTENTS	Fols. 1^r–6^v *Op. Sac.*, treated as three works: 1^r–2^v **Op. Sac. I–II** written in 3 chapters; 2^v–3^r **Op. Sac. III** headed 'Liber boetii de bono' in 2 chapters; 3^r–6^v **Op. Sac. IV–V** headed 'De duobus (*sic*) naturis et una persona cristi' in 6 chapters; 6^v–10^v Ps.-Boethius, *De disciplina scolarium*; 11^r–14^v Augustine, *De bono coniugali*; 14^v–21^r idem, *De adulterinis coniugiis*; 21^r–24^v idem, *Liber ad Dardanum presbiterum*; 24^v–30^r idem, *De predestinatione*; 30^r–37^r idem, *De bono perseverantie*; 37^r–42^v idem, *Contra mendacium*; 42^v–48^r idem, *De mendacio*; 48^{r-v} idem, part of Sermon 252; 48^v–52^v *Questiones Orosii ad Augustinum*; 53^r–90^r Augustine, *Confessions*; 90^v–204^r idem, 144 Letters (as MS London, BL, Royal 5 B. V).
GLOSS	None; a few corrections in the same or similar hand as the text.
DECORATION	Fols 1^r–108^r: initials in red and blue with nice penwork, at each of the major divisions; minor initials at chapter breaks in single colour, with opposite colour penwork. Red and blue running headers up to fol. 97^r; decoration of lesser quality after fol. 97^r. Fols 109^r–63^v: red initials, incomplete; space left for blue initials, not supplied. Fols 164^r–73^r: solid letter forms.

Fols 173ᵛ–90ᵛ: red and blue alternating initials,
but work seems incomplete. From fol. 191ʳ
initials not supplied.

PROVENANCE   English. Bought by Chetham's in 1650, from Robert Little-
                 bury, bookseller of London, for £2.

BIBLIOGRAPHY   Bernard, *CMA*, ii.7146; J. O. Halliwell, *An Account of the
                European Manuscripts in the Chetham Library, Manchester,
                Manchester, 1842, p. 3, no. 6682; Ker *MMBL*, iii.339–41;
                Weijers omits.

OSCOTT

ST MARY'S COLLEGE LIBRARY

* 160. Oscott, St Mary's College, RVZ–I1, 118
Topica Aris.   s. xi

Parchment; 2 fols; front and back flyleaves to J. Bunderius, *Compendium*,
Antwerp, 1555. No measurements; 22 lines surviving. This is the only known
MS of *Topica Aris.* prior to the mid-twelfth century. (For fragments of *Topica
Aris. IV* embedded in *Div.* see Minio-Paluello below.)

CONTENTS: *Topica Aris.* II.1–2 'in]esse. In accidentibus' to 'aut non esse'
                 (31/4–35/26).

GLOSS   None.

DECORATION   None.

PROVENANCE   Continental (Ker).

BIBLIOGRAPHY   Ker, *Pastedowns*, no. 784; L. Minio-Paluello, 'Note sull' Aris-
                totele latino medievale X. — I *Topici* nel X–XI secolo', in
                idem, *Opuscula: The Latin Aristotle*, Amsterdam, 1972, pp.
                357–76.

OXFORD

BODLEIAN LIBRARY, f. 1602

The University Library, founded c. 1320 and augmented by Humfrey, duke of Gloucester, 1439–44, was re-established by Sir Thomas Bodley in 1602. A few of the manuscripts from the medieval library may be identified, but most are new acquisitions in and after 1602: some from other institutions (e.g., Exeter Cathedral), some from sixteenth-century private collections, but the majority from the diverse libraries of medieval England; they had been on the market for seventy years and more, and had long lost their original *ex libris*. The fonds Bodley is the foundation collection, with further acquisitions continuing until 1860. In 1789 the finest classical and biblical manuscripts were put on display in the Auctarium, on the south side of the library quadrangle. These books still retain their Auct. classification. The other fonds which concern us here—from Savile (1620) to Lyell (1949)—are noted below as they occur. Five of these fonds—Ashmole, Canonici, Digby, Laud, Rawlinson—are described in the Quarto Catalogues, written by Black, Coxe and Macray, 1845–80. The entire collection is covered by the seven volumes of the *Summary Catalogue* (*SC*), vol. I being the historical introduction and conspectus of shelf-marks. The *Summary Catalogue* gives a number to every manuscript that was in the Library by 1915 and provides a description of those not included in the Quarto Catalogues. The fonds Lyell has its own catalogue.

Bernard, *CMA*, I.i.1840–3126; W. D. Macray, *Annals of the Bodleian Library Oxford*, 2 edn, Oxford, 1890, reprinted Oxford, 1984; *A Summary Catalogue of Western Manuscripts in the Bodleian Library at Oxford*, ed. F. Madan, H. H. E. Craster et al. and (vol. I) R. W. Hunt, 7 vols, Oxford, 1895–1953; Ker, *MMBL*, iii.582–86; *Duke Humfrey's Library and the Divinity School 1488–1988*, Bodleian Library exhibition June – August 1988, Oxford, 1988.

ASHMOLE (1692)

Elias Ashmole (d. 1692) gave the Ashmolean Museum a substantial collection of books and manuscripts, which was augmented by the libraries of Anthony Wood (1695) and John Aubrey (1697). In 1860 the manuscripts in this collection were transferred to the Bodleian Library.

Bernard, *CMA*, I.i.6491–6547, 6616–8465; W. H. Black, *Catalogue of the Manuscripts Bequeathed unto the University of Oxford by Elias Ashmole, Esq., M.D., F.R.S.*, Oxford, 1845, index volume by W. D. Macray, Oxford, 1866 [= Quarto X]; R. W. Hunt, 'The Cataloguing of Ashmolean Collections of Books and Manuscripts', *Bodleian Library Record*, 4, 1952, pp. 161–70; *SC*, I, pp. l–lii.

161. MS Oxford, Bodleian Library, Ashmole 1285
DCPhil. s. xiii 1/2

Parchment; i + 379 + i fols; page 180x125mm. 14 volumes of s. xii/xiii bound together at the time of Edward I.
D: text 122–35 x 85–100mm; 20–31 lines, increasing towards the end of the text; *DCPhil.* well-written in one good, small hand. Metres in three and four cols to fit into space.
Binding: medieval boards covered with red leather; straps lost.

CONTENTS　　　　Fol. 1ʳ contents list (mid-s. xiii cursive).
A: 2ʳ–4ʳ treatise on the Church, *inc.* 'Duplex est ecclesia militans scilicet et triumphans'; *expl.* 'et eos benedixit.'; 4ʳ⁻ᵛ *De corpore et nomine primi hominis*, *inc.* 'Corpus ade de octo partibus factum fuit'; *expl.* 'Collige fiet adam'; 5ʳ⁻ᵛ patristic *sententiae*.
B: fols 8ʳ–19ᵛ patristic *sententiae* on the good life.
C: fols 20ʳ–46ᵛ Hymnary with intercalated commentary.
D: fols 50ʳ–89ʳ *DCPhil.*
E: fols 90ʳ–100ᵛ arithmetic and computistica; 101ʳ–106ᵛ John de Sacro Bosco, *De sphera*.
F: fols 107ʳ–16ᵛ John de Sacro Bosco, *De computatione temporis*; 117ᵛ metrics.
G: fols 118ʳ–82ᵛ Galen, *Tegne*, glossed; Theophilus, *Liber de negotio urinarum*; Egidius, *De urinis*; Hippocrates, *Aphorisms*, *Liber pulsuum*, *Liber prognosticorum*.
H: fols 185ʳ–95ᵛ Fragment of a monastic rule (Salter).
I: fols 198ʳ–235ᵛ Treatise, 'Cum in claustro quadam die cum fratribus considerem', ed. A. Wilmart, *Revue Bénédictine*, 46, 1934, pp. 296–344; 235ᵇ chanson,

upside down, with notation.

J: fols 236ʳ–94ᵛ Homilies, letters (incl. Aelred, *Speculum caritatis*, and *Disputatio contra cuiusdam epistolam de monachorum regula*).

K: fols 295ʳ–305ʳ homilies and homiletic material.

L: fols 308ʳ–25ᵛ homilies and homiletic material.

M: fols 326ʳ–33ʳ homilies and homiletic material.

N: fols 334ʳ–375ʳ homilies on Joel, Hosea, Amos and Jonah; 376ʳ–77ʳ capitula of *Speculum caritatis* (s. xiv).

GLOSS   D: none.

DECORATION   D: simple red initials beginning each prose; rubrication at the beginning of each line of metres.

PROVENANCE   English. 'Liber quondam fratris Hugonis de Wendouere' (fol. 1ᵛ: s. xivⁱⁿ). 'Liber ecclesie sancte Marie de Suwerke' (fol. 166ᵛ: same hand). Belonged to St Mary Overy, OSA, in Southwark, where Hugh of Wendover had been a canon.

BIBLIOGRAPHY   Black and Macray, *Ashmole*, cols 1044–50; H. E. Salter 'An Arrouasian General Chapter' in *English Historical Review*, 52, 1937, pp. 267–79 (= H); Ker, *MLGB*, p. 180; *PA*, iii.390 (G only).

162. MS Oxford, Bodleian Library, Ashmole 1524
Mus.

s. xii 1/2

Parchment and paper; viii (paper) + 171 + viii (paper) fols; six books bound together but not trimmed—all different sizes. Titles, colophons and chapter-headings in red.

C: parchment; page 250x160mm; text 175x105mm; 41 lines; one hand.

CONTENTS   A (s. xii): fols 1ʳ–48ᵛ patristica; (40ᵛ–44ᵛ) Honorius Augustodunensis, *Elucidarium*, *expl.* imperf.

B (s. xiiiⁱⁿ): fols 49ʳ–56ᵛ Peter of Poitiers, *Compendium historiae in genealogia Christi* (Stegmüller 6778).

C (s. xii 1/2): fols 57ʳ–102ʳ *Mus.*, glossed.

D (s. xiii/xiv): fols 107ʳ–41ᵛ Laurence of Aquileia,

dictamen (107^r–8^v); material relating to Ramsey Abbey (Hunts.), partly in French.

E (s. xvi; paper): fols 142^r–58^v, tabulated summary of world history.

F (s. xv; paper): fols 160ra–70^v Richard Rolle, *The Form of Living*; 171^r Middle English verses.

GLOSS Fols 57^v–93^r quite extensive user's gloss in minute script (s. xii 2/2 – xiii 1/2).

DECORATION Competent Romanesque initial with foliage, slightly shaded in red (fol. 57^v). Thereafter plain red minor initials only. Some beautifully drawn diagrams, e.g., fol. 62^v.

PROVENANCE Unknown.

BIBLIOGRAPHY Black, cols 1431–36; *PA*, iii.336 (= B); White, in Gibson, pp. 162–205; Bower, no. 68.

AUCT.

In 1789 the finest classical and biblical manuscripts were put on display in the Auctarium, on the south side of the library quadrangle. These books still retain their Auct. classification.

163. MS Oxford, Bodleian Library, Auct. F. 1. 15
DCPhil., Vita III   s. x 2/2

Parchment; i + 93 fols; page 375x250mm; 26 lines in A and B, ruled for gloss.

A: main text 255x135mm; comm. (outer marg.) 255x60mm; one lovely hand throughout.

Neumes in metres I.m.i (fol. 5^r), I.m.v (12^v), II.m.ii (18^v), III.m.vi (35^v), III.m.x (42^v), III.m.xi (fol. 45^v), III.m.xii (47^v), IV.m.iii (54^r), IV.m.iv (57^v), IV.m.vii (64^v).

Tituli to bk I only; colophons to bks I–IV only. Binding: s. xi 2/2; white

leather on boards.
A very fine early book.

CONTENTS   A: fol. 1ʳ ***Vita III*** (damaged); 1ʳ⁻ᵛ another *accessus* (badly damaged); 1ᵛ–4ᵛ Lupus, *De metris* (damaged); 5ʳ–77ʳ ***DCPhil.***, glossed; 77ᵛ donor's note in Latin and Anglo-Saxon.
B: fol. 78ʳ donor's note in Latin and Anglo-Saxon; 79ʳ–92ʳ Persius, *Satires*, glossed.

GLOSS   Fols 5ʳ–8ʳ, 39ᵛ–40ʳ, 66ᵛ–71ʳ, 72ʳ⁻ᵛ extensive, systematic marginal and interlinear gloss. Gloss related to text by Latin and Greek letters and Tironian notes. fols 8ᵛ–16ᵛ interlinear glosses.

DECORATION   Fine line-drawn initials with interlace and animal-masks at the beginning of each book, cf. MS Cambridge, Trinity B. 14. 3 (289). Display script and minor initials in silver (oxidized), purple, red, green. Line-drawing of lion passant (fol. 78ʳ: s. xi).

PROVENANCE   A & B were written in St Augustine's, Canterbury; presented separately by Bp. Leofric (d. 1072) to Exeter cathedral (cf. fols 77ᵛ–78). Given to the Bodleian by the Dean and Chapter of Exeter in 1602.

BIBLIOGRAPHY   *SC*, 2455; R. W. Chambers, M. Foerster and R. Flower, *The Exeter Book of Old English Poetry*, London, 1933, pp. 28–30 (notes 101 and 102); Ker, *MLGB*, p. 83; T. A. M. Bishop, *English Caroline Minuscule*, Oxford, 1971, no. 9, pl. VII; *PA*, iii.37; Temple, *Anglo-Saxon Manuscripts*, no. 37; Bolton, pp. 52–53; Troncarelli, *Boethiana*, no. 85; M. B. Parkes, *Pause and Effect*, Aldershot, 1992, pl. 72. See pl. 7.

164. MS Oxford, Bodleian Library, Auct. F. 3. 13
Mus.
                                                    s. xiii 2/2

Parchment; iii + 229 fols; page 250x175mm.
B: text 170x95mm; 37 lines; one scribe. Greek (fol. 67ᵛ) has partial Latin interlinear translation.

CONTENTS   Fol. iii^v contents-list for whole MS in s. xiv hand.

A (s. xiii): fols 1^r–66^v Euclid, *Elementa*; (49) Ptolemy, *Centiloquium*.
B (s. xiii 2/2): fols 67^r–90^v **Mus. I–IV**.8, line 17 'ab hac si octauam'.
C (s. xiii/xiv): fols 91^r–103^v *Canones toletanae*; 104^v Bernard Sylvester, *Experimentarius*, prologue.
D (s. xiii 1/2): fols 105^r–114^v astronomy and astrology including (105^r) Gerard of Cremona, *Theorica plane-tarum*; (110^r) *De quadrante, inc.* 'Heec (*sic*) tabula docet in quo loco', with delightful marginal illustra-tions for measurement of tall buildings.
E (s. xiii 1/2): fols 115^r–75^v astronomy and astrology including (115^r) Campanus Novariensis; (152^r) Alca-bizin, *inc.* 'Primo differentia inesse'; (166^r) Albumazar, *Liber revolucionum*.
F (s. xiii 1/2): fols 176^r–200^r Alfraganus, trans. by John of Spain; (194^r) Martianus Capella, *De nuptiis* viii (both heavily glossed).
G (s. xiii): fols 201^r–20^v Arzachel, *inc.* 'In nomine domini scito quod annus lunarum'; (219^v) calendrial rules.

GLOSS   B: late marginal notes in pencil.

DECORATION   B: initials in blue, with very elaborate internal and external red penwork flourishing. No capitula or diagrams, although space has been left.

PROVENANCE   Kenilworth Priory, Warwicks.; *ex dono* master John Alward, fellow of Exeter College (fol. 224^v: d. 1457). Also: Johannes Lemyngton, Canones astrologii, Willelmus capellanus, Ricar-dus Boteler (fols 225^v–26^r).

BIBLIOGRAPHY *SC*, 2177; L. Thorndike, *A History of Magic and Experimental Science*, 2 vols, New York, 1923, ii.123; Saxl and Meier, III.i.389; Leonardi, no. 140; Emden, *BRUO*, p. 29; Ker, *MLGB*, p. 105; *PA*, iii.510 (A–C), 520 (E–F); Bower, no. 69.

165. MS Oxford, Bodleian Library, Auct. F. 5. 28
Op. Sac. I–II

s. xiii[ex]

Parchment; i + xl + 227 fols (fols 208–9 are the same leaf); page 235x163mm.
A (s. xiii 2/3): text 140x75mm; no. of lines varies.
B (s. xiii[ex]): text 2 cols, each 136x48mm; 48 lines; ruled for commentary.
A and B united in the later s. xiv (Oriel catalogue of 1375).

CONTENTS A: fols ii[r]–xli, 1[r]–144[v] astronomy and geometry: Euclid,
Jordanus Nemorarius, Ptolemy (well listed in *SC*). Diagrams
(cf. *PA*, iii.415 and pl. xxxv).
B: fols 145[r]–224[v] theology, philosophy and medicine:
(145[r]) Ps.-Boethius, *De disciplina scolarium* (Weijers
O[1]); (153[r]) *Liber de causis*; (158[r]) Nicholas of Amiens,
Ars catholice fidei; (164[r]) *De spiritu et anima*;
(170[va]–72[rb]) *Op. Sac. I–II*: first fourteen lines of *II*
only, and undifferentiated from *I*; (172[r]) Gundissalinus,
De unitate et uno; (173[r]) idem, *De divisione philosophie*; (186[v]) Walther 11565; (186[v]) Alfarabi, *De
assignanda causa*; (187[v]) William of Conches, *Drag-
maticon*; (209[v]) Rasis, *De phisionomia*; (213[r]) Galen,
Anatomia de homine; Aristotle, *De celo et mundo; De
sensu et sensato; De memoria et reminiscentia; De
somno et vigilia; De longitudine et brevitate vitae* (=
Parva naturalia).

GLOSS A few scattered notes to *Op. Sac.*

DECORATION None. Space left for rubrication, but rarely added.

PROVENANCE Oriel College; *ex dono* of master John Cobbuldik, a. 1337;
appears in the 1375 catalogue of Oriel College library (Shadwell, p. 67: 2⁰ folio *latera*); A and B united in the s. xv contents-list (fol. 225[v]). John Dee (cypher, fol. ii[r]).

BIBLIOGRAPHY *SC*, 3623; C. L. Shadwell, 'The Catalogue of the Library of
Oriel College in the Fourteenth Century', in C. R. L. Fletcher,
ed., *Collectanea, I*, Oxford, 1885, pp. 57–70, with facsimile at
p. 67; Saxl and Meier, III.i.278; Emden, *BRUO*, pp. 449–50;
AL, ii.798; Ker, *MLGB*, p. 149; *PA*, iii.415 (A only); W. J.
Courtenay, 'The Fourteenth-Century Booklist of the Oriel

College Library', *Viator*, 19, 1988, pp. 283–90; R. J. Roberts
and A. G. Watson, *John Dee's Library Catalogue*, London,
1990, M. 13, p. 16, pl. VIb; Burnett, *Adelard*, no. 81.

166. MS Oxford, Bodleian Library, Auct. F. 6. 4
DCPhil.   s. xiii 1/4

Parchment; iii + 276 fols (fol. 61 doubled); page 195x100mm.
A (s. xiii 1/4): text 160x60mm; 29–34 lines.
B (s. xiv 1/4): text 150x73mm; 34 lines.
Legal hand; fat, tall, narrow book.

CONTENTS   A: fols 1ʳ–61aʳ *DCPhil.*; 61aᵛ–61bᵛ various Latin notes, two
                mazes leading to the 'domus Dedali'; verses on the signs of
                the Zodiac; a hymn beginning *In terram Christus expuit*.
                B: fols 62ʳ–268ʳ Trivet, *Commentary on DCPhil.*;
                268ᵛ–276ᵛ blank except for a few s. xv notes in short-
                hand.

GLOSS   Some glosses and notes, e.g., fols 1ʳ⁻ᵛ, 42ʳ⁻ᵛ (extensive), 53ᵛ.

DECORATION   Blue initials with red ink flourishing throughout. Occasional
                pretty and unusual brown, slightly ornamental, initials with
                pale red highlighting. Some plain red initials.

PROVENANCE   'Liber Thomae Corsaeri presbiteri ex dono Radulphi Blore
                quondam canonici de Osney' (1543: fol. iiʳ; cf. fols 1ʳ, 274ᵛ).
                Donation note of Thomas Allen (fol. iiiᵛ).

BIBLIOGRAPHY   *SC*, 2150; Ker, *MLGB*, p. 140; R. J. Dean, 'The Dedication of
                Nicholas Trevet's Commentary on Boethius', *Studies in Philol-
                ogy*, 63, 1966, pp. 593–603 (598); A. G. Watson, 'Thomas
                Allen of Oxford and his Manuscripts' in *Medieval Scribes,
                Manuscripts and Libraries*, eds M. B. Parkes and A. G. Wat-
                son, London, 1978, p. 310; M. B. Parkes, *Pause and Effect*,
                Aldershot, 1992, pl. 73; Minnis, *Chaucer*, p. 35.

167. MS Oxford, Bodleian Library, Auct. F. 6. 5
Vita I, DCPhil. c. 1130–40

Parchment; viii + 80 fols; page 190x112mm; text 132x65mm; 27 lines; ruled in drypoint; one scribe throughout. Running headers.

CONTENTS	Fol. vii^r *Vita I*; vii^v–75^v *DCPhil.*
GLOSS	Occasional later annotations.
DECORATION	Author-portrait with wax tablets within *C(armina)*, fol. vii^v, and full-page miniature of Philosophy expelling the Muses (fol. viii^v), possibly by the artist of MS London, BL, Lansdowne 383 (the Shaftesbury Psalter); both using gold. Good minor initials (red, blue, green: single colour or combinations) throughout.
PROVENANCE	Attributed to Winchester or Hereford on the basis of the illumination; given to the Bodleian in 1611 by William Harwood, prebendary of Winchester.
BIBLIOGRAPHY	*SC*, 1856; Saxl and Meier, III.i.291; *PA*, iii.103 and pl. x; *Survival*, no. 124; Kauffmann, *Romanesque*, no. 49; *English Romanesque*, ed. G. Zarnecki et al., London, 1984, no. 31; Troncarelli, *Boethiana*, no. 86.

168. Oxford, Bodleian Library, Auct. III Q. 5. 5
Div. s. xiii mid

Parchment; page 220x155mm; text 120x75mm; 21 lines; one even hand.
4 leaves: front pastedown, front flyleaf (fol. iii), end flyleaf, end pastedown (now mostly torn away; impression of text left on back board). Contemporary German stamped binding.
Once a nice working copy.
Host book is an incunable of Gratian's *Decretum* (1480, first edition; Adam of Rottweil, in Venice).

CONTENTS	Front pastedown text is *PL*, 64:884B6–D12; flyleaf in the beginning of the book is *PL*, 64:887B11–888C4; flyleaf at the

end of book is *PL*, 64:881A10–882B11. Back pastedown is too damaged to permit identification.

GLOSS   Interlinear gloss; some marginal annotations, s. xiii – s. xiv.

DECORATION   Red and blue paraph signs. Face; pointing hand.

PROVENANCE   Unknown.

BIBLIOGRAPHY   *Proctor*, 4420.

BODLEY

The fonds Bodley is the foundation collection, with further acquisitions continuing until 1860.

169. MS Oxford, Bodleian Library, Bodl. 309
Arith.   s. xi 3/4

Parchment; iii (modern) + 168 fols; page 350x230mm; text 2 cols, each 270x80mm; 39 lines; more than one, very characteristic, hand of c. 1075. Blind-stamped binding.
A valuable book: nice, big, practical, monastic production.

CONTENTS   Fol. 2^r (s. xii 1/2) three letters of Pope Honorius II; 2^v s. xii poem, *Porticus est Rome*, Walther 14284; 3^v–61^v Bede, *De ratione temporum*; 62^r–110^v short treatises on ecclesiastical computation (includes Bede's *De computo, De divisione temporum*, excerpts from Macrobius, *Saturnalia*, I.xii–xv, and other treatises titled *De pascha, De sollennitatibus, De ratione paschae*); 111^r–31^v list of years from 152 BC to AD 1421 (the notes of events begin at AD 734; continue in one hand until 1075, largely concerning Benedictine Abbey of Holy Trinity, Vendôme; contemporary hands continue notes, obits etc. until the Battle of Crecy, AD 1346); 131^v–37^v computistica; 137^v–41^v weights and measures; 141^v–42^r tables in Greek; 142^r–46^v calendar for the year; 147^r–48^r Genealogy of the kings of France from the mythical Faramund to Philip I (1060–1108), then to Louis IX (1226–70); 148^v fortune-telling table; 149^r–64^v **Arith.**, *inc.* imperf. I.17 (36/9), 'cabit. Hic quoque'; *expl.* imperf. II.26 (116/4), 'longiores. ut sub'; 165^{r-v} computistica.

GLOSS   None.

DECORATION   Simple orange-red initials; chapter numbers and headings, figures and tables in orange-red; diagrams on fol. 165^r in red, green and black, with simple flourishing.

PROVENANCE   In the possession of Holy Trinity, Vendôme from c. 1075 until at least the battle of Crecy.

BIBLIOGRAPHY   *SC*, 8837. C. W. Jones, 'The "Lost" Sirmond Manuscript of Bede's *Computus*', *English Historical Review*, 52, 1937, pp. 204–19; Watson, *Oxford*, no. 76.

CANONICI (1817)

A major biblical and classical collection formed by the Venetian Jesuit, Matteo Luigi Canonici (d. 1805).

H. O. Coxe, *Catalogi codicum manuscriptorum bibliothecae Bodleianae III: codices graecos et latinos Canonicianos complectens*, Oxford, 1854 [= Quarto III]; Macray, *Annals*, pp. 299–301; *SC*, I, p. lii; J. B. Mitchell, 'Trevisan and Soranzo: Some Canonici Manuscripts from Two Eighteenth-Century Venetian Collections', *Bodleian Library Record*, 8, 1969, pp. 125–35.

170. MS Oxford, Bodleian Library, Canon. Class. Lat. 80
DCPhil.
          c. 1400

Parchment; i (modern) + i + 70 + i + i (modern) fols (5 blank sheets between fols 39–40 are not foliated in the current foliation).
A: page 260x180mm; text 185x c. 110mm; 30 lines; one hand.

B: page 260x185mm; text 175x112mm; variable no. of lines; one hand. Red chapter headings, and lines for reference in margin.
C: page 260x175mm; text 180x120mm; 42 lines; one hand. Red running headers.
A well-made book, corrected and used.

CONTENTS A: fols 2^r–19^v Galterus Anglicus, *Aesop*.
B: fols 20^r–34^v *Precepta rhetorica*, in Italian; 36^r
drawing of Christ with instruments of the Passion;
36^v–38^v dictaminal formulae with Italian headings.
C: fols 39^r–65^v *DCPhil.*

GLOSS A & B: none.
C: a very few marginal and interlinear annotations by two hands at least; pointing hands.

DECORATION A: initial with portrait of Aesop, fol. 2^r. Simple red and pale blue initials and paraph signs.
B: elaborate blue capitals with red infilling and scroll-ing. Blue paraph signs with red decoration.
C: half border with leaves (green, red, blue, mauve, gold) and initials with portrait of Boethius, very much rubbed (fol. 39^r). Ugly but ambitious initials and half-borders at beginning of each book. Red capitals with ink flourishing, and a few faded ?brown capitals with red flourishing. Rubricated.

PROVENANCE ? N. W. Italy.

BIBLIOGRAPHY Coxe, *Canonici*, col. 144; Kottler, Bo; *PA*, iii.756 (= A), 764 (= B); 757 (= C).

171. MS Oxford, Bodleian Library, Canon. Class. Lat. 138
DCPhil.   s. xiv 2/2

Parchment; i (modern) + 90 + i (modern) fols (23 & 74 doubled); page 230x192mm; text 168x105mm; 22 lines. Cursive Hebrew (pledge note?), fol. 88^v.
A well-made book.

CONTENTS   Fols 1ʳ–86ᵛ *DCPhil.*

GLOSS   Extensive marginal gloss until I.pr.v (fol. 11ʳ); then interlinear annotations by a different hand of dwindling frequency; bks III–V have very few annotations.

DECORATION   Enigmatic portrait of Boethius in initial, and half-border, in red and shades of brown, yellow, and gold, with blue touches (fol. 1ʳ). Lovely initials in gold, blue, white, red, pink, ochre at beginning of other bks. Elsewhere, blue and red initials with red and mauve flourishing.

PROVENANCE   N. E. Italy; ? Bologna.

BIBLIOGRAPHY   Coxe, *Canonici*, col. 169; Kottler, Bd; *PA*, ii.758.

172. MS Oxford, Bodleian Library, Canon. Class. Lat. 182
DCPhil.
                                                          s. xiv 2/2

Parchment; i (modern) + 66 fols; page 282x206mm; text 150x95mm; 27 lines. Running headers are outline Roman numerals of book nos.
Excellent book with wide margins; used and corrected.

CONTENTS   Fols 1ʳ–66ᵛ *DCPhil.*

GLOSS   Marginal annotations; frequent pointing hands and *nota* signs.

DECORATION   Part-border and intriguing initial in gold and various shades of pink, purple, red, blue, and green: *C(armina)* enclosing Boethius and Philosophy in prison (fol. 1ʳ); space left for initials for bks II–V, not added. Simple red and blue capitals.

PROVENANCE   North Italian, ? Venice. Soranzo collection, s. xviii (see headnote).

BIBLIOGRAPHY   Coxe, *Canonici*, col. 192; Kottler, Be; *PA*, ii.127.

173. MS Oxford, Bodleian Library, Canon. Class. Lat. 228
Top. Diff. IV   s. xv mid

Parchment; i (modern) + i (half-sheet) + 68 fols; some mouse damage; page 250x170mm; text 163x103mm; 30 lines; one clear, humanistic hand throughout. *Top. Diff.* has space left for *titulus* and ?chapter headings, not added. An uncluttered, clear, spacious book.

CONTENTS   Fols 1^r–57^v Ps.-Cicero, *Ad Herennium*; 57^v–65^v *Top. Diff. IV*; 66^v–67^r inventory of books headed *Inventario de libri di maestro Sinolfo* (mainly Latin classics).

GLOSS   A few annotations by various hands for *Ad Herennium*; none for *Top. Diff.*

DECORATION   Splendid initial and full border on fol. 1^r (gold, pink initial with blues, greens, and browns); entwined plants and life-like birds, rabbit, wild cat and a merman. Elaborate *I(n)*, fol. 8^r, in same palette as fol. 1^r. Elsewhere, very simply decorated blue and red capitals, as well as many merely ink-drawn.

PROVENANCE   Genoa. 'Arsicci et amicorum' (fol. 65^v: s. xvi); Master Sinolfo (book list).

BIBLIOGRAPHY Coxe, *Canonici*, col. 208; *PA*, ii.715.

174. MS Oxford, Bodleian Library, Canon. Class. Lat. 273
Mus.   s. xiv^{ex}

Parchment; i (paper) + ii + 73 + iv (paper) fols; page 297x203mm; text 213x120mm; 34 lines; one clear pre-humanist hand throughout. Fols ii–iii, 71–72 are erased sheets from a text written in 2 cols.

CONTENTS   Fols 1^r–62^v *Mus.*; 62^v note on the measurement of the earth; 63^r–69^v misc. musical texts. Originally followed (fols 70^r–122^v) by Odo of Cluny, *De musica*, now MS Canon. Misc. 212, fols 3–54.

GLOSS   None.

DECORATION   Author-portrait with codex in first major initial (fol. 1ʳ); minor initials blue or red with penwork flourishes; attractive diagrams in yellow.

PROVENANCE   ? Bologna; 'Stephani Biancii Bononiensis' (fol. 70ᵛ: s. xviᵉˣ).

BIBLIOGRAPHY   Coxe, *Canonici*, cols 225–26; *PA*, ii.657; Bower, no. 70.

175. MS Oxford, Bodleian Library, Canon. Class. Lat. 303
DCPhil.
                                                                              s. xiv (c. 1300)

Parchment; i (modern) + 39 + i (modern) fols; page 335x230mm; text 220x120mm; 26 lines; one big round hand throughout the text. Mutilated; initials excised.

CONTENTS   Fols 1ʳ–39ᵛ *DCPhil.*, *inc.* I.m.vi.5, 'Elusus cere[r]is fide'. *Inc.* gloss 'talis s. seminator'; *expl.* text V.pr.iv.70 'Aliter enim ac'.

GLOSS   Extensive interlinear and marginal gloss in a hand similar to and contemporary with the text; connected to text by underlined key words; ruled for gloss.

DECORATION   Of the well-illuminated initials (shades of pink, with orange and green foliage on blue ground) only one remains (fol. 24ᵛ: bk IV); red and blue capitals with blue and red flourishing; blue and red paraph signs.

PROVENANCE   Italian.

BIBLIOGRAPHY   Coxe, *Canonici*, col. 241.

176. MS Oxford, Bodleian Library, Canon. Misc. 554
Arith.
                                                                              s. xv 2/4

Parchment; ii (modern) + i (parchment, s. xv) + ii (paper) + i (parchment, excised) + 225 + ii (paper) fols; page 260x180mm.
B: text 200x130mm; 29 lines; one neat humanistic minuscule.

A, D, E written by Cando Candi, nephew of Prosdocimo de' Beldomandi, in Padua (fol. 194^r); *Arith.* in a slightly later hand.
A very useful working copy.

CONTENTS   A: fols 1^r–73^r Prosdocimo de' Beldomandi, *De geometria*, with good diagrams; 73^v–93^v idem, *Canones de motibus corporum supercoelestium.*
B: fol. 94^{r-v} Prologue to *Arith.*, *inc.* 'Prohemium in quo divisio mathematice. De substantia numeris'; *expl.* 'inequalitas ab equalitate'; 94^v–153^v **Arith.**, with last word left off.
C: fols 154^r–74^r fine coloured drawings, usually two per page, of zoomorphic constellations and planets.
D: fols 174^v–94^r Prosdocimo de' Beldomandi, *Stelle fixe verificatio completis annis Christi 1251*, followed by a table of latitudes and longitudes, but with only the place names (Ancona to Yherusalem, Çeçam), no measurements.
E: fols 196^r–225^r Ptolemy, *Liber centum verborum*, with commentary by Hali (in fact, that attributed to John of Spain or Plato of Tivoli).

GLOSS   None.

DECORATION   B: spaces left for initials, not supplied. Chapter headings etc. in red humanistic cursive. Diagrams and tables in red and brown, some with cursive rubrics, and Arabic, as well as Roman, numerals.

PROVENANCE   Padua. Bought by Coco de Rugeriis in 1566 (fols iii^v, 194^r).

BIBLIOGRAPHY   Coxe, *Canonici*, cols 856–57; Saxl and Meier, III.i.341–44; *PA*, ii.598, and pl. 57; Watson, *Oxford*, no. 373.

177. MS Oxford, Bodleian Library, Canon. Pat. Lat. 39
Op. Sac. II   s. xi/xii

Parchment; i (modern) + 120 fols (older, different foliation bottom of page;

cut; beg. fol. 13^r); page 225x136mm; text 182x105mm; 39 lines; various hands, neatly done. *Titulus* in red; red titles to many other works. A small book of solid texts.

CONTENTS	Fols 1^r–8^v Ambrose, *De paradiso* (comm. on Gen. – Exod., *expl.* imperf.); 9^r–18^v patristica; 19^r–77^r Isidore, Commentary on Genesis to Kings; 77^r–78^v Gregory the Great, Homilies 1–8 on Ezechiel, excerpts; 79^r *Op. Sac. II*; 79^v–82^r Homily on Prov. 31:10; 82^r–85^r Augustine, Excerpts from his questions on both Testaments; 85^r *Sententia sancti Hieronimi de essentia divinitatis Dei*; 85^r–87^v papal synods; 87^v–118^v patristica, including Augustine, *De doctrina Christiana* (90^v–103^v), Jerome, Cassiodorus, Isidore; 118^v–19^v Alcuin on Genesis.
GLOSS	None for Boethius; a few annotations and *nota* signs to other works.
DECORATION	Almost none. Ink-drawn *P(lantaverat)* with beast and acanthus leaves, background in red (fol. 1^r). Some rubrication; a few red capitals.
PROVENANCE	Italian.
BIBLIOGRAPHY	Coxe, *Canonici*, cols 308–9; W. Holtzmann, *Papsturkunden in England III*, *Göttingen Abhand.*, 33, 1952, p. 30; *PA*, ii.42.

DIGBY (1634)

A collection presented to the University by Sir Kenelm Digby (d. 1665), courtier, scientific amateur and man of letters.

Bernard, *CMA*, I.i.1602–1834; W. D. Macray, *Catalogi codicum manuscriptorum bibliothecae Bodleianae IX: codices a uiro clarissimo Kenelm Digby, eq. aur.*, Oxford, 1883; Macray, *Annals*, pp. 78–81; *DNB*, v.965–71; A. G. Watson, 'Thomas Allen of Oxford and his Manuscripts', in *Medieval Scribes, Manuscripts and Libraries: Essays Presented to N. R. Ker*, ed. M. B. Parkes and A. G. Watson, London, 1978, pp. 279–314.

178. MS Oxford, Bodleian Library, Digby 98
Arith. s. xii; s. xiv

Parchment and paper; 263 fols (fol. 161 missing); page 220x165mm. 8 vols bound together; 60 headings in all.
B: text 155x96mm; 36 lines; one good s. xii hand, changing at fol. 104^r to s. xiv cursive. Fols 104^r–6^v: text c. 155x c. 115mm; 45 lines.
A *collectaneum* assembled in Oxford, perhaps c. 1408, belonging to the erstwhile Wycliffite, Peter Partriche, chancellor of Lincoln (d. 1451). *Arith.* is an elegant text.

CONTENTS A (paper: s. xv^{in}): fol. 1^v table of contents (s. xv); fols 4^r–77^r various arithmetical, computational, and grammatical works.
B (parchment; s. xii): fols 78^r–85^v Euclid imperf. to IV, bk. iii; 86^r–106^r **Arith.**, *expl.* imperf. II.16, line 14, 14/99, 'generationis regula'.
C (parchment and paper [fols 133–60]; s. xv^{in}): fols 107$^{r–v}$ geometry text; 109^r–17^r Thorndike and Kibre, 1175, exposition of *Arith.* by Simon Bredon, *inc.* 'Quantitatum alia continue que'; *expl.* 'Exp. arsmetica Bredone. Deo gracia quod Partriche'; 118^r–31^v John Pecham, *Perspectiva*; notes from Euclid.
D (paper; s. xv^{in}): fols 132^r–61^v Simon Bredon on the planets; Ps.-Grosseteste, *De astrolabio*; Robert Grosseteste, *De luce*, *De colore*, *De iride*, *De potencia et actu*, *De impressionibus aeris*, *De sphera*, and two other, later works.
E (parchment; s. xiii): fols 162^r–76^v various geometrical texts; Robert Grosseteste, *De sphera*; John de Sacro Bosco, *De sphera*.
F (parchment, paper; s. xv^{in}): fols 177^r–224^v Rule of St Francis; Testament of St Francis; various letters, notes, verses and satires; disputes against Jews and Dominicans; some theological and legal tracts.
G (parchment): fols 225^r–56^v *Mirror of St Edmund Rich*; articles of faith.
H (parchment): fols 257^r–64^r English medical recipes, *Cirurgia*, 'Walteri Brit'.

GLOSS None for Boethius.

DECORATION   None for Boethius, but space left for diagrams and initials. Diagrams in Boethius only in fols 104^r–105^r.

PROVENANCE   Oxford: Peter Partriche (*ex libris*, e.g., fol. 213^v); William Maydwelle (fol. 197^v); John Dee; Thos Allen (fols 1, 4: Watson); Sir Kenelm Digby (fol. 197^v: Starks).

BIBLIOGRAPHY   Macray, *Digby*, cols 108–113; Emden, *BRUO*, pp. 1430–31 (Partriche); A. G. Watson, 'Thomas Allen of Oxford and his Manuscripts' in *Medieval Scribes, Manuscripts and Libraries*, eds M. B. Parkes and A. G. Watson, London, 1978, pp. 279–314, at 311; C. Starks, in *Hunt Memorial Exhibition*, Oxford, 1980, no. xxvi.3; *Wyclif and his Followers: An Exhibition to Mark the 600th Anniversary of the Death of John Wyclif*, Dec. 1984 – April 1985, eds A. C. de la Mare and B. C. Barker-Benfield, Bodleian Library, Oxford, Oxford, 1984, no. 79; R. J. Roberts and A. G. Watson, *John Dee's Library Catalogue*, London, 1990, M 186, p. 129.

179. MS Oxford, Bodleian Library, Digby 174
Vitae III, I, DCPhil. (2 copies)   s. ix/ s. xii

Parchment; ii (modern) + v + 252 + i (modern) fols. Thirteen booklets (s. xii/xiv) containing sixteen items put together by John of London; untrimmed, so vols of very different shapes and sizes. E–H assembled s. xii/xiii (R. W. Hunt, typescript revision of Digby catalogue, Bodleian Library).
Fol. iii (s. ix): page 240x165mm; original page width = 170mm.
B (s. xii 1/2): page 265x180mm; text 175x100mm; 22 lines; one scribe for *DCPhil.*.
C (s. xii): page 195x125mm; text 175x115mm; 50 lines; one scribe.
Dry-point ruled, no margins. Original Digby binding, brown leather with missing clasps. Fols 248^v–50^v: trials of Hebrew alphabet and practice writing, including the *Pater noster* transliterated (fol. 249^v, upside down) and 'Thomas' (248^v).
The full *DCPhil.* was once a nice, useful text with decoration; now made scruffy by the company it is keeping.

CONTENTS   Fol. iii$^{r–v}$ s. ix bifolium of **DCPhil.**, V.pr.v.32 'vero ad universitatis' to V.pr.vi.2 'omne quod', with marginal and interlinear glosses; and Lupus, *De metris*, 88–145 (not recorded by V. Brown); v^v medieval contents-list.

A: fols 1^r–2^r glosses, incl. III.m.ix (s. xii).

B: fol. 3^r ***Vita III*** and prologue to *DCPhil.* in a hand contemporary with the glossing hand; 3^v–74^v ***DCPhil.***, glossed; 74^{r-v} schemata of learning; 74^v poem of the scribe about the conclusion of the work; seven verses on seven days of creation; diagram of philosophy (as a woman's face) as source of all other disciplines including theology (Walther 19805, 14669a).

C: fols 75^r–98^v ***Vita I*** and continuous commentary on *DCPhil.*, *expl.* V.pr.iv.77 (fol. 96^v = Silk, *Commentarius*, 300/22: *signe de renvoi* fol. 98^v).

D: fols 99^r–124^r Euclid, *Demonstrationes et figurae lib. i–ix* (s. xii); 125^r–32^v idem, bks x, xi (init.).

E: fols 133^r–37^r geometrical texts.

F: fols 139^r–45^r Euclid, ibid., bk x (again); 145^{r-v} *De altimetria, sive de altitudinum mensuratione.*

G: fols 146^r–53^v Euclid, ibid., bks ii–iv.

H: fols 154^r–59^v Euclid, ibid., *Pars libri vi et propositiones*, bks vii–x; 160^r–73^v bks i–xiii + beginning of xiv with diagrams; 174^{r-v} Jordanus Nemorarius, *Opusculi pars de ponderositate* (with diagrams).

I: fols 174^v–78^r Archimedes, *De curvis superficiebus*; 178^v *Commentarius in propositiones septem tractatus Archimedis*; 179^r–81^v Jordanus Nemorarius, *Liber de speculis.*

J: fols 182^v–95^r three tractates on proportion.

K: fols 196^r–200^v Hermann of Reichenau, *Liber de mensura astrolabii*; 200^v–10^v Gerbert, *Liber de utilitatibus astrolabii.*

L: fols 211^r–42^v treatise on logic.

M: fols 243^v–46^v theological sentences.

GLOSS

B: Frequent interlinear and marginal glosses in at least two hands, one of which is contemporary with the text, the other s. xiii; gloss connected to the text by reference signs.

DECORATION

B: English illumination, s. xiii^{ex}. Mainly blue initials with red flourishing; a few red initials with blue flourishing; small red capitals; rubricated. Large illuminated miniature of Christ pantocrator enthroned and wounded, red, blue, brown, green, and gold (s. xiii 3/4). Moon and sun above a golden throne, and Boethius kneeling in gesture of prayer (fol. 11ʳ). Illustrates the text 'O stelliferi conditor orbis' (fol. 11ᵛ).

PROVENANCE   John of London (d. 1370), to St Augustine's, Canterbury (fol. 3ʳ); Thomas Allen (fol. vᵛ); John Dee, 1625–26, M 100.

BIBLIOGRAPHY   Macray, *Digby*, cols 184–86; *SC*, 1775; Silk, *Commentarius*, pp. li–lii, frontispiece and pp. 3–300 (using this text as his base); C. R. Dodwell, *The Canterbury School of Illumination*, Cambridge, 1954, p. 123; *Bodleian Library Record*, 5, 1956, pl. 13b; L. M. de Rijk, *Logica modernorum*, Assen, 1962–67, II.i.76–77, pp. 264–390; Ker, *MLGB*, p. 46; Courcelle, pp. 408, 411, pl. 100; A. B. Emden, *Donors of Books to S. Augustine's Abbey, Canterbury*, Oxford, 1968, pp. 11–12; *Medieval Scribes, Manuscripts and Libraries*, eds M. B. Parkes and A. G. Watson, p. 290, n. 54; *PA*, iii.281 and (fol 11ᵛ) 457 and pl. xli; H. L. L. Busard, *The Latin Translation of the Arabic Version of Euclid's 'Elements' Commonly Ascribed to Gerard of Cremona*, Leiden, 1983, MS D; Troncarelli, *Boethiana*, no. 89; Burnett, *Adelard*, no. 85; R. J. Roberts and A. G. Watson, *John Dee's Library Catalogue*, London, 1990, M 100, p. 121.

D'ORVILLE (1804)

The library of Jacques Philippe d'Orville (d. 1751), classical scholar and professor in the University of Amsterdam.

Macray, *Annals*, p. 282; *SC*, IV, pp. 37–38.

180. MS Oxford, Bodleian Library, D'Orville 102.
DCPhil. (2 copies)   s. xiii; s. xiv 2/2

Parchment; ii + 60 fols (some damage).
A (s. xiv 2/2): page 270x190mm; text 165x107mm; 28 lines; rubbed; one hand

throughout *DCPhil.*
B (s. xiii): page 240x160mm; text 190x80mm; 26 lines; drypoint ruling; one
scribe.

CONTENTS	A: fols 1ʳ–54ʳ ***DCPhil.***
	B: fols 55ʳ–58ᵛ ***DCPhil.***, IV.pr.vi.13 'praede]stinatione divina' to V.pr.i.4 'sed quod tu', with *scholia*.
GLOSS	A: none.
	B: see contents.
DECORATION	A: painted major red, blue, turquoise, mauve, green, brown, pink initials at beginning of each book of *DCPhil.* Minor initials in blue and red with a little red and mauve flourishing. Borders at beginning of each book.
	B: orange-red initials to begin each new section. Orange-red rubrication.
PROVENANCE	Bologna or Venice.
BIBLIOGRAPHY	*SC*, 16980; Kottler X; *PA*, ii.140.

181. MS Oxford, Bodleian Library, D'Orville 153
DCPhil.
1438

Paper; i (modern) ii + 134 fols (a number of added half- or part-sheets); page
212x140mm; text 148x65mm; 20 lines; wide space for gloss; one hand
throughout. Dated colophon, fol. 132ᵛ.
A striking book for personal use.

CONTENTS	Fols 1ʳ–132ᵛ ***DCPhil.***
GLOSS	Copious notes on inserted leaves; sporadic but extensive marginal gloss inexpertly linked to text and interlinear annotations in a hand similar to the scribe's.
DECORATION	Decorated initials in monochrome in ink of main text, large at the beginning of books I–III, simply decorated with ink fillings.

PROVENANCE   Germany.

BIBLIOGRAPHY *SC*, 17031; Watson, *Oxford*, no. 443.

182. MS Oxford, Bodleian Library, D'Orville 154.
DCPhil.
c. 1300

Parchment; iii (paper) + 49 fols; page 158x114mm; text 119x80mm; 26 lines; rubbed in many places; one scribe. Red headings and colophons to bks of *DCPhil.*
A home-made flavour throughout.

CONTENTS   Fols 1ʳ–46ʳ *DCPhil.*, *expl.* imperf. 'nam cum omne iudicium', V.iv.118.

GLOSS   No gloss; a few sporadic annotations.

DECORATION   Red initials with simple red flourishing. Rubrication.

PROVENANCE   England.

BIBLIOGRAPHY *SC*, 17032.

183. MS Oxford, Bodleian Library, D'Orville 208
Logica vetus
s. xiii 1/2

Parchment; ii (modern) + 117 fols; page 180x138mm; text 102x58mm; 24 lines; not ruled for gloss; one hand throughout. Running headers.
A university book with wide margins.

CONTENTS   Fols 1ʳ–14ᵛ *Isag.*; 15ʳ tree of Porphyry; 15ᵛ–38ʳ *Cat.*; 38ʳ–50ʳ *Liber sex principiorum*; 50ʳ–64ʳ *De Int.*; 64ʳ–80ᵛ *Div.*; 80ᵛ–113ᵛ *Top. Diff. I–III*; 114ʳ–17ᵛ miscellaneous notes.

GLOSS   Frequent annotations by various hands throughout. *Div.*: extensive marginal gloss in one hand contemporary with the text. A few annotations, but no gloss for *Top. Diff.* A good deal of later student scrawl and drawings.

DECORATION   Red and blue initials with red and blue flourishing; rubrication.

PROVENANCE   *Sancti Martini Monasterii Wiblingensis* (fol. 1^r: s. xv), i.e., the
               Benedictine monastery at Wiblingen near Ulm. Names of
               Herthnus (or Hertlinus) and Faruus on fol. 60^v (both called
               asinus!) are nearly contemporary with the MS.

BIBLIOGRAPHY   *SC*, 17086; *AL*, 1915; Ker, *MLGB*, p. 40; Lewry, in Gibson,
               pp. 90–135 (116); Krämer, i.833.

HAMILTON (1857)

The fifty-eight Hamilton manuscripts come from Erfurt, principally from the
Benedictine and Carthusian houses which were suppressed in 1806. Acquired
c. 1826 by John Broad, they were presented to Sir William Hamilton
(1788–1856), with whom Broad had studied in Edinburgh, in 1841. On
Hamilton's death, his sons gave the collection to the Bodleian Library.

J. Broad, *Catalogus codicum manuscriptorum ex bibliotheca Hamiltoniana*,
Berlin, 1841; Macray, *Annals*, pp. 363–64; *SC*, V, pp. 11–12; *DNB*,
xxiv.227–32; Krämer, i.220–21, 230–31.

184. MS Oxford, Bodleian Library, Hamilton 46
DCPhil.   1465

Paper; ii + 370 fols (many added part-sheets); mouse damage fols 61–77; page
215x140mm.
B: text 160x80mm; 16 lines for the text, 41 for the commentary; one scribe,
perhaps Rotger Scheffer (fol. 185^v). Commentary linked to text with lemmata
in large black letters. *Tituli*, fols 85^{r-v}, 113^v, 160^v, 108^r. Dated colophon, fol.
202^v: 1465. Running headers. Binding is s. xv wooden boards; clasp missing.
A cheap personal book, but much used.

CONTENTS   A: fols 1^r–60^v excerpts from Master Ortolffus, physician
               (1^r–14^v); excerpts from Hugh of St Victor, *Didascalicon* (fols
               15^r–50^r); miscellaneous theological treatises, incl. life of St

Catherine in German.
B: fols 61ʳ–220ʳ **DCPhil.**, with German translation and Latin commentary; 220ᵛ–23ᵛ a Latin hymn to the Virgin, macaronic Latin and German hymns, musical notes to a prayer about St Catherine (221ʳ).
C: fols 226ʳ–81ᵛ Apocalypse, with extensive gloss; 282ʳ–332ᵛ short theological treatises and sermons; 333ʳ–64ᵛ Gerardus van Vliederhoven, *Cordiale de quattuor novissimis*; 365ʳ–68ᵛ miscellaneous notes.

GLOSS   *DCPhil.* has extensive interlinear gloss by at least two hands. The added commentary (in the margins and on added sheets) has been ruled for gloss, not supplied.

DECORATION   Plain orange initials and paragraph marking; rubricated. Lemmata in text underlined in orange; orange marginal headings.

PROVENANCE   ? Buchen, Saxony (colophon; Palmer). Probably Erfurt, O. Carth.

BIBLIOGRAPHY   *SC*, 24476; Palmer, in Gibson, pp. 362–409 (381–90), with plate; Watson, *Oxford*, no. 507 (B only); N. Henkel, *Deutsche Übersetzungen Lateinischer Schultexte*, Munich etc., 1988, p. 233; Krämer, i.221.

LAT. CLASS. AND LAT. MISC. (1887)

SC, I, p. xlv.

185. MS Oxford, Bodleian Library, Lat. class. d. 1
DCPhil.

s. xv mid

Paper; 79 fols; page 290x212mm; text 200x112mm; 28 lines. One hand throughout *DCPhil.*, another hand for Horace. Signs of use, incl. pointing hands. Bound between boards, half-bound with leather; two clasps, missing. A well-made book.

CONTENTS　　　Fols 4ʳ–62ʳ *DCPhil.*; 62ʳ unintelligible Hebrew words emphasized by large pointing hand; 64ʳ Greek alphabet; 65ʳ–77ᵛ Horace, *Ars poetica*, heavily glossed (gloss begins fol. 64ᵛ).

GLOSS　　　Heavily glossed by various hands in the margins and interlinearly esp. for bks I–III (beginning) and end of bk V; another glossing hand for Horace.

DECORATION　　Three miniatures all on blue and white background: bk I, Boethius in *C(armina)*, in red robe and fine fur hat, sitting reading a book (fol. 4ʳ); bk II, sailing boat in red, blue brown (fol. 13ʳ); bk III, Philosophy with book and sceptre (fol. 24ʳ). Bk IV, simpler initial in blue and blue-red flourishing (fol. 39ᵛ); good initial for bk V in blue, different shades of red, ochre (rubbed; fol. 52ᵛ). Elsewhere blue and red capitals with alternate flourishing.

PROVENANCE　　North Italian.

BIBLIOGRAPHY　*SC*, 30056; Courcelle, p. 74 and pl. 15; *PA*, ii.817.

186. MS Oxford, Bodleian Library, Lat. class. d. 35
Logica nova　　　　　　　　　　　　　　　　　c. 1300

Parchment; iii + 110 fols; missing original quire three, between fols 16–17; page 224x165mm; text 135x90–100mm; 28–34 lines; similar scribes.

CONTENTS　　　Fols 1ʳ–40ʳ *Topica Aris.* missing end of III to beginning of V (118b35–132b8); 40ʳ–54ᵛ *Soph. Elench.*; 55ʳ–90ᵛ *Prior Anal.*; 90ᵛ–107ᵛ *Post. Anal.*, *expl.* imperf. bk II 'Quare omnino eiusdem' (91a8).

GLOSS　　　Users' glosses throughout, especially to *Post. Anal.* Pointing hands; some marginal diagrams.

DECORATION　　Red and blue initials with contrasting penwork (occasionally mauve); red and blue paraph signs.

PROVENANCE   Phillipps 16238 (fol. 1ʳ); bought in 1949.

BIBLIOGRAPHY *AL*, 1916; Bodleian typescript catalogue.

187. MS Oxford, Bodleian Library, Lat. misc. a. 3, fol. 5
Topica Aris.
                                                              s. xiii

Parchment; one folio (offset traces of second leaf of bifolium); page
301x190mm; text 180x95mm; 32 lines; one scribe. Same MS as MS Oxford,
Magdalen College, lat. 271.
Host book: Zachary of Besançon, Cologne, 1535.

CONTENTS   *Topica Aris.* VIII.5–8 (166/9–169/23).

GLOSS   None.

DECORATION   Red and blue paraph signs.

PROVENANCE   Formerly a pastedown in MS Oxford, Magdalen College, C. 7.
              13.

BIBLIOGRAPHY Bodleian typescript catalogue; Ker, *Pastedowns*, no. 165; *AL*,
              1955.

188. MS Oxford, Bodleian Library, Lat. misc. e. 42
Op. Sac. I, III
                                                              s. xii mid

Parchment; i (modern) + 54 fols; one MS with two sets of flyleaves, here A
and C. Boethius text (once flyleaves for MS as a whole) has been cut down to
fit the binding, losing a substantial proportion of the leaf.
A and B: page 200x145mm.
C: (at present) fol. 53: 185x130mm; fol. 54: 185x140mm; text and
commentary fill almost the whole of extant space. Original page size perhaps
280x200mm.
Plain white sheepskin binding (English s. xv?) on re-used and worm-eaten
boards, with clasp.

CONTENTS A (s. xiii): fols 1–4 four leaves of music from a gradual of Sarum type (fols 1, 4 are in double columns and in a hand different from that of fols 2–3).
B (s. xii 2/2): fols 5–52 Geoffrey of Monmouth, *De gestis regum Britanniae*, imperf.
C (s. xii mid): fols 53^r–54^v two non-contiguous leaves from **Op. Sac. I, III,** with commentary by Gilbert of Poitiers: fol. 53^r end of *De trinitate*; *inc.* comm. 'Nam Plato et Cicero'; fol. 54^r *Quomodo substantiae*, *inc.* text imperf. '[Ha]rum duplex modus est'; *expl.* 'atque consistit'; *inc.* comm. 'Quoniam et quod concipimus'.

GLOSS None.

DECORATION Simple red, green and blue two-colour capitals.

PROVENANCE English. Belonged to William Marshall: *Liber Guil[lelmi] Mart. emptus 14 Aug. 1568 precium 3s 4d.*, fol. 54^r; Pembroke College, Cambridge, c. 1600.

BIBLIOGRAPHY *SC*, 36220; *PA*, iii.136; Häring, no. 98; N. R. Ker, 'Oxford College Libraries in the Sixteenth Century', *Bodleian Library Record*, 6, 1959, pp. 459–515 (505–6: William Marshall), repr. in *Books, Collectors and Libraries: Studies in the Medieval Heritage*, ed. A. G. Watson, London, 1985, no. 25; J. Crick, *The 'Historia Regum Britannie' of Geoffrey of Monmouth*, III, Cambridge, 1989, pp. 233–34.

LAUD (1635–40)

The major benefaction to the new Bodleian Library (and arguably its best ever) was the more than twelve hundred manuscripts given by Archbishop Laud (d. 1645), chancellor of the University 1630–41. In the years 1635–41, Laud acquired Latin, Greek and oriental manuscripts and extensive collections from southern Germany that were thrown on the market by the Thirty Years War.

Bernard, *CMA*, I.i.300–1601; H. O. Coxe, *Catalogi codicum manuscriptorum bibliothecae Bodleianae II: codices Latinos et miscellaneos Laudianos complectens*, [= Quarto II], revised reprint by R. W. Hunt, Oxford, 1973.

189. MS Oxford, Bodleian Library, Laud Lat. 49
Logica vetus   s. xi 1/4

Parchment; 177 fols; 50–51 lines.
A: page 347x290mm; text 3 columns, each 255x60–65mm; several good, similar hands.
Laudian binding; elaborate *tituli* and colophons normally in red, up to fol. 58^{vc}, thereafter omitted. Pointing hands.
A rare instance of the 'pure' Boethian text of *Cat.* (Minio-Paluello).

CONTENTS   A (s. xi 1/4): fols 1ra–3ra *Isag.*; 3ra–14ra (omitting 9^{vc}) *1 in Isag.*, 9^{vb-vc}, 10^{r-v} lower margin only; 14ra–27vb *2 in Isag.*; 27vb–28^{vc} Alcuin, *Dialogus*; 28^{vc}–32va *Cat.*; 33ra–56va *in Cat.*; 56va–58^{vc} *De Int.*; 58^{vc}–76^{rc} *1 in Int.*; 76^{rc-va} *accessus*; 76vb–96^{vc} *2 in Int.* (*expl.* imperf., 487D); 97va–100^{vc} Cicero, *Topica*; 101ra–128^{rc} *in Topica Cic.*; 129ra–46^{rc} Cicero, *De inventione* (misbound, with extensive glosses from Grillius and Victorinus [Dickey, 1968]); 146va–66^{rc} Marius Victorinus, comm. on *De inventione*, *expl.* imperf.
B (s. xiv): fols 167^{v}–76^{r} John of Hildesheim, O. Carm., *Speculum fontis vite*: *Verfasserlexikon*, iv.638–47, at 640, apparently the unique MS.

GLOSS   Few glosses to *Logic*. The only serious annotation is to *De inventione*.

DECORATION   Major initials drawn in red ink fols 1^{r}, 97^{v}. Good contemporary initials fols 1^{r}–62^{r}, red or silver (oxidised); thereafter a few poor s. xiv substitutes in red or blue ink.

PROVENANCE   Mainz (initials: Hoffmann); presented by Archbp. Laud.

BIBLIOGRAPHY   Coxe, *Laudian*, cols 24–25; *AL*, 336; L. Minio-Paluello, 'The Genuine Text of Boethius' Translation of Aristotle's *Categories*', *Medieval and Renaissance Studies*, 1, 1941–43,

p. 158; *PA*, i.30 and pl. iv; M. A. Dickey, 'Some
Commentaries on the *De inventione* and *Ad Herennium* of the
Eleventh and Early Twelfth centuries', *Medieval and
Renaissance Studies*, 6, 1968, pp. 1–41; *Survival*, no. 108 and
pl. xviii; B. Bischoff, *Paläographie des römischen Altertums
und des abendländischen Mittelalters*, Berlin, 1979, p. 47 n. 70
(on tricolumnar MSS); H. Hoffmann, *Buchkunst und Königtum
im ottonischen und frühsalischen Reich*, Stuttgart, 1986, p.
253.

190. MS Oxford, Bodleian Library, Laud Lat. 53
DCPhil., Epitaphs I–II   S. XV

Parchment; ii (modern) + 59 fols (fol. 58 double); page 272x185mm; text
175x93mm; 26 lines. Neatly produced; one scribe for *DCPhil.* Greek looks
uncertain. Laudian binding: suede, two ties (lost).
Much evidence of use, up to fol. 40ᵛ.

CONTENTS	Fol. 1ʳ former pastedown, now illegible. UV photograph shows opening lines of Latin *Gorgias*, transl. 1409 by Leonardo Bruni Aretino; 1ᵛ drawing of earth and its regions according to inhabitability (later hand); 2ʳ *Quaedam notabilia super Boetio* (hand of the gloss); 3ʳ–56ᵛ **DCPhil.**; 57ᵛ *Epitaphs I–II*, with *tituli*; 58ʳ drawing and verse about wheel of fortune (same hand as fol. 2ᵛ).
GLOSS	Extensive interlinear and marginal gloss, especially in bk I; dies out after about fol. 40ʳ; few notes to books IV–V.
DECORATION	Decorated initials in red, blue, mauve; red and blue capitals with mauve and red flourishing. Late, finely drawn pointing hands, as well as sketchy ones by a different user. The *notabilia* and *Epitaphs* have elaborate ink-drawn initials.
PROVENANCE	Italy; presented by Archbishop Laud, 1637.
BIBLIOGRAPHY	Coxe, *Laudian*, cols 26–27.

191. MS Oxford, Bodleian Library, Laud Lat. 54
Arith.
                                                                              s. xiii

Parchment; i (modern) + 55 fols; page 235x160mm; text 165x86mm; 35 lines.
Original Arabic page number at bottom centre; at top centre of each page book
number and red chapter heading, numerated; one scribe throughout. Limp
white parchment covers, with Laud's stamp in gold.
A fine book, well-produced and usable.

CONTENTS   Fols 1ʳ–54ʳ *Arith.*

GLOSS   None.

DECORATION   Primitive red, blue, and ochre decorated initials at the
                    beginning of each book (fols 1ʳ, 21ᵛ); red and blue capitals
                    with simple blue and red flourishing; diagrams in blue, red,
                    and ochre.

PROVENANCE   English. Samson Johnson (fol. 1ʳ: s. xvi); presented by Laud in
                    1635.

BIBLIOGRAPHY   Coxe, *Laudian*, col. 27; *PA*, iii.241. See pl. 8.

192. MS Oxford, Bodleian Library, Laud Misc. 457
Op. Sac.
                                                                              c. 1200

Parchment; i + 185 fols; page 348x257mm; 2 cols, except for *Op. Sac.* which
is sometimes a central text with gloss in cols to left and right, sometimes in 2
cols with much smaller left and right marginal glosses; both formats have
interlinear glosses; text measurement therefore varies widely; 40 lines. *Titulus*
to *Op. Sac. I*; space left for *tituli* to II–IV. Chapter headings in red. Laudian
leather binding.
A used book.

CONTENTS   Fol. 1ʳ calendrial verses (added s. xiii 2/2); 1ᵛᵃ–80ʳᵃ John
                    Chrysostom, *Homiliae xxxiv in epistolam ad Hebraeos*, transl.
                    Mutianus; 80ʳᵇ–99ʳᵃ Anselm, *Cur Deus homo*; 99ʳᵇ–115ʳᵃ *Vitae
                    sanctorum* (BHL 3566–67, 93, 4057); 115ʳᵃ–45ᵛᵃ Alcuin, *In*

Proverbia (129ra) *In Genesim* (143rb) *De benedictionibus patriarcharum*; 145va–63ra *Op. Sac.*; 163ra–84va *Vitae sanctorum* (*BHL* 6605, 7617, 7621, 4968).

GLOSS   Ps.-John Scot Eriugena, commentary on *Op. Sac. I–III, V* set out as a marginal and interlinear gloss (fols 145va–53^{r}, 155va–63ra) in a contemporary hand. Occasional later notes.

DECORATION   Odd, single-colour initials throughout the manuscript, in red and green. Space for major initials which are not added. Rubrication.

PROVENANCE   St Mary, Eberbach, O. Cist. (dioc. Mainz); presented by Laud.

BIBLIOGRAPHY   Coxe, *Laudian*, cols 328–29; Cappuyns, 'Opuscula Sacra'; *PA*, i.105; Troncarelli, 'Opuscula', p. 19; Krämer, i.177. See pl. 9.

LYELL (1949)

James Lyell assembled his collection of c. 250 manuscripts in the decade 1936–46, normally buying from a few trusted London booksellers. See Ker in de la Mare, pp. xv–xxix.

A. C. de la Mare, *Catalogue of the Collection of Medieval Manuscripts Bequeathed to the Bodleian Library Oxford by James P. R. Lyell*, Oxford, 1971.

193. MS Oxford, Bodleian Library, Lyell 49
Op. Sac.   s. xii 2/3

Parchment; i + 129 fols; page 235x155mm.
A: text 160x73mm; 20–23 lines ruled with stylus (glosses 31–32 lines); two or three similar hands.

B: text 175x110mm; 32 lines; one scribe.
C: text 178x100mm; 32 lines; one scribe.
D: text 180x100mm; 32 lines; one scribe.
Binding: s. xiv, plain rough white sheepskin covering wooden boards; title on front label, *Boecius Glosatus de S. Trinitate*; front fastening, central clasp (missing).

CONTENTS   A: fols 1ʳ–57ᵛ *Op. Sac.* (III & IV run together), with text of
                  second (short) version of commentary of Remigius of Auxerre,
                  as marginal and interlinear gloss.
                  B: fol. 58 reject leaf; 59ʳ–79ᵛ Remigius, Commentary
                  on *Op. Sac.* (longer version, written as continuous
                  commentary); 80ʳ blank; 80ᵛ drawing.
                  C: fols 81ʳ–100ᵛ Thierry of Chartres, Commentary on
                  Op. Sac. I–II and a fragment of III, here attributed to
                  Peter Helias, ed. Häring, pp. 62–116, 119–21.
                  D: fols 101ʳ–28ᵛ Abelard, *Theologia summi boni.*

GLOSS   See contents.

DECORATION   Two initials of entwined acanthus leaves (and beast) in shades
                  of red and brown, to treatises II and V (fols 11ᵛ, 30ʳ); other
                  ribbon-like initials in various sizes, in red, to treatises I and III
                  (fols 1ʳ, 14ᵛ); thereafter only brown ink decoration. Almost no
                  colour in rest of MS.
                  Ink drawing (s. xii) of standing woman and man,
                  offering flower; crudely made religious by addition of
                  two haloes (fol. 80ᵛ).

PROVENANCE   Monastery of St Blaise, Admont, Austria (fol. 80ᵛ), no. 382 in
                  library. Acquired by Lyell, November 1936.

BIBLIOGRAPHY *PA*, i.92; N. M. Häring, *Commentaries on Boethius by Thierry
                  of Chartres and his School*, Toronto, 1971, MS A; de la Mare,
                  Lyell, pp. 131–33; C. Jeudy, 'L'Oeuvre de Remi d'Auxerre' in
                  *L'Ecole Carolingienne d'Auxerre de Murethach à Rémi
                  830–908*, ed. D. Iogna-Prat et al., Paris, 1991, pp. 373–97
                  (379–80) and ibid., pp. 474–75 (list of MSS).

E MUS. (1655, renumbered 1728)

Manuscripts kept in the librarian's room.

Bernard, *CMA*, I.i.3491–3737; *SC*, I, pp. xiv and xxxvi.

194. MS Oxford Bodleian Library, e Mus. 134
Op. Sac.   c. 1300

Parchment; ii (modern) + 764 pages; page 228x151mm; 3 MSS bound
together.
A: text: 130x70mm; 40 lines.
B: text 2 cols, each 160x50mm; 43 lines.
C: text 2 cols, each 160x50mm; c. 44 lines.
Blind-stamped binding. *Tituli* to *Op. Sac*. in red; red chapter headings.

CONTENTS   A: pp. 1–144 Theological treatises (including various treatises
                 of Ps.-Dionysius) translated by John Scot Eriugena and
                 Johannes Sarracenus.
                 B: pp. 147–458 Anselm, various treatises including
                 Monologion, Proslogion, Cur Deus homo; Augustine,
                 De immortalitate animae, and various treatises by John
                 Damascene; 459–92^b John Damascene, *Logica*
                 preceded by a list of chapters and a *sermo de
                 philocosmis*; 492^b–516^a idem, *Introductio dogmatum
                 elementaris*; 516^a–28^a idem, *Epistola scripta ad
                 Iordanem archimandritam de Trisagio*; 528^a–49^a ***Op.
                 Sac.***, *expl.* to *IV*, 'Ibi erit gaudia sempiternum.
                 Delectatio cibus laus perpetua opus conditoris.
                 Explicit' (539^b); 549^a–52^a Gundissalinus, *De unitate et
                 uno;* 555–649 various treatises by or attributed to
                 Augustine.
                 C: pp. 651–744 Richard of St Victor, *Liber de
                 trinitate*; 745–62 Part of an index to Anselm,
                 Monologion and *Proslogion* and a list of questions.

GLOSS   A–C: none; merely a few pointing hands or marginal
                 annotations.

DECORATION   A–C: red and blue initials with blue and red flourishing; rubricated.

PROVENANCE   English; 'Liber bricii' (s. xvi: p. 529); 'Mr. John Sotwell' (late s. xvi: p. 730); given by John Newton, fellow of Brasenose, 14 June 1658 (*SC*, II.699).

BIBLIOGRAPHY *SC*, 3614.

RAWLINSON (1755)

Richard Rawlinson (d. 1755), non-juring bishop.

Bernard, *CMA*, I.i.6561–6615; W. D. Macray, *Catalogi codicum manuscriptorum bibliothecae Bodleianae*, V, i–iv: *viri munificentissimi Ricardi Rawlinson JCD…classes duas priores codicum complectens*, Oxford, 1862–98 [= Quarto V.i–ii, Rawl. A–C only]; Macray, *Annals*, pp. 231–51; *DNB*, xvi.774–76; *SC*, iii, pp. 341–76 = Rawl. G [Classics].

195. MS Oxford, Bodleian Library, Rawl. G. 38
DCPhil.
                                            c. 1200

Parchment; i (modern) + 137 fols (fol. 74 doubled; 74a is an inserted paper half-sheet); page 200x140mm; six MSS bound together. F: text 145x95mm; 34 lines; one scribe for *DCPhil.*

CONTENTS   A (c. 1200): fols 1^r–8^v Gilbert of Hoyland, four letters and (8^v–47^r) some ascetic treatises; 47^r–54^r Serlo, On the Lord's prayer, *inc.* 'Protector noster aspice deus' (Walther, 14848); 54^v–55^r Bull of Urban III concerning the Cistercians (1187), *inc.* 'Audivimus et audientes mirati sumus'; 55^r–57^r Circular letter from the abbey of Melrose concerning the death of Jocelin, bp. of Glasgow (1199).
B (s. xiii): fols 58^r–73^r Cicero, *De senectute*.
C (s. xii 4/4): fols 74b^r–89^r Plato, *Timaeus*, transl. Chalcidius.
D (s. xiii): fols 90^r–97^v Ps.-Grosseteste, *De Aseneth* (S.

H. Thompson, *The Writings of Robert Grosseteste*, Cambridge, 1940, p. 242).
E (s. xiii): fols 98ʳ–102ʳ Theological excerpts, some concerning St Cuthbert.
F (c. 1200): fols 103ʳ–35ᵛ **DCPhil.**, *expl.* imperf. 'in sua natura pependitur', V.pr.vi.102. Final leaf lost.

GLOSS   F: virtually none, but text corrected.

DECORATION   F: simple red initial with green flourishing (fol. 103ʳ); simple silver (oxidized) or red capitals, many missing.

PROVENANCE   A–C at least were owned by Henry Spelman, who has signed fols 1ʳ, 55ʳ, 58ʳ, 74aᵛ.

BIBLIOGRAPHY   *SC*, 14769; Palmer, in Gibson, pp. 362–409 (405, n. 46).

196. MS Oxford, Bodleian Library, Rawl. G. 39
DCPhil., Op. Sac.   s. xii 2/2

Parchment and paper; 141 fols (foliated 142 as fols 6 & 7 are one leaf); parchment damaged, fols 51–56; page 216x133mm; text 170x71mm; 44 lines; largely one scribe, although some metres added later. Fols 8–56 were part of a larger collection which once included Cicero, *De inventione* (now MS Rawl. G. 34); two last fols. damaged; *tituli* to all treatises except for *De trinitate*. Book nos in red as running headers. Rawlinson binding.

CONTENTS   Fols 1ʳ–7ᵛ (paper) blank; 8ʳ–39ᵛ **DCPhil.**, *expl.* imperf. V.pr.vi.105 'etiam non evenire potuissent. Quid'; 40ʳ–56ᵛ **Op. Sac.**, *inc.* imperf. 'pater inquiunt deus', I.1, line 7; 57–141 (paper) blank.

GLOSS   Extensive interlinear contemporary gloss; some marginal gloss for *DPhil.* only; pointing hands in red or brown. *Op. Sac.* has only a few marginal annotations.

DECORATION   *DCPhil.* has simple but pretty initials in single colours or combinations of red, green, blue; dragon flourishing, beginning bk III (fol. 19ʳ); metre and prose marks at the margins;

rubricated; diagram of world temperature zones, fol. 23ᵛ.
Op. Sac. has fewer, but more elaborate, decorations.
Very nice initial (pale blue, purple, green, red) begins
each treatise.

PROVENANCE   ? English.

BIBLIOGRAPHY *SC*, 14770; *PA*, iii.276; Palmer, in Gibson, pp. 362–409 (405,
              n. 46); Troncarelli, *Boethiana*, no. 90; Troncarelli, 'Opuscula',
              p. 18.

197. MS Oxford, Bodleian Library, Rawl. G. 41
DCPhil.
                                                          s. xii 1/2

Parchment; ii (modern) + iii + 109 fols; page 213x145mm; text 148x55mm;
22 lines; ample space for gloss; colophon after bk III (fol. 62ʳ); one French
scribe throughout. Rawlinson binding. Much used by different readers. Price
mark, fol. 107ʳ, *precium huius libri. II equites.*
A very attractive, used and useful book.

CONTENTS   Fol. ivʳ fragment of commentary on III.m.ix (s. xiv cursive);
              1ʳ–104ᵛ *DCPhil.*

GLOSS   Extensive marginal and interlinear glosses, contemporary, in
              same or similar hand to text; rubricated; some later gloss by at
              least two other hands; extracts from the French translation of
              Jean de Meung added in s. xv to bk I.

DECORATION   Gold *C(armina)* with red, green, and blue intertwined leaves
              and beasts' heads; elsewhere, very pretty combinations of red,
              green, gold, blue, and ochre initials with animal or flower-
              shaped decoration at beginning of every prose and metre. Text
              and gloss rubricated.

PROVENANCE   Probably French. *Ex libris* of St Martin, Louvain (fols vᵛ, 106ᵛ:
              s. xv).

BIBLIOGRAPHY *SC*, 14772; V. L. Dedeck-Héry, 'Boethius' *De consolatione* by
              Jean de Meun', *Mediaeval Studies*, 14, 1952, pp. 165–275; *PA*,

iii.123; Palmer, in Gibson, pp. 362–409 (366–67, 405, n. 46); Troncarelli, *Boethiana*, no. 91.

198. MS Oxford, Bodleian Library, Rawl. G. 49
Logica vetus   s. xiii

Parchment; ii (modern) + 105 fols. Two vols bound together by s. xiv (*expl.*, fol. 102^r).
A: page 195x135mm; text 105x65mm; 24–26 lines; one neat scribe. Pointing fingers, caricatures etc.
B: page 188x130mm; text 105x65mm; 20–26 lines; two or three neat book hands.
A much used schoolbook.

CONTENTS   A: fols 1^r–9^r ***Isag.***; 9^r–27^v ***Cat.***; 28^r–40^r ***De Int.***; 40^v–67^r ***Top. Diff.*** **I–III**, *expl.* imperf. 'Themistio ab oppositis' (1205A); 67^r–78^r ***Div.***; 78^v s. xiii table of contents of A and of four other MSS of logic and grammar.
              B: fols 79^r–89^r *Liber sex principiorum*; 89^r–102^r ***Top. Diff.*** **IV**; 102^r 'Expliciunt topica boycii et omnes libri veteris logices v. porfirius cum libro praedicamentorum et peryarmenias cum libro sex principiorum etiam divisionum etiam topicorum boicii'.

GLOSS   A & B: extensive s. xiii/xiv glosses by two major hands; frequent pencil marks and annotations; tree diagrams; tables.

DECORATION   A: blue or red initials with alternate flourishing (fols 1^r, 28^r, 40^v, 59^r, 67^r, 70^v). Finicky, self-colour capitals, slightly flourished (e.g., 60^v).
              B: plain red capitals with clumsy attempts at slight flourishing (fols 79^r–102^r).

PROVENANCE   English; *Reverendo patri suo G. de Balgameshelle scolaris Occonie* (fol. 100^v: c. 1300).

BIBLIOGRAPHY *SC*, 14780; Emden, *BRUO*, p. 98.

199. MS Oxford, Bodleian Library, Rawl. G. 187
DCPhil.
                                                                          s. xiv 2/2

Parchment and paper; vi (modern) + 122 fols; page 420x265mm; text 2 cols, each 58mm wide, varying heights; ruled for gloss; lines variable; one hand throughout. Gloss on three sides around each of 2 col. text. Space left in commentary (for diagram?), fol. 3ʳ; *Correctum est ad unguem totum per fratrem Beati Egidii, qua anima requiescat in pace* (fol. 54ʳ). *Titulus* to Trivet in red (fol. 1ʳᵃ). Running headers and bk numbers. Rawlinson binding.

CONTENTS   Fols 1ʳ–54ʳ *DCPhil.*, with Trivet's commentary; 54ᵛ diagrams; 55–122 (paper) blank.

GLOSS   Trivet. Few other annotations (mainly corrections). A few pointing hands.

DECORATION   Red or blue initials with mauve and red simple flourishing; blue and red paraph signs; rubricated; eight nice astrological diagrams, fol. 54ᵛ .

PROVENANCE   Italian. Thos Hearne; Rawlinson, 11 April 1720.

BIBLIOGRAPHY   *SC*, 14904; Kottler, R; Minnis, *Chaucer*, p. 35. See pl. 10.

SAVILE (1620)

Sir Henry Savile (d. 1622), warden of Merton, provost of Eton, editor of Chrysostom, founded the Savilian chairs of astronomy and geometry in the University of Oxford. He complemented these with a substantial donation of mathematical books and manuscripts to the Bodleian Library.

Bernard, *CMA*, I.i.6561–6615; *DNB*, xvii.856–59; *SC*, II, p. 1094.

200. MS Oxford, Bodleian Library, Savile 20
Arith.
                                                                          s. xii 1/2

Parchment; 64 fols; page 245x158mm; text 172x65mm; 32 lines; one scribe throughout. Late s. xiv binding, white leather on boards with two clasps (one lost). Front pastedown, Zach. 5.8–7.10; end flyleaf, Hag. 2.16–Zach. 3.7 (s. xiii).

CONTENTS Fols 1^r–64^v *Arith.*: pages missing at 18/19 (I.xxiii–xxvi: pp. 48.17–53.10) and 20/21 (I.xxviii–xxix: pp. 58.16–61.4); 2$^{r–v}$ list of capitula added, s. xiii.

GLOSS None.

DECORATION Two good gold initials, with line-drawn gold foliage (fols 1^r, 25^r); otherwise competent, slightly flourished red initials. Nice diagrams in red and yellow.

PROVENANCE Friars Minor of Doncaster (Yorks.) in the late s. xiv (*ex libris* on pastedown inside front cover). Later owned by Christopher Saxton (fol. 1^r: d. 1596), from whom the book passed to John Dee in 1597 (fol. 1^r, with Dee's cypher).

BIBLIOGRAPHY *SC*, 6566; *DNB*, xvii.874 (Saxton); Ker, *MLGB*, p. 58; *PA*, iii.122; R. J. Roberts and A. G. Watson, *John Dee's Library Catalogue*, London, 1990, DM 124, pp. 17, 24, 177.

SELDEN (1659)

John Selden (d. 1654), lawyer and scholar, after whom the west end of the Old Library is named.

Bernard, *CMA*, I.i.3134–3490; Macray, *Annals*, pp. 110–23; *DNB*, xvii.1150–62; *SC*, II, pp. 594–95.

201. MS Oxford, Bodleian Library, Selden Supra 25
Arith., Mus.   s. xii 1/2; s. xii 4/4; s. xiv

Parchment; i + 246 fols; fols 39–44 damaged by fire; page 210x140mm.
A (s. xii 4/4): text 160x80mm; 29 lines; chapter headings in red.

B (s. xii 1/2): text 156x92mm; 29 lines.
C (s. xiv): text 170x105mm; 43 lines; plain red and blue chapter headings.
A, B, C, each written by one scribe, different for each.
Binding: blind-stamped brown leather on boards, rebacked, with clasps
(missing), s. xv 2/3; bound at Canterbury by John Kemsyn.

CONTENTS A: fols 1ʳ–43ʳ **Arith.** (fols 43ʳ–44ʳ *Saltus Gerberti*).
B: fols 45ʳ–75ᵛ **Mus.** (up to III c. 6).
C: fols 76ʳ–92ʳ **Mus.** (continuation from III c. 6 to
end).
D: fols 94ʳ–96ʳ Hermann of Reichenau, *Compositio
astrolabii*; 96ᵛ–102ʳ idem, *De utilitatibus astrolabii*;
102ʳ–3ᵛ *De componendo horologico instrumento*;
104ᵛ–6ʳ diagram and description of astrolabe, together
with astronomical excerpts from Bede, *De natura
rerum*; 106ᵛ–14ʳ *De abaco*; 114ʳ–15ʳ notes for con-
structing a sundial, an astronomical globe, roofs and
ceilings; 115ᵛ a diagram of musical tunes and bells;
118ᵛ–28ᵛ Gerbert, *Geometry* (to c. xiii).
E: fols 130ʳ–62ᵛ Martianus Capella, *De nuptiis*, bks
1–2; 163ʳ–74ᵛ idem, *De astronomia*, bk 8, *inc.* 'Mun-
dus igitur' (c. 814); *expl.* 'luminis sui' (c. 881).
F: fols 175ʳ–76ᵛ Cicero, *Somnium Scipionis*; 177ʳ–211ᵛ
Macrobius, *In somnium Scipionis*.
G: fols 212ʳ–44ᵛ Robert Grosseteste, *De arte computi*.

GLOSS A: some user's marginal and interlinear notes and corrections
by a contemporary hand, and in later hands. Pointing hands.
B: few marginal annotations.
C: none

DECORATION A: entwined beasts drawn in ink against blue initials with red
flourishing (fol. 1ʳ); Ink-drawn **S** with acanthus leaves, with
red and green filling (fol. 20ʳ). Blue and red capitals with red
and blue flourishing. Red and brown diagrams and tables.
B: decorated blue and red capitals at beginning of each
bk; small red and blue capitals with blue and red
flourishing; diagrams in red, green, yellow ochre.
C: plain red and blue capitals; no diagrams, no separa-
tion between books.

PROVENANCE   St Augustine's, Canterbury, pressmark (fol. 1^r: s. xv). W.
             Patten (fol. 1^r: s. xvi).

BIBLIOGRAPHY *SC*, 3413; James, *ALCD*, no. 1019; Ker, *MLGB*, p. 46; C. R.
             Dodwell, *The Canterbury School of Illumination*, Cambridge,
             1954, p. 123; Leonardi, no. 146; *PA*, iii.202 (A), 121 (B), 203
             (E); White, in Gibson, pp. 162–205 (195, n. 56); Bower, no.
             71.

OXFORD COLLEGES

For the six medieval colleges and the three sixteenth-century foundations that
concern us here see the relevant volumes of *The History of the University of
Oxford*, Oxford, 1984–92, I: ed. J. I. Catto; II, eds J. I. Catto and R. Evans;
and III, ed. J. McConica, 1986. Note particularly M. B. Parkes, 'The Provision
of Books', in *History*, ii.407–83 and N. R. Ker, 'The Provision of Books', in
History, iii.441–77. Only Balliol has a modern catalogue (Mynors). Otherwise
see H. O. Coxe, *Catalogus codicum MSS qui in collegiis aulisque Oxonien-
sibus hodie adseruantur*, Oxford, 1852 [= Coxe, I–II].

ALL SOULS COLLEGE, f. 1437

Bernard, *CMA*, I.ii.44–45; Ker, *MLGB*, pp. 143–44; N. R. Ker, *Records of All
Souls College Library*, Oxford, 1971; E. Craster, *The History of All Souls
College Library*, London, 1971; A. G. Watson, *A Descriptive Catalogue of the
Medieval Manuscripts of All Souls College*, forthcoming.

202. MS Oxford, All Souls' College, aa. 3. 8 (formerly SR 29, fol. 4)
Isag.   s. xiii^{ex}

Parchment; one bifolium; page 255x190mm; text 110–122x70mm; 17–19 lines;
ruled for gloss; one scribe.
Former host book: Innocent IV, Venice, 1491.

CONTENTS   Fol. 1ʳ⁻ᵛ *Isag.* 'Chrisaorie' [Cgrisarori: *sic*] to 'quidem appel-
latum' (5/1–6/17); 2ʳ⁻ᵛ 'species quidem' to 'quae erant'
(25/4–27/9).

GLOSS   Extensive marginal users' gloss in at least three hands. Marginal tree diagrams.

DECORATION   Blue initials with red flourishing; red and blue paraph signs.

PROVENANCE   Probably English.

BIBLIOGRAPHY   Ker, *Pastedowns*, no. 2; Watson, *All Souls*, Appendix I(A) 2.

203. Oxford, All Souls' College, SR 77. c. 3
Prior Anal.
s. xiii

Parchment; 2 fols, heavily cut down; page now 170x100mm; 25 & 19 lines;
ruled for gloss; one neat scribe. Front and back pastedowns of Antididagma,
Louvain, 1544.

CONTENTS   *Prior Anal.* Front I.20: 'haec' to 'Si autem' (46/23–47/25).
Back I.16: 'C contingat' to Et in con[tingenti' (38/5–27).

GLOSS   Systematic commentary with lemmata, in a cursive hand.

DECORATION   Red and blue paraph signs.

PROVENANCE   English or French.

BIBLIOGRAPHY   *AL*, 1993; Watson, *All Souls*, Appendix I(Bi) 37.

BALLIOL COLLEGE, f. 1263.

For the first century of the Balliol library, culminating in an elegant recon-
struction of the inventory of c. 1385, see Mynors, pp. xi–xvi. The fifteenth
century saw a purpose-built library building (1431), a Fellows' book-list

(1465–70) and the major benefaction by William Gray, bishop of Ely (1454–78), who 'gave or bequeathed more than half the surviving library of medieval Balliol' (Mynors, p. xxix). In the mid-seventeenth century Gerard Langbaine, provost of Queen's, drew up a catalogue of the Balliol manuscripts, now MS Bodleian Library, Wood donat. 4 (*SC*, 8617).

Bernard, *CMA*, I.ii.166–468; Coxe, I; R. A. B. Mynors, *Catalogue of the Manuscripts of Balliol College Oxford*, Oxford, 1963; Ker, *MLGB*, pp. 144–45; *History*, i.292–95.

204. MS Oxford, Balliol College, 10
Op. Sac.   s. xii 4/4

Parchment; i (modern) + 133 + i (modern) fols; page 345x223mm; text 2 cols, each 255x71mm; 40 lines; frame-ruled in pencil; one good scribe. Extended colophon to *Op. Sac. V* (fol. 125ra). Binding: s. xvii Balliol, tooled 'rough leather' (suede). Greek (e.g., fols 120^{v}–21^{r}) has superscript Roman transliteration. Books and chapters have early Arabic nos as running headers.

CONTENTS   Fol. 1^{v} s. xii contents list; 2ra–113rb Augustine, *De trinitate*; 113va–25ra *Op. Sac. I–V* (I–II run together; lacuna in V lines 13–36); 125ra–26ra Lupus, *De metris*; 126ra–31ra Jerome, *Contra Luciferianum*, with (131rb) Walther 3214, added s. xiii; 132ra–33vb (flyleaves) two non-consecutive leaves from a late s. xiii antiphonal.

GLOSS   Glosses to *Op. Sac. III* (fols 116^{v}–17^{r}) only.

DECORATION   Very good major and minor initials with delicate leaf ornaments in red, green and ochre.

PROVENANCE   English. *Ex dono* William Gray, bishop of Ely (1454–78), fol. 1^{v}.

BIBLIOGRAPHY Bernard, *CMA*, I.ii.246; Mynors, *Balliol*, p. 8: *AT*, no. 119.

205. MS Oxford, Balliol College, 141
DCPhil., Epitaphs II–III   s. xv 1/4

Parchment; i (modern) + 58 + i (modern) fols; page 255x180mm; text
165x110mm; 32 lines; one competent scribe for Boethius. Binding: s. xvii
Balliol, tooled 'rough leather' (suede).
A rather late example of a standard *DCPhil.* with ample margins for gloss,
which have been well used.

CONTENTS	Fols 1ʳ–50ʳ *DCPhil.*, *inc.* I.m.ii.1; 50ʳ⁻ᵛ *Epitaph III*; 50ᵛ *Epitaph II*; 51ʳ–56ʳ Ps.-Aristotle, *Liber de pomo* (*AL*, 2052).
GLOSS	Extensive and systematic marginal and interlinear gloss in small clear cursive hand.
DECORATION	Blue initials with red penwork flourishing throughout Boethius. No other decoration.
PROVENANCE	English (script). *Ex dono* master John Burton, sometime fellow of Balliol and vicar of St Nicholas, Bristol (d. before February 1499).
BIBLIOGRAPHY	Bernard, *CMA*, I.ii.205; Emden, *BRUO*, p. 319; *AL*, 2052; Mynors, *Balliol*, p. 121.

206. MS Oxford, Balliol College, 253
Logica vetus et nova   s. xiii 3/4

Parchment; i (modern) + 269 + i (modern) fols; page 295x188mm; text
145x82mm; 28 lines; double-panel ruled for gloss; one good hand to fol. 267ʳ.
Binding: s. xvii Balliol, tooled 'rough leather' (suede). Red and blue running
headers. Price mark. xˢ (fol. 2ʳ: s. xv).
An excellent academic book of logic with wide margins.

CONTENTS	Fols 1ʳ–10ᵛ *Isag.*; 10ᵛ–27ᵛ *Cat.*; 27ᵛ–37ᵛ *De Int.*; 37ᵛ–45ᵛ *Liber sex principiorum*; 46ʳ–80ʳ *Top. Diff.*; 80ᵛ–92ʳ *Div.*; 92ʳ–160ᵛ *Topica Aris.*; 160ᵛ–211ᵛ *Prior Anal.*; 211ᵛ–45ʳ *Post. Anal.*; 245ʳ–67ʳ *Soph. Elench.*; 268ʳ–69ᵛ (flyleaves) s. xiii fragment of *Digest*, glossed.

GLOSS The margins are full of notes by various scribes of s. xiii–xv, except *Top. Diff.*, which has many fewer annotations; a s. xiv hand in the margins of *De Int.* added what seems to be a commentary, *inc.* 'In hoc libro philosophus intendit determinare de enunciacione ubi premittit prohemium in quo tangit'; a similar commentary (although not so complete) has been added to *Cat.* also. Glosses usefully characterized by Mynors.

DECORATION Excellent small historiated initials of teachers and pupils, with gold, at the beginning of each treatise; abstract initials to begin each book. Blue and red capitals with alternate penwork; red and blue paraph signs.

PROVENANCE Paris (Branner). 'liber ballioli' (fol. 267^v: ?s. xv).

BIBLIOGRAPHY Bernard, *CMA*, I.ii.392; *AL*, 356; L. Minio-Paluello, *Classical Quarterly*, n.s. 5, 1955, pp. 108–18 (*Topica Aris.*, *Soph. Elench.*); Mynors, *Balliol*, pp. 275–77; Branner, *Manuscript Painting in Paris during the Reign of Saint Louis: A Study of Styles*, Berkeley, 1977, pp. 116, 117, 125 n. 27, cat. 235; L. Minio-Paluello, 'Note sull'Aristotele latino medievale X:I "Topici" nel X–XI secolo', in idem, *Opuscula: The Latin Aristotle*, Amsterdam, 1972, pp. 357–76; *AT*, no. 673; N. R. Ker, 'The Books of Philosophy Distributed at Merton College in 1372 and 1395' in idem, *Books, Collectors and Libraries: Studies in the Medieval Heritage*, ed. A. G. Watson, London, 1985, pp. 331–78 (340).

207. MS Oxford, Balliol College, 306
Arith., Mus.   s. x; s. xii 2/2

Parchment; i (modern) + 92 + i (modern) fols (part-sheets added for diagrams); two vols bound together since later s. xii.
A (s. x): page c. 190 x c. 80mm; text 210x135mm; 38 lines; one very small, neat Carolingian hand. Colophon, 'LEGI OPUSCULUM MEUM' (fol. 21^r).
B (s. xii 2/2): page c. 280 x c. 198mm; text 195x130mm; 40–44 lines; small but messy s. xii hand.
Binding: s. xvii Balliol, tooled 'rough leather' (suede). No *capitula*; some titles added in s. xv hand. Valuation note: 'precium vi^s' (fol. 6^r, s. xvi).
A rather scruffy, used book, but used with care nevertheless.

CONTENTS   Fols 1^r–4^v (flyleaves: s. xiv) hagiography.
             A: fol. 5^r vocabulary of about 400 s. xii Tironian
             notes, about half with explanatory glosses; 5^v–41^r
             Arith., lacuna at II.48 (152/11–156/23); 41^v Saltus
             Gerberti; 42^r–45^v arithmetical notes (s. xiii^{ex} inserted
             sheet, folded to make 4 leaves).
             B: fols 46^r–89^r **Mus.**; 89^v and 90^r–91^v (flyleaves: s.
             xiii) legal questions; 92^r (former cover-lining) fragment
             of a commentary on Judges (s. xiv).

GLOSS   A: scattered annotation of s. xii 2/2; a few later notes.
             B: note on bk II.11 (fols 88^v–89^r); numbered chapters,
             scattered s. xii 2/2 annotation; a few later notes.

DECORATION   A: plain ink initials in brown and red.
             B: **O(**mnium**)** red with brown infilling (46^r). Very few
             plain blue capitals; otherwise space left for capitals,
             mostly not supplied. Diagrams adequate but not ele-
             gant.

PROVENANCE   French. Balliol *ex libris* (fol. 5^r: s. xiv); ? *ex dono* Simon
             Bredon, canon of Chichester 1372 (Mynors, p. xiv).

BIBLIOGRAPHY Bernard, *CMA*, I.ii.278; Emden, *BRUO*, pp. 257–58; Mynors,
             Balliol, pp. 324–25; White, in Gibson, p. 186 (Simon Bredon);
             Bower, no. 72.

208. MS Oxford, Balliol College, 317
Mus.
                                                              s. xii 2/3

Parchment; i (modern) + i + 72 + i (modern) fols (one leaf lost after fol. 66);
page 250x160mm; text 160x85mm; 32 lines; one good hand. Binding: s. xvii
Balliol, tooled 'rough leather' (suede). Greek written in red with Roman
interlinear transliteration (fol. 5^r). Pledge note, fol. 72^v, 'Memoriale pro duobus
voluminibus de Fisica, scilicet, Practica Alexandri de Aylestre, et glosis super
viaticum ejusdem contra magistrum Petrum de Cusincton.'

CONTENTS   Fols 2^r–3^v diagrams concerning music, relating to fols 59^v–60^r;
             4^r–72^r **Mus.**, each book preceded by list of *capitula*; lacks

V.i–ii 351/10 – 354/6 'ptolo]mei divisio' – 'quadruplaeque'.

GLOSS   Scattered annotations throughout in ink and pencil; nota signs
                 and a few marginal notes in s. xiv hand.

DECORATION   Unusual major initials with abstract decoration, red, blue,
                 purple, green, brown, some with gold (fols 4^r [excised] 21^r,
                 35^v, 48^r). Minor initials, capitals, and careful diagrams, mostly
                 in red and green, a few blue and purple-brown. Space left for
                 other diagrams not supplied.

PROVENANCE   English; *ex dono* master Peter of Cossington, d. 1276 (fol. 2^r:
                 s. xiii^{ex}).

BIBLIOGRAPHY   Mynors, *Balliol*, pp. xii, 334–35; Emden, *BRUO*, pp. 530–31;
                 AT, no. 54; Bower, no. 73.

CORPUS CHRISTI COLLEGE, f. 1517.

Bernard, *CMA*, I.ii.1468–1720; Coxe, II; Ker, *MLGB*, p. 145; *History*, iii.17–29
and (books) 458–60.

209. MS Oxford, Corpus Christi College, 59
DCPhil.   s. xiii mid

Parchment; i + 120 fols (fol. 60 doubled); page 223x130mm.
D: text 145x82mm; 32 lines; various hands, but one scribe for *DCPhil.*
Binding: leather on boards, two clasps (missing). Red running titles to chap-
ters.

CONTENTS   A: fols 1^r–4^r miscellaneous theological notes.
                 B: fols 5^r–58^r Alan of Lille, *Anticlaudianus*.
                 C: fols 58^v–71^v 14 short moral treatises and verses.
                 D: fols 72^r–111^v *DCPhil.*, glossed
                 E: fols 112^r–19^r various short hymns and verses.

GLOSS   D: extensive interlinear and marginal commentary of Remigius of Auxerre, sometimes added on separate leaves (e.g., fol. 107^r) in one main hand contemporary with the text (Bolton).

DECORATION D: simple red or green capitals and initials; poorly rubricated. *Anticlaudianus* has extensive allegorical illustrations.

PROVENANCE Lanthony, Gloucs. (local devotions, fol. 67^r etc.). *Ex dono* Henry Parry, 1619 (fol. 3^r). 'Radulphus de Longo-campo fecit expositionem in hoc opus habere in bibliotheca collegii de Balliolo. habetur in hoc opus ibidem bis semel cum glossa interlineari' (fol. 4^v; see Mynors, *Balliol*, p. 127).

BIBLIOGRAPHY Bernard, *CMA*, I.ii.1526; Coxe, *Corpus*, pp. 21–22; Ker, *MLGB*, p. 112; Bolton, pp. 39, 60; *AT*, no. 231; M. T. Gibson, N. F. Palmer, and D. R. Shanzer, 'Manuscripts of Alan of Lille, "Anticlaudianus" in the British Isles', *Studi Medievali*, 3 ser., 28, 1987, pp. 905–1001, no. 27 (detailed description); Minnis, pp. 109–11; idem, *Chaucer*, p. 94.

210. MS Oxford, Corpus Christi College, 74
Vitae III–V, DCPhil.   s. xi 1/4

Parchment; v (modern) + ii + 64 + iv (modern) fols; page 210x126mm; text 153x65mm; 28 lines; one scribe. Later running headers.

CONTENTS Fol. i^{r-v} *Vitae III–V*; i^v Atticus, *Epistola formata* (P. Hinschius, *Decretales pseudo-Isidorianae*, Leipzig, 1863, p. 291); i^v–ii^r Lupus, *De metris, expl.* imperf. 'iura tonantis', line 145; 1^r–61^v *DCPhil.*

GLOSS   Extensive marginal and interlinear commentary by Remigius of Auxerre in contemporary, possibly the same, hand as the text; at least two more users, one contemporary (e.g., fol. 51^r) other later (fols 11^v–12^r: ?s. xv); some Greek annotations in pencil.

DECORATION Drawing of the tree of knowledge with philosophy at the top (fol. i^r); in the same hand, two diagrams of the virtues (fol 62^v); simple red, blue, and green capitals and initials.

PROVENANCE   Richard Browne (fol. 63^v).

BIBLIOGRAPHY Bernard, *CMA*, I.ii.1541; Coxe, *Corpus*, p. 27; Bolton, p. 58;
                      Troncarelli, *Boethiana*, no. 88; Minnis, *Chaucer*, p. 94.

211. MS Oxford, Corpus Christi College, 118
Mus., Arith.   s. xii 2/4; s. xiv 2/2

Parchment; ii (modern) + 118 + ii (modern) fols (incl. half-sheets for dia-
grams); page 210x135mm.
Two vols bound together in ?s. xiv.
A (s. xii 2/4): text 160x88mm; 36 lines.
B (s. xiv 2/2): text 168x90mm; 36 lines.
Rebound and recut 1931.

CONTENTS   A: fols 3^r–56^v *Mus.*
                      B: fols 57^r–101^v *Arith.* incl. tables (100^v) and diagrams of
                      tree of sciences (100^r) and of proportion of geometry,
                      arithmetic, consonancy and harmony (101^r); 101^v–13^v
                      Simon Bredon, on *Arith.* of Boethius; 113^v four diagrams of
                      proportions of geometry, arithmetic, consonancy, harmony.

GLOSS   *Mus.* has marginal gloss, ?s. xv.

DECORATION   *Mus.* red and green initials; rubrication; tables and diagrams,
                      some on extra leaves (fols 27^{r-v}, 47^{r-v}).
                      Arith. red and blue initials with alternating pen
                      flourishing; rubrication.

PROVENANCE   English. 'Dominus Robert Greene de Welbe' (fol. 118^r: s. xv);
                      John Dee.

BIBLIOGRAPHY Bernard, *CMA*, I.ii.1585; Coxe, *Corpus*, p. 41; White, in Gib-
                      son, pp. 186–87; *AT*, nos 35, 367; Bower, no. 74; R. J. Roberts
                      and A. G. Watson, *John Dee's Library Catalogue*, London,
                      1990, M. 142, p. 125 (with note on R. Greene).

212. MS Oxford, Corpus Christi College, 224
Arith., Mus. (2 copies) s. xii 3/4; s. xiii

Parchment; 190 fols; page 215x135mm; several books, each written by a different, well-schooled hand. Medieval binding of white leather on boards.
A (s. xii 3/4): text 175x90mm; 40 lines.
B (s. xiii): text 138x80mm; 37 lines.
D (s. xiii): text 172x92mm; 26 lines.

CONTENTS	A: fols 2ʳ–41ᵛ **Arith.** B: fols 42ʳ–69ʳ Alfraganus, *Theorica planetarum et stellarum*, transl. by John of Spain (dated in margin, fol. 69ʳ, 13 Feb. 1225); 69ᵛ–111ᵛ **Mus.** I–IV only, with diagrams at end; 112ʳ–13ʳ musical diagrams. C: fols 114ʳ–41ʳ Euclid, *Geometry* (corrected, diacritical marks added). D: fols 142ʳ–88ᵛ **Mus.**, colophon, *Longobardorum invidia non finita. Explicit Musia* (*sic*).
GLOSS	D: contemporary marginal gloss.
DECORATION	A: mainly plain red initials, but fols 18ᵛ–19ʳ initials in blue, red, green, brown; rubrication; tables and diagrams. B: alternate red and blue initials with a little pen flourishing; red and blue paraph signs; tables, figures, diagrams. D: red, blue and occasionally green initials; plain, bigger initials beginning each book. Brown penwork initials with intertwined acanthus leaves etc. at fols 142ʳ, 161ᵛ; many diagrams and tables.
PROVENANCE	St Mary's abbey, York (*ex libris* fol. 2ʳ: s. xiii); John Dee (fol. 1ʳ).
BIBLIOGRAPHY	Bernard, *CMA*, I.ii.1691; Coxe, *Corpus*, p. 89; Ker, *MLGB*, p. 217; *AT*, no. 70; Bower, no. 75; R. J. Roberts and A. G. Watson, *John Dee's Library Catalogue*, London, 1990, M 167, p. 127.

213. MS Oxford, Corpus Christi College, 490, nos 23 & 24
Soph. Elench.   s. xiii

Parchment; 2 fols, heavily cut down; page now 150x125 & 150x120mm; 18
lines (no. 23), 5 lines (no. 24); ruled for gloss; one scribe.
Host book: C. Dionysius (in Latin), Lyons, 1543.

CONTENTS   No. 23: *Soph. Elench.* 'syllogizavit' to 'aliae' (54/23–55/21)
                  and 'levissimus' to 'contradictione o[mnes' (56/4–25).
                  No. 24: *Soph. Elench.* 'autem' to 'modo' (47/17–24)
                  and 'dictionem' to 'inanimatum' (46/13–20).

GLOSS   Heavy marginal and interlinear gloss.

DECORATION   None.

PROVENANCE   Unknown.

BIBLIOGRAPHY   Ker, *Pastedowns*, no. 698; *AL*, 1973.

214. MS Oxford, Corpus Christi College, 490, no. 112
Topica Aris.   s. xiii

Parchment; 1 fol., heavily cut down; page now 160x136mm; 16 lines; ruled
for gloss; one scribe.
Host book: Machiavelli, Montbéliard, 1599 (SH. VII. 54).

CONTENTS   *Topica Aris.* VI.6 'alicui et' to 'ad videndum' (126/23–129/4).

GLOSS   Consistent contemporary marginal and interlinear gloss; point-
                  ing hands. A few later notes.

DECORATION   Blue and red paraph signs.

PROVENANCE   Unknown.

BIBLIOGRAPHY   Ker, *Pastedowns*, no. 1618; *AL*, 1973.

EXETER COLLEGE, f. 1314.

Bernard, *CMA*, I.ii.817–52; Coxe, I; Ker, *MLGB*, p. 146; *History*, i.299–302.

215. MS Oxford, Exeter College, 28
DCPhil.

s. xiv

Parchment; iv + 312 fols (fol. 249 doubled); page 355x235mm.
A (s. xiv): text 2 cols, each 272x82mm; 54 lines; one scribe.
B (s. xiii): text 2 cols, each 280x90mm; 44 lines; one scribe.
C: (s. xiv^ex): text 2 cols, each 270x78mm; 52 lines; frame ruled; one scribe.
A folio-size schoolbook; all the Boethius texts are in the same hand.

CONTENTS — Fol. 1^v s. xv contents-list of entire volume.
A: fols 2ra–68va William Wheteley, commentary on Ps.-Boethius, *De disciplina scolarium*; 68va–205vb idem, commentary on *DCPhil.* (200rb–5vb list of chapters and conclusions; 206ra–49^r Anon., *Quaestiones in DCPhil.*, *inc.* 'Carmina qui condam. Quia in isto libro, qui est liber Boecii de consolacione'; *expl.* 'temporum successione set earundem similitate; Amen. Expliciunt questiones super quintum librum Boecii de consolacione philosophie. Mando lectori post mortem gaudia celi. Ut det scriptori roget Deum ore fideli quod sol.reve.'
B: fols 250ra–84vb sermon collection 'Filius matris', *inc.* prol. addressed to W. dei gratia N. ecclesie dispensatori, 'Quoniam nonnullos nostri temporis'.
C: fols 285ra–89rb Augustine, *De praedestinatione et gratia Dei*; 289rb–93rb idem, *Sermo de patientia*; 293rb–94va idem, *Sermo in natali S. Mariae Magdalenae*; 294va–96vb Grosseteste, *De veritate*; 296vb–305rb idem, *De libero arbitrio*; 306ra–7vb idem, *De Dei scientia, voluntate, misericordia, et justitia et praesentia localiter.*

GLOSS — A: William Wheteley, intercalated. Otherwise very few annotations; pointing hands; running footers and headers of bk numbers.

DECORATION   A: a few blue initials with red infilling and scrolling; mostly
              simple red and blue capitals; red and blue paraph signs; lem-
              mata underlined in red.
              B: blue initials with red penwork, red initials with
              purple penwork; rubrication; lemmata underlined in
              red.
              C: space left for initials, not supplied.

PROVENANCE   English. 'emptus scolaribus de Stapleton Hall, cum bonis
              magistrorum Henrici Whitefeld & Johannis Landreyn', mid to
              late s. xiv (fol. 1ᵛ).

BIBLIOGRAPHY Bernard, *CMA*, omits; Coxe, *Exeter*, pp. 10–11; Emden,
              BRUO, pp. 1090 (Lanreyn), 2030–31 (Wheteley), 2037–38
              (Whitefeld); Courcelle, pp. 322, 415; Weijers, no. 63; P. O.
              Lewry, 'Four Graduation Speeches from Oxford Manuscripts',
              Mediaeval Studies, 44, 1982, pp. 138–40.

JESUS COLLEGE, f. 1571.

Bernard, *CMA*, I.ii.2020–2126; Coxe, II.

216. MS Oxford, Jesus College, 4
Mus.   s. xii 1/2

Parchment; i (modern) + 107 + i (modern) fols; page c. 230x c. 140mm; three
vols bound together.
A (s. xii 1/2): text 180x87–115mm; 31–38 lines; several scribes.
B (s. xii 1/2): text 190x115mm; 37 lines, ruled with stylus; same or similar
hand throughout.
C (s. xii): text 190x100–115mm; 31–38 lines; one scribe.
Ex-flyleaf: neumed liturgical fragment (fol. 107: s. xii).
Late s. xii white leather binding, repaired s. xix 2/2; labelled on cover: 'An-
selmi opus. 17'.

CONTENTS   A: fols 1ʳ–57ᵛ Anselm, five opuscula and (54ᵛ) *Monologion*
              1–6 (*expl.* 'nullum bonum' [Schmitt I.20, line 1]).

B: fols 59^r–77^r **Mus.**, I–II.31 (265/30), *expl.* 'sit autem descriptio'; 77^v–78^r ruled but blank; 80^r–95^r anonymous treatise on geometry (*inc.* '(G)eometricales tractanti diuersitates premonstrandum est quas ipsius artis tractatus spondeat utilitates'; *expl.* 'apud Germanos unum rastum vel rastam efficiunt' [95^r]); 95^v '(C)alcus est pars minima omnium ponderum constans'; *expl.* 'calcos ccclxxxiiii'.

C: fols 96^r–106^v homiletic material, incl. Gospel of Nicodemus (96^v).

GLOSS None.

DECORATION A: simple red, green, ochre capitals; space left for headings, etc., not supplied.

B: space left for major initials, *tituli* and diagrams which are not supplied; simple red or green minor initials, almost entirely omitted; no chapter headings.

C: three red capitals.

PROVENANCE Pershore Abbey, Worcs.; 'Liber Anselmi archiepiscopi G[ilberti] P[rioris]' (fol. 1^r), 'liber gill' pr[ioris]' (fol 58^r): both s. xii.

BIBLIOGRAPHY Bernard, *CMA*, omits; Coxe, *Jesus*, p. 2; Ker, *MLGB*, p. 150; N. R. Ker, 'Sir John Prise' in idem (ed. A. G. Watson), *Books, Collectors and Libraries: Studies in the Medieval Heritage*, London, 1985, pp. 471–96 (484, 489); Bower, no. 76.

217. Oxford, Jesus College, E. 4. 11 (Gall.)
Prior Anal.

s. xiii^{ex}

Parchment; 2 fols (front and back flyleaves); page 176x122mm; text 119x68mm; 27–28 lines; one scribe.
Host book: Cosmas Guymier, *Pragmatica sanctio*, Paris, 1503.

CONTENTS Fol. 1^{r-v} (front) **Prior Anal.** 'Differt enim' to 'non de tota' (67/20–70/16); 2^{r-v} **Prior Anal.** 'Quoniam autem' to 'ut sit' (20/6–23/1).

GLOSS   Dense marginal and interlinear gloss in two contemporary
                 hands.

DECORATION   Red and blue capitals with blue and red flourishing; red and
                 blue paraph signs.

PROVENANCE   English or French.

BIBLIOGRAPHY   *AL*, 1975.

MAGDALEN COLLEGE, f. 1458.

Bernard, *CMA*, I.ii.2126 (sic)–2372; Coxe, II; Ker, *MLGB*, pp. 146–47;
History, ii.610–14 and (books) 461.

218. MS Oxford, Magdalen College, lat. 19
Mus.   s. xii 1/4

Parchment; ii (modern) + 80 fols; page 240x155mm; text 180x117mm; 29
lines; drypoint ruling; one neat hand. *Titulus* in red. Greek (fol. 2ᵛ) with
interlinear Latin translation. Binding: s. xvii, suede with two ties (broken).
Chapter headings in red.
A very smart monastic MS.

CONTENTS   Fols 1ᵛ–78ʳ *Mus.*; 78ʳ⁻ᵛ *De mensura fistularum, inc.* 'Si fistula
                 equalis grossitudinis fuerit et maior minorem in sua
                 longitudine bis habuerit'; *expl.* 'tono concordant'.

GLOSS   None.

DECORATION   Good single-colour initials in red or green. Clear diagrams in
                 red and occasionally green.

PROVENANCE   ? English.

BIBLIOGRAPHY   Bernard, *CMA*, I.ii.2160; Coxe, *Magdalen*, p. 15; Bower, no.
                 77.

219. MS Oxford, Magdalen College, lat. 196
DCPhil.

1459 ?

Parchment; 73 fols, not foliated, water-damaged; page 300x213mm; text 230x113mm; 2 cols; 24 lines; written by Thomas Candour (back pastedown). Binding: contemporary blind-stamped leather on boards; clasp missing; chain mark on front cover. Blue running headers and paraph signs added later. Texts of **Bo**(ethius) and **Phi**(losophia) marked in red.
Once a lovely copy, now badly damaged.

CONTENTS   Fols 1ʳ–73ʳ *DCPhil.*, last page missing: *expl.* imperf.
                  V.pr.vi.172, 'vicia colite vir[tutes]'.

GLOSS   Marginal and interlinear gloss in one hand same as or similar
                  to the text.

DECORATION   Italian s. xv 2/2. Elaborate illuminated initials all excised;
                  lovely capitals with flourishing in gold, red, green, blue, grey.
                  Red annotation of prose and metre; rubrication.

PROVENANCE   English. Master John Neele (d. 1498), chaplain to William
                  Waynflete, bp. of Winchester.

BIBLIOGRAPHY   Bernard, *CMA*, I.ii.2337; Coxe, *Magdalen*, p. 90; Emden,
                  BRUO, p. 1341; *Hunt Memorial Exhibition*, xxii.3, p. 96;
                  Watson, *Oxford*, no. 834; *AT*, no. 575.

220. MS Oxford, Magdalen College, lat. 267, nos 41 & 56
in Cat., Cat.

s. xii

Parchment; 2 bifolia; page 217x164mm; text 180x117mm; 30 lines; one scribe. Four fols which were nos 1, 4, 5, 8, of a quire, perhaps the second, of one MS.

CONTENTS   No. 41: *in Cat.* (*PL*, 64:167C–172A).
                  No. 56: *Cat.* caps 8, 10–15 (26/10–29/12;
                  35/16–41/10).

GLOSS   Users' marginal and interlinear annotation and underlining.

DECORATION   Plain red initials; offset, self-coloured capitals.

PROVENANCE   English or French.

BIBLIOGRAPHY *AL*, 1978.

221. MS Oxford, Magdalen College, lat. 271, nos 16 & 17
Prior Anal.   s. xiii – s. xiv

Parchment; 2 fols; page 312x205mm; text 177x98mm; 32 lines; one scribe.
Same as MS Bodleian Library, Lat. misc. a. 3, fol. 5.
Host book: Ambrosius Autpert, Cologne, 1536.

CONTENTS   *Prior Anal.* I.15–16 (33/22–36/9) and I.41–45 (82/1–85/20).

GLOSS   None.

DECORATION   Red and blue initials with contrasting penwork; red and blue
              paraph signs.

PROVENANCE   English or French.

BIBLIOGRAPHY Ker, *Pastedowns*, no. 167; *AL*, 1981.

222. Oxford, Magdalen College, E. 21. 12
Soph. Elench., Topica Aris.   s. xiii^{ex}

Parchment; 1 fol. & 1 bifolium (fol. 2 imperf.); once front and back pastedowns of host book, now detached but bound in; page 310x195mm; text
185x90mm; 41 lines; one scribe.
Host book: Valerius Maximus, Paris, 1536.

CONTENTS   Fol. 1^{r-v} (front) *Soph. Elench.* 'utrum ut' to 'prius habens'
              (39/28–44/15); 2^r blurred, but text prior to 2^v *Soph. Elench.*
              'bo]num' to 'e contrario' (50/17–52/13); 3^{r-v} *Topica Aris.*
              III.2–3 'omnia' to 'eligenda' (50/19–57/7).

GLOSS   None for *Soph. Elench.* Marginal gloss in dense cursive for *Topica Aris.*; some later users' notes.

DECORATION   Blue and red paraph signs.

PROVENANCE   Unknown.

BIBLIOGRAPHY Ker, *Pastedowns*, no. 168; *AL*, 1983.

MERTON COLLEGE, f. 1264.

Bernard, *CMA*, I.ii.469–807; Coxe, I; F. M. Powicke, *The Medieval Books of Merton College*, Oxford, 1931; Ker, *MLGB*, pp. 147–48; *History*, i.295–99; ii.459–62.

223. MS Oxford, Merton College, 145
Op. Sac.
s. xiv

Parchment; i + 103 fols; page 253x176mm; text 2 cols, each 200x60mm; 44 lines; one scribe. Binding: Merton blind-stamped suede, two ties. *Tituli* to *Op. Sac.*
A solid personal workbook.

CONTENTS   Fol. 1^v s. xv contents list; 2ra–49vb John Damascene, *De fide orthodoxa*; 50ra–67vb idem, *Logica*; 68ra–80ra idem, *Elementarium*; 80ra–87rb idem, *Epistola de trisagio*; 87rb–100rb *Op. Sac.*; 100rb–102ra Gundissalinus, *De unitate et uno*; 102rb commentary on *Rorate coeli* (Isai. 45.8).

GLOSS   Scattered notes to Damascene; very occasional notes to *Op. Sac.*

DECORATION   None. Space left for a few small initials, not supplied.

PROVENANCE   Given to Merton by master John Raynham, a former Fellow (d. by Nov. 1376).

BIBLIOGRAPHY   Bernard, *CMA*, I.ii.612; Coxe, *Merton*, p. 62 ;
                     Powicke, *Merton*, no. 353, p. 134. Emden, *BRUO*, p.
                     1570.

224. MS Oxford, Merton College, 260
Op. Sac. III   s. xv 2/3

Parchment; iii + 169 fols; page 205x145mm; text 162x117mm; 21 lines for
Op. Sac.; good professional cursive written by Manby (fols 2^r–34^r; scribal
colophon, fol. 34^r) and Chapeleyn (fols 100^r–53^r). Binding: s. xvii, Merton,
tooled 'rough leather' (suede); two ties.

CONTENTS   Fols 2^r–25^v Ps.-Albert the Great, *De modis significandi*;
                     25^v–34^r Ps.-Albert the Great, *De passionibus sermonum*;
                     34^v–61^v Francis Meyronnes, *De modis significandi*; 62^r–95^v
                     Duns Scotus, commentary on *De Int.*; 96^r–99^v blank; 100^r–53^r
                     idem, commentary on *Soph. Elench.*; 153^v–57^r *Inc.* 'Quoniam
                     in quibusdam naturalibus corporibus'; 157^r–58^v ***Op. Sac. III***;
                     159^r–68^v Thomas Aquinas, *De ente et essentia*, *expl.* imperf.

GLOSS   None; few signs of use, though it has many reader aids.

DECORATION   Blue with red penwork flourishing. Red textual divisions in
                     margins; rubrication; lemmata underlined in red.

PROVENANCE   Bought by the Fellows of Merton in 1452 (Powicke).

BIBLIOGRAPHY Bernard, *CMA*, I.ii.727; Coxe, *Merton*, pp. 102–3; Powicke,
                     Merton, no. 925, p. 197; Burnett, *Glosses*, p. 172.

225. MS Oxford, Merton College, 309
in Topica Cic.   s. x/xi

Parchment; iv + 201 + iii fols; page 262x190mm; four vols bound together.
A (s. xiii 2/2): text 142x78mm; 24 lines; panel-ruled for gloss; one scribe;
catchwords.
B (s. xiii mid): text c. 140x80mm; 19 lines; panel-ruled for gloss; one scribe.

C: (s. xiii 2/2): text 2 cols, each 212x70mm; c. 68 lines; one very small cursive hand.

D (s. ix/x): text 220x110mm; 31 lines; at least three small Caroline hands. *Tituli* in rustic capitals and colophons to *in Topica Cic.*.

Tituli and colophons, 'conditor operis emendaui' (fols 149ᵛ, 177ʳ, cf. 184ᵛ).

Binding: s. xvii, Merton, tooled 'rough leather' (suede).

CONTENTS	A: fols 1ʳ–88ᵛ Priscian, *Institutiones* xvii–xviiii.157 (Passalacqua, no. 469), with users' glosses; unpaginated leaf with pencil notes on the recto. B: fols 89ʳ–98ᵛ Donatus, *Ars Maior* iii, glossed. C: fols 99ʳᵃ–112ʳᵇ Peter of Spain, *Absoluta* (Hunt B; here attributed to Petrus Helias). D: fols 114ᵛ–15ʳ commentary on the *Benedicite*; 115ʳ–18ᵛ Cicero, *Topica* (fragment) with some glosses; 118ᵛ–21ʳ *Communis speculatio de rethoricae et logicae cognatione*; 121ʳ–22 *Locorum rethoricorum distinctio*; 123ʳ–201ᵛ ***in Topica Cic.*** with some contemporary annotation. End flyleaf (iiiʳ) diagrams of hierarchy of spheres etc.
GLOSS	A: fairly extensive contemporary and later marginal and interlinear glosses. Many signs of use, pointing hands etc. B: extensive marginal and interlinear gloss in at least two hands. C: some marginal notes, diagrams, faces, animals, etc. A wonderfully *used* schoolbook. D: scattering of contemporary marginal and interlinear notes and diagrams. Text carefully corrected.
DECORATION	A: a few red and blue initials with alternate penwork; small blue or red capitals; red and blue paraph signs; faces etc. B: none; space left for initials, not supplied. C: blue initials with red flourishing; blue and red paraph signs. D: simple red and brown initials and capitals. Gallows paraph signs.
PROVENANCE	Bequeathed to Merton by master John Raynham, a former Fellow (d. by November 1376); *ex dono* fol. 115ᵛ.

BIBLIOGRAPHY Bernard, *CMA*, I.ii.776; Coxe, *Merton*, p. 122 ; Powicke, *Merton*, no. 101; Emden, *BRUO*, p. 1570; R. W. Hunt, 'Absoluta*: The Summa of Petrus Hispanus on *Priscianus Minor*', in *Collected Papers on the History of Grammar in the Middle Ages*, ed. G. L. Bursill-Hall, Amsterdam, 1980, pp. 95–116.

226. Oxford, Merton College, E. 3. 5 (a)
Soph. Elench.

s. xiii

Parchment; 2 bifolia; page 280x208mm; 157x80mm; 22 lines; ruled for double gloss; one good scribe. Once part of MS Merton lat. 268 (*Post. Anal.*).
Host book: Jacobus de Arena, 1541.

CONTENTS *Soph. Elench.* 'has ad absconsas' – 'quoniam huic' (29/7–39/21).

GLOSS Marginal gloss in two cols in each margin; some interlinear gloss; one scribe.

DECORATION Red initial with blue and red infilling and penwork; red and blue paraph signs.

PROVENANCE Unknown.

BIBLIOGRAPHY *AL*, 1985; cf. *AL*, 1979, 1940.

227. MS Oxford, Merton College, E. 3. 12
DCPhil.

s. x/xi

Parchment; two consecutive leaves from a MS another leaf of which is a pastedown in York Minster Library (MS 7. N. 10: currently untraceable). Here used as pastedowns, now detached.
Page now 215x180mm and 212x174mm; original c. 280 x c. 210mm; text c. 180x102mm (originally); 18 lines (originally 19); drypoint ruling; ruled for gloss; one expert scribe for text and gloss. Gloss related to text by symbols and Greek letters.
Once a very fine copy.

CONTENTS   *DCPhil.* V.pr.iv.91–119, '[pu]ra mentis acie contuetur' (missing line 105) to 'ut suam quisque'; and V.pr.iv.120 – V.m.iv.35. 'potestate perficiat' to 'Tum mentis vigor excitus' (missing line 17).

GLOSS   Extensive and systematic contemporary marginal and interlinear gloss. A few ?s. xv interlinear notes.

DECORATION   Plain red capitals, some oxidized.

PROVENANCE   Probably continental. 'Unidentified host book' (Ker), although York Minster fragments bound in an *Aesop* printed Leipzig, 1564. Identified by H. W. Garrod, fellow of Merton from 1901.

BIBLIOGRAPHY   Ker, *Pastedowns*, p. 179, n. 2.

NEW COLLEGE, f. 1379.

Bernard, *CMA*, I.ii.965–1287; Coxe, I; Ker, *MLGB*, p. 148; R. W. Hunt, 'The Medieval Library', *New College Oxford, 1379–1979*, ed. J. Buxton and P. Williams, Oxford, 1979, pp. 317–45; *History*, ii.460–62.

228. MS Oxford, New College, 264
DCPhil.
                                                             s. xiv 1/4

Parchment; 267 fols; page 370x248mm; text 2 cols, each 272x90mm; 60 lines. One scribe for *DCPhil.* Oxford 'rough leather' binding (suede on cardboard), s. xvii. Red and blue bk nos as running headers.
A typical late schoolbook.

CONTENTS   Fols 2ᵛ–5ʳ fragments of philosophical questions on interpreting dreams etc.; 5ᵛ–8ᵛ letter of William Wheteley to Roger, bp. of Salisbury; 9ʳᵃ–10ʳᵃ idem letter to Henry of Mansfeld, dean of

Lincoln; 10^r–257^v **DCPhil.** (text begins 14rb) with an opulent, intercalated commentary of William Wheteley, rector of the church of Yatesbury; 252^r no. of questions for each book and the total; 253^r–59^v various items, mostly by William Wheteley, incl. *Tractatus de signis pronosticis sterilitatis, expl.* imperf.; 262^r–65^v hymns to St Hugh of Lincoln, with intercalated commentary, written in 1316 by a clerk of Lincoln grammar school.

GLOSS   A few marginal annotations; marked with scholastic terms (e.g., *argumentum, expositio*; some running footers of question discussed.)

DECORATION   Splendid illuminated initials with full and three-quarter bor-ders, in blue, green, pink, orange, white and gold with elabo-rate flourishing in plant and animal patterns at beginning of each book and list of capitula to *DCPhil.* and at 253^r and 255^v. A variety of simple and elaborate blue and red capitals some-times with flourishing. Rubricated; red and blue paraph signs; lemmata underlined in red. Diagram of phases of the moon, fol. 39^v.

PROVENANCE   William Reed, bp. of Chichester, from Master Nicolas of Sandwich. Reed presented it to the chained library at New College: 'Liber collegii beate Marie Wynton in Oxon.' (fol. 2^r).

BIBLIOGRAPHY   Bernard, *CMA*, I.ii.1228; Coxe, *New College*, pp. 93–94; Em-den, *BRUO*, pp. 1639–40 (Reed), 2030–31 (Wheteley); Cour-celle, pp. 322, 415; Hunt, 'Medieval Library', pp. 320–21; *AT*, no. 276.

229. MS Oxford, New College, 265
DCPhil.   s. xiv

Parchment; ii + 60 fols; page 257x182mm; text 155x110mm; 27 lines; one scribe with even, rotunda hand. Catchwords. Greek very unsure. Oxford 'rough leather' binding, s. xvii (suede with two ties). Bk nos (in Roman numerals) as running headers; red headings to bks.

A well-produced, spacious book.

CONTENTS	Fols 1ʳ–59ʳ **DCPhil.,** *inc.* imperf. 'ac torvis inflammata' (I.pr.i.28).
GLOSS	Annotated (s. xv mid) by Andrew Holes, fellow of New College and Thomas Candour; transliteration of the Greek.
DECORATION	Fine illuminated initials, in acanthus leaf pattern, in blue, pink, grey, brown, white, black and gold at beginning of each bk; blue and red capitals with red and blue flourishing; letters dotted with yellow.
PROVENANCE	Central Italy; ? Florence.
BIBLIOGRAPHY	Bernard, *CMA*, I.ii.1229; Coxe, *New College*, p. 94; Kottler, No; Hunt 'Medieval Library', pp. 326–27; *Hunt Memorial Exhibition*, xxii.4, p. 96; *AT*, no. 912.

230. MS New College, 364/1 no. 32 (Y. 15. 12)
Top. Diff.

s. xiii mid

Parchment; one folio; page 175mm wide; text 85mm wide; panel ruled for gloss; one small hand.

CONTENTS	*Top. Diff.* III–IV (*PL*, 64: 1204C–6B).
GLOSS	Extensive contemporary and later annotation.
DECORATION	Major initial in red and blue, with flourishing. Red and blue paraph signs.
PROVENANCE	Unknown.
BIBLIOGRAPHY	Ker, *Pastedowns*, no. 1726 (fragment no. 31 is an unidentified philosophical text, not Boethius).

231. Oxford, New College, B. 30. 6
Prior Anal.   s. xiii

Parchment; 2 fols, forming front pastedown of host; page 225x160mm; text 127x74mm; 30 lines; ruled for gloss; one scribe. Running headers in red; marginal indexing letters.
Host book: Josephus (in Greek), Basel, 1544.

CONTENTS   *Prior Anal.* I.5–6 'album lapis' to 'affirmativa inerit' (14/25–16/23) and I.17 'non inesse' to 'demonstratio. Man[ifestum' (39/24–41/22).

GLOSS   Extensive contemporary marginal and interlinear glosses.

DECORATION   Blue intials with red penwork; red and blue paraph signs (two types).

PROVENANCE   Unknown.

BIBLIOGRAPHY   Ker, *Pastedowns*, no. 717; *AL*, 1990.

QUEEN'S COLLEGE, f. 1341.

Coxe, I; Ker, *MLGB*, p. 149; *History*, ii.459–62.

232. MS Oxford, Queen's College, 315
Op. Sac. IV, DCPhil. I-II   s. xiii

Parchment; 210 fols; page 290x190mm; text 190x120mm; 31 lines; one scribe. Binding: s. xv red leather on boards with two clasps. Running headers to the Anselm.
A well-made book.

CONTENTS   Fols 1ʳ–186ᵛ Anselm, *Opera varia* (12 items including *De veritate, De libero arbitrio, Cur Deus homo, Proslogion, Monologion*); 187ʳ–90ʳ *Op. Sac. IV*; 190ʳ–202ᵛ Ps.-Boethius, *De disciplina scolarium*; 202ᵛ–10ᵛ *DCPhil.*, *expl.* imperf. 'cum coniugis pudore cum', II.pr.iii.21.

GLOSS   Some late s. xiv dry point notes at the end of Anselm and beginning of Boethius and a few pointing fingers. Boethius shows no sign of use.

DECORATION   Red and brown initials with alternate flourishing; red paraph signs.

PROVENANCE   Unknown.

BIBLIOGRAPHY   Coxe, *Queen's*, p. 75; Weijers, Q (pp. 58–59).

233. MS Queen's College 78. E. 12
Top. Diff., Isag.

s. xiv

Parchment; two bifolia; now front and back flyleaves to printed book in s. xvi binding.
A (front flyleaves): severely cut down; text 81mm wide; 2 cols; ruled with outer col. for gloss; one scribe.
B (back flyleaves): page 235x185mm; text 158x80mm; inner col. of text, allowing space for gloss in outer col.; 28 lines; one scribe.
Host book is a Psalter commentary, Geneva, 1562, printed by Henri Etienne II for Ulrich Fugger of Augsburg: see Adams, *s.v.*, Bible 1441.

CONTENTS   A: *Top. Diff.* III and IV (*PL*, 64: 1202A–3A, 1215A–16A).
                  B: *Isag.*, (11/2–18/13).

GLOSS   Extensive user's gloss in several hands for both A and B.

DECORATION   A: red and blue flourished initials and paraph signs.
                  B: red and blue paraph signs.

PROVENANCE   Given to Queen's by Edmund Grindall, archbishop of Canterbury (1575–83).

BIBLIOGRAPHY   Ker, *Pastedowns*, no. 1671; *AL*, 1999; H. M. Adams, *Catalogue of Books Printed on the Continent of Europe, 1501–1600, in Cambridge Libraries*, 2 vols, Cambridge, 1967, I, p. 145.

234. MS Queen's College, Guardbook 389B (nos 29–30)
in Topica Cic.   s. xii[in]

Parchment; one folio cut in two and cropped; text 105mm wide; one col.;
beautiful Anglo-Norman hand.

CONTENTS   *in Topica Cic.* II (*PL*, 64: 1065C–67B).

GLOSS   None.

DECORATION   Offset initials.

PROVENANCE   Unknown.

BIBLIOGRAPHY   *AL*, 1997 (MS listed as Queen's 389).

TRINITY COLLEGE, f. 1555.

Although Trinity College is on the site of Durham College, there is no conti-
nuity with the pre-Reformation library. Sir Thomas Pope (d. 1559), the
founder of Trinity College, established a chained library which included
twenty-six manuscripts, some from the royal collection.

Bernard, *CMA*, I.ii.1938–2019; Coxe, II; *History*, ii.42–45 and (books) 460–61;
R. Gameson and A. Coates, *The Old Library, Trinity College, Oxford*, Trinity
College Exhibition Catalogue, 14–25 Nov. 1988, Oxford, 1988.

235. MS Oxford, Trinity College, 1
Mus.   s. xv mid

Parchment; i + 88 fols; page 220x140mm; text 150x95mm; 28 lines; one hand
throughout.
Trinity College binding, s. xix 1/2. *Tituli.*

CONTENTS   Fols 1[r]–85[r] *Mus.*; 85[v]–86[r] blank; 86[v]–87[r] some arithmetical
                  rules of calculation in the same hand.

GLOSS   None.

DECORATION   Blue and red initials with red flourishing (fols 1^r,12^v); blue capitals with red flourishing throughout. Diagrams, figures, and red chapter headings only up to fol. 40^v, although space is left for the rest.

PROVENANCE   English. *Ex dono* Thomas Pope.

BIBLIOGRAPHY   Bernard, *CMA*, I.ii.1942; Coxe, *Trinity*, p. 1; *AT*, no. 558; Bower, no. 78.

236. MS Oxford, Trinity College, 17
DCPhil., Arith.
                                                              s. xii

Parchment; i (modern) + ii + 158 fols; page 180x128mm.
A: text 128x73mm; 28 lines; running headers.
B: text 142x76mm; 32 lines.
C: text 158x70mm; 29 lines; written by Rogerus Levita (fol. 142^v).
D: text 150x55mm; 41 lines.
Different hand for each treatise. Trinity College binding, s. xix 1/2.
MS of *Arith.* (B) inserted into one of *DCPhil.* (A) when the four vols that make up this MS were bound together.

CONTENTS   A: fols 1^r–42^v ***DCPhil.*** I–IV.pr.vii.9 'ratio et'.
                      B: fols 43^r–89^v ***Arith.***
                      A: fols 90^r–98^v ***DCPhil.*** IV–V (an exact continuation from fol. 42^v).
                      C: fols 99^r–142^r Arator, *Historia apostolica, expl.* 'gratia palmam'; 142^v *Versus de Aratore* (cf. *CSEL*, 72, p. xxix).
                      D: fols 143^r–56^r *Liber de physiognomia.*

GLOSS   *DCPhil.* marginal glosses in at least two hands; Grossetestian signs and glosses; chapter and bk no. at top of page in the glossator's hand, *DCPhil.* IV–V. *Arith.* has a few later annotations. Many signs of use.

DECORATION   A: plain red, blue, green initials; partly rubricated.

B: simple red ink capitals up to fol. 46ʳ; from 46ᵛ no
capitals; diagrams scrappily added by a different, less
professional, hand.
C: a few simple red capitals.
D: red and blue slightly flourished initials.

PROVENANCE   *Iste liber est de Oxon'* (fol. 143ʳ); perhaps from Oxford Fran-
ciscan convent.

BIBLIOGRAPHY   Bernard, *CMA*, I.ii.2008; Coxe, *Trinity*, p. 7; S. H. Thompson,
'Grosseteste's Concordantial Signs', *Medievalia et Humanis-
tica*, 9, 1955, p. 35; Ker, *MLGB*, p. 142.

237. MS Oxford, Trinity College, 47
Logica vetus, Topica Aris., Arith., Mus.   s. xii 1/2

Parchment; i + 183 fols; page 270x190mm. Several MSS bound tightly
together in Trinity College s. xix 1/2 binding, so as to make them homoge-
neous.
Isag. text 190x120mm; 41–46 lines; one small, neat hand.
Cat. text 190x120mm; 41–46 lines; same hand as *Isag.*
De Int. text 190x120mm; 41–46 lines; same hand as *Isag.*
Top. Diff. text 201x133mm; 42 lines; one regular hand.
Topica Aris., fols 19ʳ–26ᵛ, text 215x125mm, 48 lines; one hand similar to *Isag.*
Topica Aris., fols 27ʳ–47ʳ, text 205x120mm; 50 lines; two or three small
hands.
Arith. text 192x115mm; 44 lines; two small hands.
Mus. text 192x115mm; 51 lines; same hands as arith.
Chapter titles in red. Greek in *Mus.* is omitted (fol. 72ʳ).
A very fine, useful book of its type, well produced, in a number of small
hands.

CONTENTS   Fols 1ᵛ–4ᵛ *Isag.*; 5ʳ–10ʳ *Cat.*; 10ʳ–13ᵛ *De Int.*; 14ʳ–18ʳ *Top.
Diff. I–II, *expl.* 'atque subiecto' (*PL*, 64:1186D), with marginal
table; 19ʳ–47ʳ *Topica Aris.*; 48ʳ–70ʳ *Arith.*; 71ᵛ–103ᵛ *Mus.*,
preceded by list of capitula; 104ᵛ–38ʳ Euclid, *Elements*, trans.
Adelard of Bath, version II, glossed; 139ʳ–80ᵛ Euclid, *Elements*, trans. Adelard of Bath, version I; 181ʳ–82ᵛ (end-papers)

commentary on Lev. 19:19–26:19; Deut. 1:6–3:27 (s. xii/xiii).

GLOSS

Isag., Cat., Top. Diff., Topica Aris. all have a very few contemporary marginal notes, with slightly more in *De Int.. Arith.* has a quite extensive marginal gloss; *Mus.* has a little marginal gloss by at least two hands, quoting (87ᵛ) Manegold [of Lautenbach] and Adelard [of Bath]; *Top. Diff.* has subject headings.

DECORATION

Isag., Cat., De Int. have handsome, plain capitals in green and red (slightly oxidized). Space left for major initials in *Top. Diff.* but not supplied. *Topica Aris.* has brown self-coloured capitals up to fol. 26ᵛ; space left for initials, tables, etc., not supplied. Fols 27ʳ–47ʳ of *Topica Aris.* has plain red capitals and headings etc. *Arith.* and *Mus.* have green, red, blue capitals, occasionally with simple flourishing; good red and green tables and diagrams. Diagrams and headings missing in *Mus.*, fols 100ʳ–3ᵛ.

PROVENANCE

French, ? Chartres. Merton College; bequeathed by master Bryce de Sharstead (d. 1327: Powicke). In Oxford s. xv (pledge note, fol. 1ʳ). *Ex dono* Thomas Pope (fol. 180ᵛ).

BIBLIOGRAPHY Bernard, *CMA*, I.ii.1967; Coxe, *Trinity*, p. 19; F. M. Powicke, *The Medieval Books of Merton College, Oxford*, Oxford, 1931, no. 56, p. 50; *AL*, 379 and *suppl. alt.*, pp. 26–29 (*Topica Aris.*); Emden, *BRUO*, p. 1681; *Hunt Memorial Exhibition*, ix.5, p. 46; White in Gibson, pp. 162–205 (182–84, 202); N. R. Ker, 'The Books of Philosophy Distributed at Merton College' in idem, *Books, Collectors and Libraries: Studies in the Medieval Heritage*, ed. A. G. Watson, London, 1985, pp. 331–78 (353); Burnett, *Adelard*, no. 93; Gameson and Coates, p. 36; Bower, no. 79; H. L. L. Busard and M. Folkerts, *Robert of Chester's (?) Redaction of Euclid's 'Elements': the So-Called Adelard II Version*, 2 vols, Basel etc., 1992; P. Stirnemann, 'Où ont été fabriqués les livres de la glose ordinaire dans la première moitié du XIIᵉ siècle?', in F. Gasparri, ed., *Le XIIᵉ siècle: tournant et renouveau 1120–1150*, Paris, forthcoming, 1994.

238. Oxford, Trinity College, I. 7. 14
Soph. Elench.   s. xiii[ex]

Parchment; 1 fol.; page 260x172mm; text 155x92mm; 32 lines; ruled for gloss; one scribe.
Host book: Sarum Missal, London, 1523.

CONTENTS   *Soph. Elench.* c. 32 'Amplius non danda' to 'de qua oratio' (54/5–57/14).

GLOSS   Dense marginal and interlinear annotations in at least two hands.

DECORATION   Blue initials with red flourishing and infilling; red paraph signs.

PROVENANCE   Unknown.

BIBLIOGRAPHY   Ker, *Pastedowns*, no. 807a; *AL*, 2004.

WORCESTER

WORCESTER CATHEDRAL LIBRARY

Some 250 manuscripts from the medieval chapter library remain *in situ*, many in late medieval bindings. The manuscripts were carefully reviewed in the 1620s by the King's librarian, Patrick Young.

Bernard, *CMA*, II.i.696–926; J. K. Floyer and S. G. Hamilton, *Catalogue of Manuscripts Preserved in the Chapter Library of Worcester Cathedral*, Oxford, 1906; I. Atkins and N. R. Ker, *Catalogus librorum manuscriptorum bibliothecae Wigornensis made in 1622–1623 by Patrick Young, Librarian to King James I*, Cambridge, 1944; Ker, *MLGB*, pp. 205–15; Ker, *MMBL*, iv.669–89.

239. MS Worcester Cathedral, F. 66
Logica vetus et nova

s. xiii 2/3

Parchment; 224 fols; page 270x190mm; text 135x80mm; 29 lines; one scribe; fols 1, 223–24 are flyleaves of different works in same or similar hand. Modern binding.
A fine academic book with spacious margins; cf. MS Worcester Cath. F. 165.

CONTENTS   Fols 2^r–10^r ***Isag.***; 10^v–24^r ***Cat.***; 24^r–32^r ***De Int.***; 32^v–39^v *Liber sex principiorum*; 39^v–47^v ***Div.***; 48^r–75^v ***Top. Diff.***; 76^r–127^r ***Topica Aris.***; 133^r–50^v ***Soph. Elench.***; 151^r–98^v ***Prior Anal.***; 199^r–222^v *Post. Anal.*

GLOSS   Heavily annotated and corrected; marginal and interlinear gloss in various hands—one at least contemporary with the scribe, the rest (at least four) from s. xiv–xv. *Div* has no annotations; *Topica Aris.* is sparsely annotated; *Soph. Elench.* again heavily glossed with the main hand from fols 1–31 appearing again; the thick annotations continue to the end of the book.

DECORATION   Fine first initials (except for *De Int., Top. Diff.*) in blue and red infilling and flourishing; coloured initials stop after fol. 26^v and resume on fol. 133^r; red and blue paraph signs until fol. 26^r, reappearing on fols 133–50. Caricature sketches of men at arms and angel-like figures, fols 34^v, 67^v, 68^r.

PROVENANCE   ? English. 'Iste liber est fratris thome palmar' (front flyleaf), d. after 1415.

BIBLIOGRAPHY   Floyer and Hamilton, pp. 31–32; ? Emden, *BRUO*, pp. 1421–22.

240. MS Worcester Cathedral, F. 165
Logica vetus

s. xiii

Parchment; 146 fols; page 330x230mm; text 150x75mm; 20–21 lines; one scribe. Bound on boards in white; remains of bosses on back.
A well-used textbook; cf. MS Worcester Cath. F. 66.

CONTENTS   Fols 3^r–17^v *Isag.*; 18^r–46^v *Cat.*; 47^r–65^v *De Int.*; 66^r–80^v *Liber sex principiorum*; 81^r–97^v *Div.*; 98^r–144^v *Top. Diff.*

GLOSS   Very much glossed in at least four hands (incl. tree diagrams and interlinear gloss) until *Div.* when glosses become infrequent and die out. Glosses resume for *Top. Diff.* (fol. 98^r), which is mostly glossed in one s. xiv hand with pointing fingers and frequent caricatures of faces.

DECORATION   Large red and blue initial with infilling and scrolling begins each new work. Red and blue paraph signs.

PROVENANCE   ? English.

BIBLIOGRAPHY   Floyer and Hamilton, p. 94.

241. MS Worcester Cathedral, Add. 67 nos 49 a & b (X. G. 11) *DCPhil.*

s. xii^{ex}/xiii^{in}

Parchment; two folios, cut down; page 153x123mm; text 80mm wide; originally, probably 2 cols (one survives); 22 & 28 lines visible; wide margins for gloss; one neat, open hand.
Once formed part of the binding of a printed book, Cologne, 1572.

CONTENTS   *DCPhil.* III.pr.x.94 – III.m.x.4 and III.pr.xi.1 – III.pr.xi.49.

GLOSS   None.

DECORATION   One coloured initial on each folio, in green or red, with slight flourishing.

PROVENANCE   Unknown.

BIBLIOGRAPHY   Ker, *Pastedowns*, no. 1864; Ker, *MMBL*, iv.680; Troncarelli, *Boethiana*, no. 92.

YORK

YORK MINSTER LIBRARY

Only a few manuscripts from the medieval library survive *in situ*. The present collection of about 100 manuscripts, the great majority from English houses, was well established by the later s. xvii and augmented in the s. xviii.

Bernard, *CMA*, II.i.1–57,65; Ker, *MMBL*, iv.691–826.

242. MS York Minster XVI. A. 8
Op. Sac.
s. xii[ex]

Parchment; iii (modern) + 92 + iii (modern) fols (fol. 70 doubled); some water and mouse damage; page 300x205mm; text 215x135mm; 20 lines for Boethius, 39 lines for the commentary; one good scribe throughout; s. xiv heading fol. 1[r]; catchwords. Rebound 1820. *Tituli* in red.
A nice, clear useful text, confidently produced and ruled.

CONTENTS	Fols 1[r]–2[r] *Inc.* 'Omnium que rebus percipiendis' (Gilbert's second prologue); *expl.* 'theologicis communicaverunt esse deceptos'; 2[v]–88[v] *Op. Sac. I–III, V, IV*; 88[v]–91[v] part of Gilbert's list of proof-texts from his trial at Rheims, *inc.* 'Quod divina natura id est divinitas'; *expl.* 'Tercia pars, quare et quibus et unde et quomodo scribat aperit'.
GLOSS	I–III, V: Gilbert of Poitiers, *expl.* to commentary on V (fol. 85[v]); see contents. Evidence of reading by a later hand, who corrected the text in pencil in the margins.
DECORATION	Space left for initials both to begin each tract and in the text, but none added. Lemmata in commentary underlined in red.
PROVENANCE	English.
BIBLIOGRAPHY	Bernard, *CMA*, II.i.39; M. L. Colker, 'The Trial of Gilbert of Poitiers, 1148: A Previously Unknown Record', *Mediaeval Studies*, 27, 1965, pp. 152–83: section D: Gislebertus; N. R. Ker, 'The Handwriting of Archibishop Wulfstan' in idem,

Books, Collectors and Libraries: Studies in the Medieval Heritage, ed. A. G. Watson, London, 1985, pp. 9–26 (10n); Ker, *MMBL*, iv, pp. 692–93.

DUBLIN

TRINITY COLLEGE, f. 1591

Initially, the College manuscripts (which may have been quite numerous) were shelved among the printed books. With the acquisition of Archbishop Ussher's library in 1661, the manuscripts were catalogued separately. A comprehensive list was published by Bernard in 1697. The library was reorganized in the mid-eighteenth century (cupboards A–G); later acquisitions were classified H–L in 1815.

M. L. Colker, *Trinity College, Dublin: Descriptive Catalogue of the Mediaeval and Renaissance Latin Manuscripts*, 2 vols, Aldershot etc., 1991, with historical introduction by W. O'Sullivan.

* 243. MS Dublin, Trinity College, 248
Top. Diff. I–II　　　　　　　　　　　　　　　　　　　　　　　s. xiii 1/2

Parchment flyleaves to canonistic MS of mid-s. xvi; i^r–ii^v, iv^r–v^v fols; page c. 291x205mm; text 181x90mm; 28 lines; single scribe; frame-ruled for gloss.

CONTENTS　　　　Fols i^r–ii^v, iv^r–v^v are fragments of ***Top. Diff.* I–II**, *PL*, 64:1182C–1189C: 'cognicione procepta sit usu atque exercitatione – uel propter eas aliquid'; lacuna at 1185A 'de sillogismo dicere' to 1187B 'termini eorum'.

GLOSS　　　　　　Plentiful.

DECORATION　　Smudged historiated initial in blue and white on ground of blue and gold shows Boethius in black monastic garb, writing at desk; nearby is a fantastic beast with human head and peaked hat (fol. i^r). Minor initial, blue with red flourishing (fol. i^r).

Elsewhere initials in combinations of red and blue.

PROVENANCE   English. Ussher BBB.9; C. 1. 26.

BIBLIOGRAPHY Bernard, *CMA*, II.ii.163; Colker, pp. 438–39.

* 244. MS Dublin, Trinity College, 303
Op. Sac. I–III, V   s. xii/xiii

Parchment; 100 fols; page c. 206x141mm; text c. 195x103mm; 34 lines; one
scribe, writing above top line.

CONTENTS   Fols 1ʳ–95ᵛ *Op. Sac. I–III, V*, with intercalated commentary of
              Gilbert of Poitiers; fols 96ʳ–100ʳ Memorandum of the trial of
              Gilbert at Rheims, 1148 (ed. M. L. Colker, *Mediaeval Studies*,
              27, 1965, pp. 170–83).

GLOSS   Gilbert of Poitiers.

DECORATION   Space left for initials, not supplied.

PROVENANCE   English. Henry Savile of Banke; perhaps John Dee, DM. 13.
              C. 3. 21.

BIBLIOGRAPHY Bernard, *CMA*, II.ii.252; Häring, *Commentaries*, pp. 24–25;
              Häring, no. 41; R. J. Roberts and A. G. Watson, *John Dee's
              Library Catalogue*, London, 1990, DM. 13 and p. 58; Colker,
              pp. 597–98.

* 245. MS Dublin, Trinity College, 441
Arith., Op. Sac. I–III, V   s. xiv 1/2

Parchment; 271 fols; page 163x122mm; text c. 125x c. 80mm (pages have
been severely trimmed); c. 40 lines; frame ruling; catchwords; mixture of
secretary and anglicana letter-forms. *Titulus*, fol. 1ᵛ.

CONTENTS   Fol. 1ʳ contents list; 2ʳ–44ᵛ *Arith.*; 45ʳ⁻ᵛ Gerbert, Commentary
              on *Arith.* (Bubnov, pp. 32–35); 46ʳ–60ʳ *Op. Sac. I, II, V, III*;

60^{r}–271^{r} 108 short items, mainly mathematical and astronomical.

GLOSS S. xiv–xv notes; notes by John Dee.

DECORATION Initials in red or blue, some capitals marked with red. Rough
sketches, fols 14^{v} (face), 31^{r}, 78^{v}.

PROVENANCE English. 'Liber W. Dussyng' (fol. 1^{r}; s. xv: Venn); John Dee,
18 January 1553 (fol. 2^{r}). D. 4. 27.

BIBLIOGRAPHY Bernard, *CMA*, II.ii.186; M. Esposito, 'Classical Manuscripts
in Irish Libraries Part I', *Hermathena*, 19, 1920, pp. 123–40
(137); J. Venn and J. A. Venn, *Alumni Cantabrigienses*, Cambridge, 10 vols, 1922–1954, I.ii, p. 78; Thorndike and Kibre,
623 (Gerbert) 1186; R. J. Roberts and A. G. Watson, *John
Dee's Library Catalogue*, London, 1990, M. 137 and p. 124;
Colker, pp. 871–83.

* 246. MS Dublin, Trinity College, 1442
Arith. s. xii

Parchment; 6 fols; page c. 270x c. 202mm; text c. 235x c. 160mm; 2 cols; 41
lines, hard point ruling; single hand, Irish minuscule.

CONTENTS Fols 1ra–6vb *Arith.* **II.**19–44 (104/11) 'Omnesque se triangulis
antecedent. Quare perfecte ut arbitror – contrarie quam in
arithmetica medietate' (145/4).

GLOSS None.

DECORATION Initials filled with yellow and/or red, many oxidized.

PROVENANCE Irish. H. 2. 12, no. 7.

BIBLIOGRAPHY M. Esposito, 'Classical Manuscripts in Irish Libraries Part I',
Hermathena, 19, 1920, pp. 123–40 (138); Colker, p. 1249.

* 247 MS London, University of London Library (Senate House), 932
Top. Diff. I
                                                                    s. xiii mid

Parchment; 2 consecutive fols (front and back flyleaves); page 147x124mm
(front slightly trimmed); text 92x60mm (front), 120x64mm (back); 21 lines
(front), 28 lines (back); pencil ruled for gloss; one scribe. Limp vellum
wrapper with ties (missing).
Host book: Leonhartus Lycius, *Praecepta vitae honestae* etc., E. Voegelin,
Leipzig, 1562.

CONTENTS   *Top. Diff. I*: i^r 'ambigu]itatemque adducta' to 'non est' (*PL*,
                  64:1174C–75A); i^v 'ut ita' to 'orationibus inue[niantur' (*PL*,
                  64:1175B–D); ii^r 'aliae uero' to 'inhaereat' (*PL*,
                  64:1176C–77B); ii^v 'inue]niantur. Nam' to 'inueniri' (*PL*, 64:
                  1175D–76C).

GLOSS   Contemporary marginal and interlinear gloss.

DECORATION   Red and blue initials with contrasting infilling and flourishing;
                  red and blue paraph signs.

PROVENANCE   Bought by Neil Ker.

BIBLIOGRAPHY None.

Plates

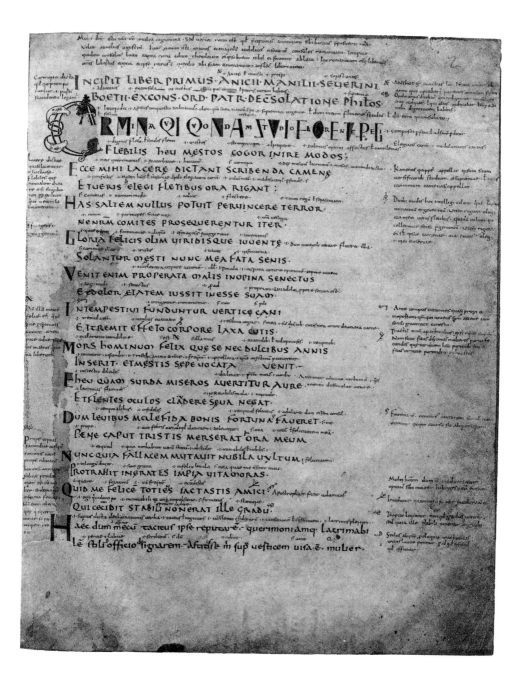

Pl. 1. MS CAMBRIDGE, TRINITY COLLEGE, O. 3. 7, fol. 2ʳ.
c. 1000. *DCPhil*. Note *tituli*, references-signs linking text to gloss, and
the contrast between the interlinear gloss (translating from one Latin
word to another) and the marginal (commenting on the wider meaning).

Pl. 2. MS LONDON, BRITISH LIBRARY, ADD. 19585, fol. 11^r.
s. xiv. Trivet's commentary to *DCPhil*. I. m. 1–8. Northern Italian.

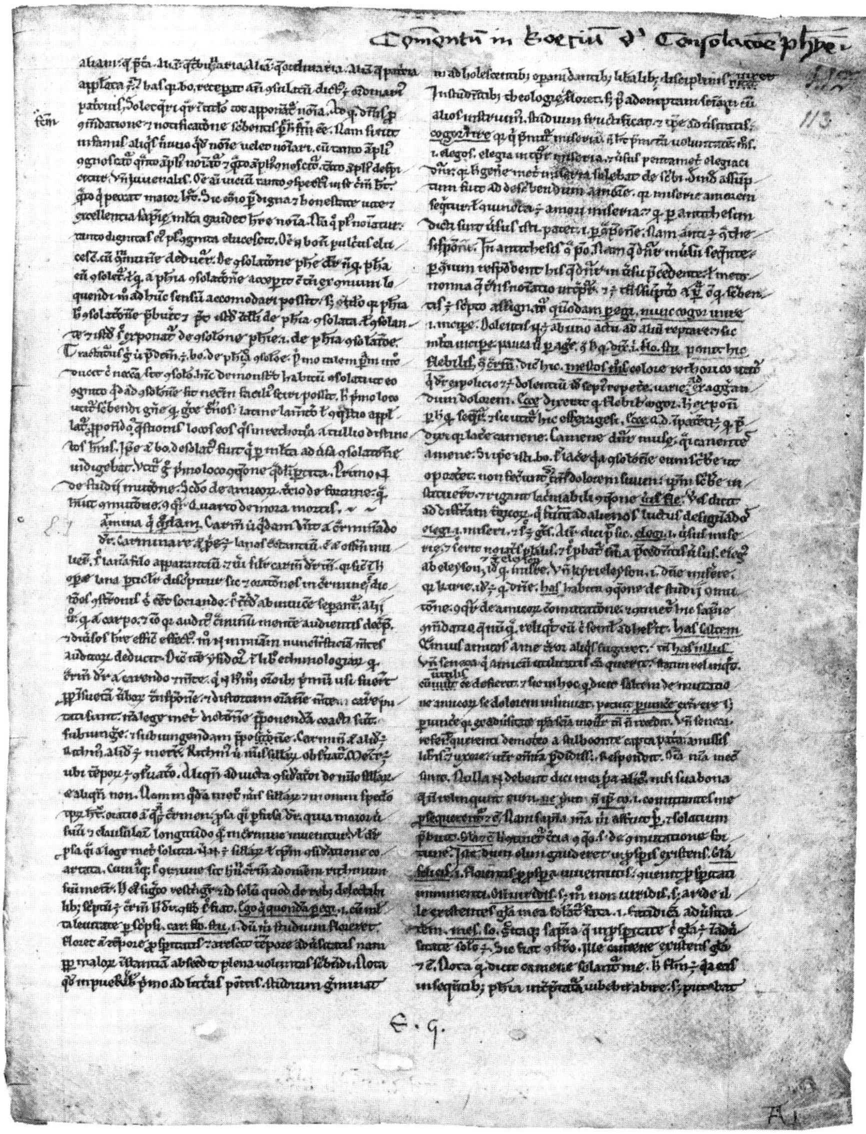

Pl. 3. MS LONDON, BRITISH LIBRARY, ADD. 19968, fol. 113ʳ.
s. xii. Continuous commentary on *DCPhil.*, with lemmata.

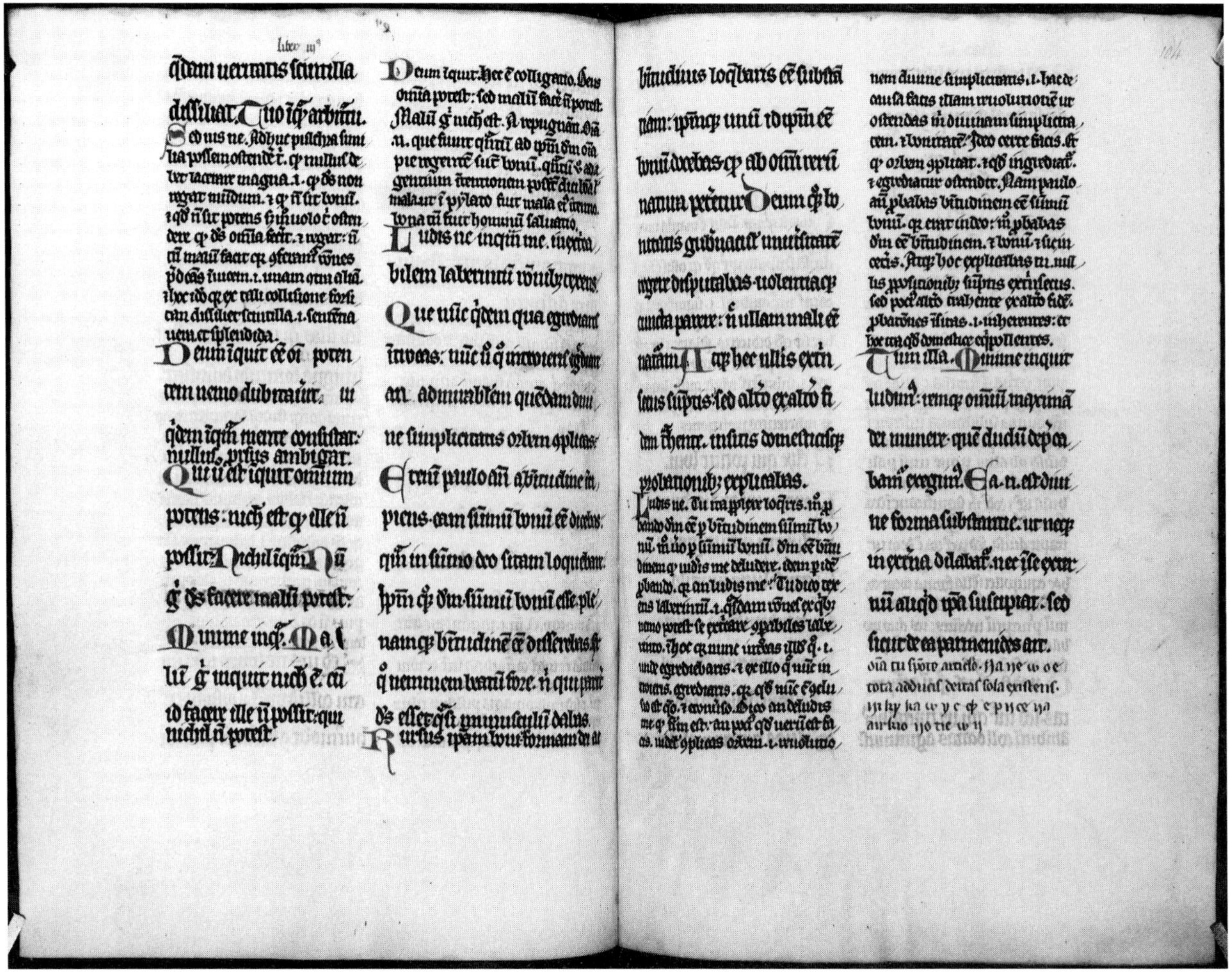

Pl. 4. MS LONDON, BRITISH LIBRARY, EGERTON 628, fols 103v–104r.
s. xiii 2/2. Intercalated commentary of Ps.-William of Conches on the *DCPhil.*

PL. 5. MS LONDON, BRITISH LIBRARY, HARLEY 3082, fols 45ᵛ–46ʳ.
s. xii 2/2. *Op. Sac. II*, with gloss of Gilbert of Poitiers.

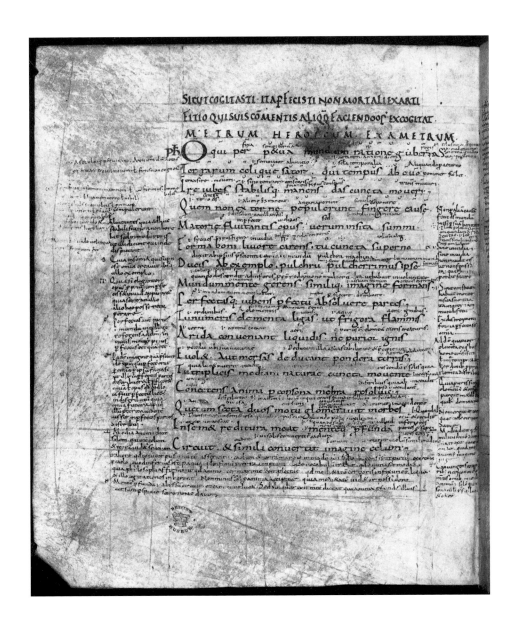

Pl. 6. MS LONDON, BRITISH LIBRARY, HARLEY 3095, fol. 46ᵛ.
s. ix. *DCPhil*. III. ix. 1–17, with at least two layers of Carolingian gloss. Note the two lines of summary at the top, the identification of the metre, Ph(ilosophia) taking up the dialogue (line 4), and the four lines of scansion at the top of the page. French.

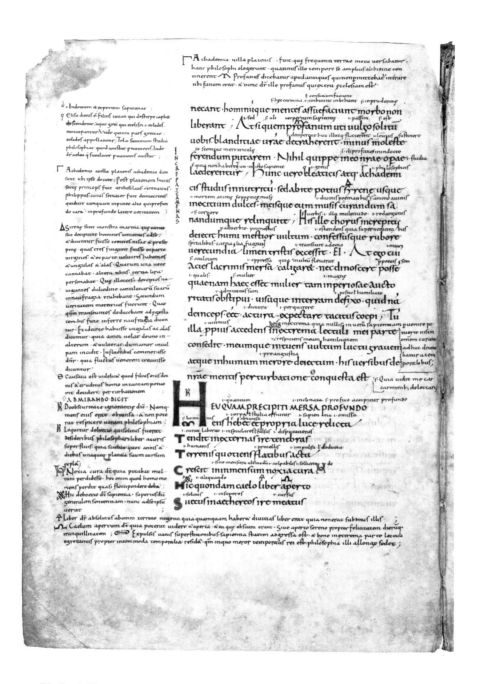

Pl. 7. MS OXFORD, BODLEIAN LIBRARY, AUCT. F. I. 15, fol. 6ᵛ. c. 1000. *DCPhil.*, with extensive gloss. A rare example of a secular text with a strictly planned gloss. Note the subject-heading 'increpat camenas'. St Augustine's, Canterbury.

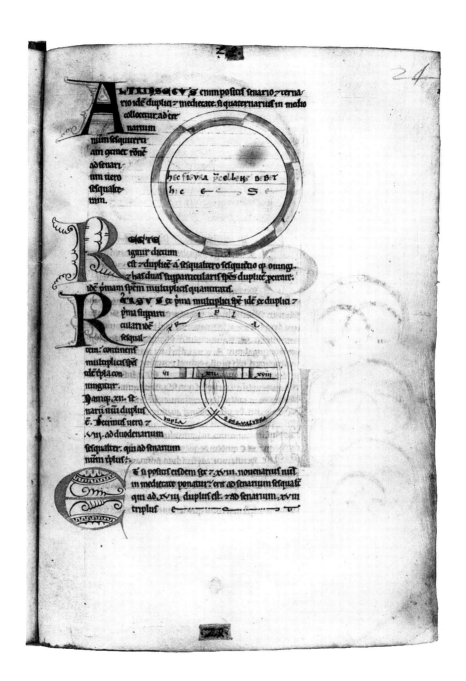

Pl. 8   MS OXFORD, BODLEIAN LIBRARY, LAUD LAT. 54, fol. 24ʳ.
s. xiii. *Arith.* with diagrams in red, blue and ochre. Note Arabic
numerals as running headers and page numbering.

Pl. 9. MS OXFORD, BODLEIAN LIBRARY, LAUD MISC. 457, fol. 145ᵛ.
s. xii 4/4: St Mary, Eberbach. Carolingian commentary on the *Op. Sac.*

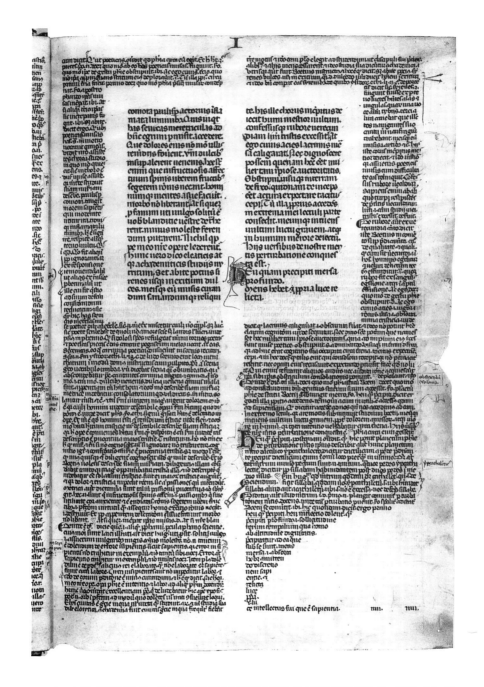

Pl. 10. MS OXFORD, BODLEIAN LIBRARY, RAWLINSON G. 187, fol. 3ʳ. s. xiv 2/2. *DCPhil.* in two columns, with Trivet's commentary surrounding; written to resemble a law text. Note marginal headings, pointing hands and face.

Indices

Numbers in the various indices refer to entries rather than to pages.

Index of Boethian Texts

156, 158, 161, 163, 166, 167,
170, 171, 172, 175, 179 (x 2),
180 (x 2), 181, 182, 184, 185,
190, 195, 196, 197, 199, 205,
209, 210, 215, 219, 227, 228,
229, 232, 236, 241

Boethius, *De differentiis topicis*
8, 25, 27, 30, 31, 35, 43, 56,
58, 88, 99, 105, 106, 125, 127,
139, 146, 148, 151, 155, 173,
183, 198, 206, 230, 233, 237,
239, 240, 243, 247

Boethius, *De divisione*
13, 27, 30, 31, 32, 35, 43, 56,
58, 87, 88, 99, 100, 106, 125,
146, 148, 168, 183, 198, 206,
239, 240

Boethius, *Introductio in syllogis-*
mos categoricos
No example in vol. 1.

Boethius, *De musica*
6, 49, 54, 95, 106, 120, 129,
132, 133, 143, 145, 157, 162,
164, 174, 201, 207, 208, 211,
212 (x 2), 216, 218, 235, 237

Boethius, *Opuscula sacra*
3, 4, 10, 19, 22, 26, 28, 36, 39,

40, 41, 45, 48, 50, 64, 67, 68,
83, 123, 124, 131, 133, 138,
144, 149, 159, 165, 177, 188,
192, 193, 194, 196, 204, 223,
224, 232, 242, 244, 245

Boethius, *De syllogismis*
categoricis
106, 146

Boethius, *De syllogismis*
hypotheticis
106, 146

Boethius, *In Topica Ciceronis*
77, 133, 189, 225, 234

Epitaphs
3, 51, 190, 205

Porphyry, *Isagoge*, trans. Boethius
13, 19, 23, 27, 30, 31, 32, 35,
43, 56, 58, 87, 88, 99, 100,
106, 125, 146, 148, 150, 183,
189, 198, 202, 206, 233, 237,
239, 240

Vitae Boetii
3, 28, 63, 108, 118, 124, 141,
163, 167, 179, 210

Index of Dates

Index of Provenance

General Index